Changing the Faces of Mathematics

Perspectives on African Americans

Series Editor

Walter G. Secada
University of Wisconsin—Madison
Madison, Wisconsin

Editors

Marilyn E. Strutchens
University of Maryland
College Park, Maryland

Martin L. Johnson
University of Maryland
College Park, Maryland

William F. Tate
University of Wisconsin—Madison
Madison, Wisconsin

National Council of Teachers of Mathematics
Reston, Virginia

Copyright © 2000 by
The National Council of Teachers of Mathematics, Inc.
1906 Association Drive, Reston, VA 20191-1502
(703) 620-9840; (800) 235-7566; www.nctm.org
All rights reserved

Second printing 2004

Library of Congress Cataloging-in-Publication Data

Perspectives on African Americans / editors, Marilyn Strutchens, Martin L. Johnson,
William F. Tate.
         p. cm. — (Changing the faces of mathematics)
    Includes bibliographical references.
    ISBN 0-87353-461-1
         1. Mathematics—Study and teaching—United States. 2. Afro-American
students—Education. I. Strutchens, Marilyn, date. II. Johnson, Martin L. III. Tate,
William F. IV. Series.

    QA13 .P462 2000
    510′.71′073—dc21

                                                                                        00-023972

Printed in the United States of America

Contents

Preface vii

Martin L. Johnson
University of Maryland, College Park, Maryland

Introduction 1

Marilyn E. Strutchens
University of Maryland, College Park, Maryland

**PART 1
FOCUS ON
RESEARCH
RELATED TO
TEACHING AND
LEARNING**

1. Confronting Beliefs and Stereotypes That Impede the Mathematical Empowerment of African American Students 7

Marilyn E. Strutchens
University of Maryland, College Park, Maryland

2. Teacher Expectations and Their Effects on African American Students' Success in Mathematics 15

Kathy M. Cousins-Cooper
North Carolina Agricultural and Technical State University, Greensboro, North Carolina

3. Reaching All Students Mathematically through Questioning 21

Dorothy Y. White
University of Georgia, Athens, Georgia

4. A High Level of Challenge in a Collaborative Setting: Enhancing the Chance of Success for African American Students in Mathematics 33

Rosalie A. Dance
University of the Virgin Islands, Saint Thomas, Virgin Islands

Karen H. Wingfield
Frank W. Ballou Senior High School, Washington, D.C.

Neil Davidson
University of Maryland, College Park, Maryland

5. African American Students' Success with School Mathematics 51

Vivian R. Moody
University of Alabama, Tuscaloosa, Alabama

6. Race Consciousness, Identity, and Affect in Learning Mathematics: The Case of Four African American Prospective Teachers 61

Norma C. Presmeg
Florida State University, Tallahassee, Florida

PART 2
FOCUS ON INSTRUCTIONAL AND CURRICULAR MODIFICATIONS AIMED AT AFRICAN AMERICAN STUDENTS

7. The Use of "Call and Response" Pedagogy to Reinforce Mathematics Concepts and Skills Taught to African American Kindergartners 73
   Maurice M. Martinez
   North Carolina University at Wilmington, Wilmington, North Carolina

8. Lessons Learned from the "Five Men Crew": Teaching Culturally Relevant Mathematics 81
   Lillie R. Albert
   Boston College, Chestnut Hill, Massachusetts

9. Teaching Mathematics to the Least Academically Prepared African American Students 89
   Laura Brooks Smith
   North Carolina Central University, Durham, North Carolina

   Lee V. Stiff
   North Carolina State University, Raleigh, North Carolina

   Melinda R. Petree
   William G. Enloe High School, Raleigh, North Carolina

10. African American Students Conduct Mathematical Research 97
    Miriam M. Stokes
    Atlanta Public Schools, East Point, Georgia

11. Culturally Relevant Mathematics Teaching at the Secondary School Level: Problematic Features and a Model for Implementation 107
    Lesley Wagner
    University of Wisconsin—Madison, Madison, Wisconsin

    Francine Cabral Roy
    University of Wisconsin—Madison, Madison, Wisconsin

    Elena Ecatoiu
    University of Wisconsin—Madison, Madison, Wisconsin

    Celia Rousseau
    University of Wisconsin—Madison, Madison, Wisconsin

12. STEP: An Enrichment Model for African American High School Students 123
    Elaine B. Hofstetter
    State University of New York—New Paltz, New Paltz, New York

    Elaine Kolitch
    State University of New York—New Paltz, New Paltz, New York

    Karen N. Bell
    Marymount College, Tarrytown, New York

13. Fostering Multicultural Connections in Mathematics through Media 135

Michaele F. Chappell
University of South Florida, Tampa, Florida

Denisse R. Thompson
University of South Florida, Tampa, Florida

14. Using Flags to Teach Mathematics Concepts and Skills 151

Joan Cohen Jones
Eastern Michigan University, Ypsilanti, Michigan

15. African Networks and African American Students 157

Claudia Zaslavsky
New York, New York

PART 3
FOCUS ON SPECIFIC METHODOLOGIES

16. Struggling toward Diversity in Graduate Education: A Reflective Exercise 169

Howard C. Johnson
Syracuse University, Syracuse, New York

Peter T. Englot
Syracuse University, Syracuse, New York

17. Changing the Faces of Mathematics Ph.D.'s: What We Are Learning at the University of Maryland 179

Duane A. Cooper
University of Maryland, College Park, Maryland

18. Developing Future Mathematicians 193

Janis M. Oldham
North Carolina Agricultural and Technical State University,
Greensboro, North Carolina

PART 4
FOCUS ON FUTURE MATHEMATICIANS AND MATHEMATICS EDUCATORS

Summary 201

William F. Tate
University of Wisconsin—Madison, Madison, Wisconsin

ACKNOWLEDGMENTS

Many people have contributed to the development of *Changing the Faces of Mathematics: Perspectives on African Americans*, including teachers, students, mathematics educators, and mathematicians. We appreciate all their efforts. Even though we cannot thank everyone individually, the editors want to make the following special acknowledgments.

We want to thank the reviewers of the manuscripts for their sincere and constructive feedback.

Thomasenia Lott Adams	Beatrice Lumpkin
Sunday A. Ajose	Carol Malloy
Harriett C. Bebout	Norma C. Presmeg
Jennie Bennett	Gary L. Reglin
George W. Bright	Neva Rose
Blanche Brownley	Walter Secada
Patricia F. Campbell	Isaiato Sessoms
Michaele F. Chappell	Marian W. Smith
Roberta L. Dees	Ann Victoria Stewart
Paula Ducket	Christine D. Thomas
Edgar Edwards, Jr.	Deborah Najee-Ullan
James D. Gates	Erna Yackel
Gloria F. Gilmer	Claudia Zaslavsky
Genevieve Knight	

We would also like to thank the Editorial Panel of the National Council of Teachers of Mathematics Changing the Faces of Mathematics series for its support throughout the process.

Walter C. Secada, Series Editor	Judith Hankes
Carol A. Edwards	Judith Jacobs
Luis Ortiz-Franco	Marilyn E. Strutchens
Gerald R. Fast	

Our thanks, as well, go to the editorial and production staffs at the NCTM Headquarters Office, who turned a collection of manuscripts into a finished monograph.

Preface

We are constantly reminded that students in the United States perform less well than students in other countries in mathematics and science (Third International Mathematics and Science Study, TIMSS). In the United States, National Assessment of Educational Progress (NAEP) data report that students continue to fall short of the standards set for them. When specific groups of U.S. children are considered, it becomes clear that, at best, small progress has been made over the past five years. This is especially true when the mathematical performance of African American students is examined in detail. Unfortunately, it continues to be the case that African American children lag significantly behind white and Asian students in their mathematics performance. Since our goal should be for all children to perform at a high level, it makes good sense that this situation be studied and real solutions be identified.

Major questions need to be answered. How do we improve the mathematics performance of African American students? What factors keep African American children from demonstrating high performance? Is it the curriculum, teaching, classroom environment, or some other combination of factors? Perhaps all the above contribute to this problem.

Recent research has identified teaching procedures that appear to foster deep and meaningful mathematical learning in a variety of classrooms, many of which actually contain African American students. Classrooms can be found in which students are engaged in meaningful problem solving, in meaningful social discourse, and in constructing their own meaningful mathematics. The findings of this research should be studied carefully. Too often it is assumed that research findings based on the performance of students who represent the majority of the population apply and are transferable to classrooms that include high African American populations, but that is not always true. For this reason, research actually involving African American students should provide important insights and help all of us to better understand the factors that both facilitate and impede learning.

A laudable goal for mathematics educators is to determine what situations or teaching and learning environments foster a high level of mathematics achievement among African American students. As we search, we must examine many interrelated parts of this equation: the curriculum, the way teachers teach, and the conditions under which students are expected to learn. The National Council of Teachers of Mathematics has published *Standards* documents to guide school curricula, provide a framework for effective teaching, and establish models for assessment. Curricular materials slowly are becoming available that are based on the Standards, and many teachers are becoming prepared to teach the new materials. Can we then assume that teachers of African American children are among those who are prepared with new approaches and new technologies, or is it more likely that teachers of African American children still teach as they did twenty or thirty years ago? Perhaps this question cannot be answered; however, we know that nationally there is much work to be done in preparing the teaching force to teach in ways that develop students who can compute and solve problems in mathematics.

Our goal is to make it possible for all students to perform at a very high level in mathematics, hence, we must find ways for this to occur. We must look at the reports presented in this volume as one source of ideas, since they reflect the actual performance of African American children. There is much more to be learned about teaching and instructional models that foster good learning within classrooms with significant numbers of African American children. Many current procedures and positions that state that all mathematics must be "culturally based" must be questioned and examined. Although cultural contexts that are rich with mathematics surely will help children learn, this does not suggest that students cannot learn mathematics in situations not embedded into a cultural context. We must study ways to foster discourse within the mathematics classroom. Students must be able to solve problems and then evaluate their solution strategies with the teacher and their peers within a comfortable and safe classroom environment.

We must help African American students believe that they can indeed become good mathematics students, so they will not become discouraged when they always see themselves compared with groups who have achieved at a higher level. African American students need to be told sometimes that they are performing at a high rate and are improving, for such attention should be given when students who begin far behind their peers make significant progress. However, this kind of confidence-building effort requires the participation of teachers who really believe that all students can learn good, usable mathematics and who can plan and design learning experiences that challenge all students .

The twenty-first century will demand an even higher level of mathematics performance than we currently have. We must accept the challenge to help African American students, and all students, become contributing participants in the world of the future. It is hoped that the contents of this volume will open new avenues of thought and provide compelling evidence that approaches, strategies, and teaching techniques exist that are effective with African American children.

Martin L. Johnson
University of Maryland

Introduction

In 1993, the National Council of Teachers of Mathematics created a task force on multiculturalism and gender in mathematics. That task force recommended the publication of a six-volume series of books that would help make the slogans of "mathematics for all," and "everybody counts" realities. The Council approved that recommendation. This series of books is called Changing the Faces of Mathematics. Each volume in the series has a different focus. An overview volume has a general conceptual and theoretical focus. Five other books look at issues involving gender equity; African Americans; Latinos; American Indians; and Asian and Pacific Islanders.

Three important commonalties cut across all six volumes. First, the chapters are "principled practice" in their orientation. This means the chapters are at the intersection of research (broadly construed to include teachers' own action research) and practice (also broadly construed to include the concerns of curriculum specialists, program developers, and policy makers). Second, many of the chapters address a broad range of audiences: teachers and lead teachers, district curriculum supervisors, department chairs and principals, program and professional developers, and other administrators. Third, the volumes contain a balanced set of manuscripts that are written to help people recognize and avoid the re-creation of stereotypes along the lines of unidimensional analyses.

The purpose of this volume of the series is to focus on equity issues in mathematics education regarding African American students. As stated in the preface, African American students have not been given commensurate opportunities to succeed in mathematics education. Thus, it is appropriate to have a book devoted to looking critically at successful and unsuccessful teaching practices related to African American students.

Chapters 1 through 4 focus mainly on issues related to teaching: pedagogy, teacher expectations, teacher-student discourse, and teachers' beliefs about African American students. In chapter 1, Strutchens expresses the importance of challenging teachers' counterproductive beliefs and practices regarding the mathematics education of African American students and the need to expose teachers to positive practices that will enhance the learning of African American students. In chapter 2, Cousins-Cooper discusses the effects of teacher expectations on African American students' achievement and gives suggestions for practice. In chapter 3, White illustrates what happened in a classroom when a teacher changed her practices to meet the needs of all her students by changing the focus and type of questions that she asked during her mathematics instruction in a manner that led to extending her students' mathematical thinking. In the next chapter, Dance, Wingfield, and Davidson describe a classroom of predominantly African-American students in an inner-city public high school that might provide a model for change to increase the participation of African American students in advanced mathematics.

Chapters 5–6 focus on perspectives of African American students. In chapter 5, Moody uses the case-study approach to discuss the perspectives of two African American female students who have been successful in mathematics. Moody's goal is to give us insights into why these students have succeeded and to challenge us to think about ways that we can foster successful African American mathematics students. In chapter 6, Presmeg also uses case studies to enlighten the reader about some of the factors that aid prospective African American teachers in coping with the stresses they frequently encounter in predominantly white universities.

Chapters 7–12 focus largely on specific instructional techniques for African American students in grades prekindergarten to 12. In chapter 7, Martinez discusses the use of Call-and-Response (a pedagogy grounded in aural and oral communication), cultural patterns of religious and secular group behavior, and the use of hands, fingers, and rhythmic "tapping" to reinforce previously learned number sequences and relationships with prekindergartners and kindergartners. In chapter 8, Albert outlines the lessons she learned from her students after an open discussion about a mathematics research project. She reflects on the changes—such as taking into consideration the cultural ideas, interests, and experiences of her students—that occurred in her curricular and pedagogical practices after this encounter with her students.

In chapter 9, Smith, Stiff, and Petree discuss the success they had with using problem-solving vignettes (PSVs) (problem situations designed to engage students in real-life activities) to enhance African American students' ability to achieve success in the study of algebra. According to Smith, Stiff, and Petree, the least academically prepared African American students in a large, urban school system were able to study more-worthwhile mathematics topics, better understand those topics, and develop better attitudes toward mathematics when taught using PSVs. In chapter 10, Stokes and Graham look at the success African American students have experienced through research projects that require students to communicate mathematically, make mathematical connections, explore careers in mathematics, and make different mathematical and interdisciplinary connections. Stokes tells how teachers can implement the ideas in their own classrooms and throughout their school district.

In chapter 11, Wagner, Roy, Ecatoiu, and Rousseau discuss the need for mathematics instruction to reflect pedagogical strategies that meaningfully integrate culture into the classroom. Such strategies include highlighting diverse cultures' contributions to the development of mathematics, the role of mathematics in society and culture, and an awareness of the influence of the students' culture on their mathematics learning. They also provide an example of how to incorporate real-life issues in an upper-level, secondary school mathematics course.

In chapter 12, Hofstetter, Bell, and Kolitch discuss the Science and Technology Entry Program (STEP), which assists historically underrepresented or economically disadvantaged secondary school students—namely, African American, Latino, and Native American Indian/Alaskan Native students. The purpose of the STEP project is to prepare these students for entry into postsecondary degree programs in scientific, technical, and health-related fields and licensed professions, such as architecture, dietetics, certified public accounting, dentistry, nursing, social work, and veterinary medicine. In this chapter, the project's methods of intervention and its successes are discussed.

Chapters 13–15 focus on specific methodologies that can be used across grade levels. In chapter 13, Chappell and Thompson look at the importance of fostering multicultural connections in mathematics through media. They discuss a framework for selecting different forms of culture-inclusive media and provide an annotated bibliography of resources. In chapter 14, Jones presents the notion of using flags to teach mathematical concepts and skills. She discusses an interdisciplinary, multicultural curricular unit, entitled "Flags of Sub-Saharan Africa," that has been successful with preservice and in-service teachers and their students.

In chapter 15, Zaslavsky focuses on African networks and their use in the mathematics classroom. She describes traditional networks of several African people and offers suggestions for classroom activities related to graph theory.

Chapters 16–18 provide a perspective on African Americans in higher education. They look at future mathematicians and mathematics educators. In chapter 16, Johnson and Englot discuss the struggle of diversifying graduate education. They present their views related to affirmative action in higher education, discuss demographic data about participation in higher education, offer their own interpretations of the data, describe some ways that they have acted on their beliefs about the subject, and discuss next steps that might be taken.

In chapter 17, Cooper describes the University of Maryland's mathematics department's successful enrollment of twenty-two black graduate students, most of whom are pursuing the Ph.D. He shares how the University of Maryland has been able to foster the mathematical development of the graduate students and how the graduate students survive the rigorous program. He also offers some suggestions for other institutions striving to obtain larger numbers of African American students.

In chapter 18, Oldham discusses the effort of faculty at North Carolina A&T State University to improve instruction in upper-level mathematics courses in order to give their mathematics majors the opportunity to learn and understand mathematics—better preparing them for graduate school in the mathematical sciences and keeping them in the pipeline. She describes the obstacles that they have encountered in trying to develop a "mathematics culture" among the students.

Tate, as a person with knowledge of school policy as well as a mathematics educator, ends the volume with a critical look at the major ideas of the book and insight into where we should go from here.

Marilyn E. Strutchens
Editor

Part 1

Focus on Research Related to Teaching and Learning

Confronting Beliefs and Stereotypes That Impede the Mathematical Empowerment of African American Students

Marilyn E. Strutchens

For more than two decades, researchers have been puzzled over the disproportionately low achievement and underrepresentation of African American students compared to white students in mathematics. Many hypotheses have been offered as reasons for this underachievement and underrepresentation: The gap is the result of economic disparities between the two ethnic groups that can be traced back to a legacy of slavery and other forms of oppression that African Americans have suffered (Ornstein and Levine 1984; Singham 1998); various social pathologies, such as unstable families, lack of parental involvement, and negative peer pressure within the African American community, are at fault (Irvine and York 1993; Ogbu 1986); and some argue that the gap is a result of genetic differences between African Americans and whites (Jensen 1969; Owen, Froman, and Moscow 1981). None of these ideologies have been conclusively verified, although fallacies within the genetic premise have already been noted (Bodmer and Cavalli-Sforza 1973; Ginsburg and Russell 1981). Ginsburg and Russell found that African American children and children from at-risk environments bring to the preschool and kindergarten classroom settings the same basic intellectual competencies in mathematical thought as their white counterparts. Thus, as conjectured by Ginsburg and Russell, there must be other factors, such as motivational problems, expectations of failure, and inadequacies of the educational system, causing the differential levels of achievement among white Americans and African Americans.

One likely factor is the differential treatment of African American students within the educational system. Researchers (Oakes 1990; Slavin 1987) have indicated that African Americans and other ethnic groups are the predominant groups placed in lower-level academic classes and that students placed in these classes often receive substandard instruction that does not adequately prepare them to function in society. The pedagogy typically faced by African American students is very directive, controlling, and debilitating (Chunn 1988; Haberman 1991). This is in contrast to the kind of mathematics teaching advocated by the National Council of Teachers of Mathematics, with its emphasis on active learning, deep understanding of concepts, and the development of problem-solving and reasoning skills (National Council of Teachers of Mathematics [NCTM] 1989). Indeed the teacher survey of the 1992 NAEP indicated that teachers of African American students were more likely to use multiple-choice testing, which concentrates on lower-level skills, than teachers of white students (Silver, Strutchens, and Zawojewski 1997).

Equally alarming, African American students are less likely to have teachers who have strong mathematics content knowledge. The Council of Chief State School Officers (CCSSO) commissioned a survey of a nationally representative sample of elementary and secondary school teachers to gather statistics on teacher preparation by student race and ethnicity (Weis 1994). This survey indicated that only 47 percent of mathematics teachers in classes with high-minority enrollments had a degree in mathematics or mathematics education. In contrast, more than 60 percent of the teachers in mathematics classes with less than 10 percent minority students majored in mathematics. Teacher content preparation is a likely factor related to the low achievement in mathematics of African American students.

Although discrepancies in mathematics achievement are complex, at least some of the inequities might be addressed by changing the pedagogy, the competency, and the mind-set of the person that should have the most influence over what goes on in the mathematics classroom, the teacher. It is the author's contention that in order to change African American students' achievement, preservice and in-service teachers must become more aware of stereotypes and beliefs that hinder them from providing equitable mathematics instruction to African American students. In this chapter, I will discuss debilitating stereotypes and beliefs held by mathematics teachers of African American students and how to counter those beliefs. I will also provide suggestions that might be shared with preservice and in-service teachers regarding effective mathematics instruction for African American students.

DEBILITATING STEREOTYPES AND BELIEFS

Teachers' negative beliefs about African American students tend to perpetuate the disproportionate failure of African American students in school.

Naturalistic expectations are those formed by teachers on their own (through interaction with students, examination of school records, knowledge of older siblings, and so forth). Studies of naturalistically formed expectations have regularly found that teachers treat students differently on the basis of their perceptions of the students' potential. In her review of the literature related to teacher expectations and student achievement, Irvine (1985) listed eleven studies that used teachers' ratings of their perceptions of African American students in comparison to their ratings of white students. She concluded that teachers, particularly white teachers, had more negative attitudes and beliefs about African American children than about white children with regard to such variables as potential for success in college, initial impression, deviant behavior, ability, and certain personality characteristics. However, it was also noted by Irvine that although the information provided by these studies is useful, it is not clear how these attitudes and beliefs influence teacher-student interaction in the classroom.

A more recent study investigated the distinctions elementary school teachers make in explaining academic failure among African Americans, Vietnamese, and Hispanic students (Irvine and York 1993). Lack of parental support was the primary reason given for academic failure among African American students. In contrast, the primary reason given for the failure of Vietnamese and Hispanic students was language difficulty. Attributing African American students' failure to a lack of parental support may lead teachers to believe that they can not effect positive change in African American student achievement. As a result of this sense of helplessness, teachers' interaction with African American students is characterized by lowered expectations, ineffective teaching, and reinforced racial stereotypes (Irvine and York 1993). Teachers' negative beliefs about African American students tend to perpetuate the disproportionate failure of African American students in school.

Delpit (1992) stated that many culturally diverse children are placed in situations where the teacher assumes deficits in students rather than locating and teaching to their strengths. In mathematics this behavior is exemplified by the assumption that some students are only capable of learning mathematics if they are told step-by-step procedures for solving problems. They are not thought of as being able to analyze and solve problems on their own. Moreover, teacher education students often view student diversity as a problem rather than a resource (Paine 1989). Preservice teachers frequently have limited views of student differences. Further, their conceptions of diversity are highly individualistic, focusing on personality factors like motivation and ignoring contextual factors like cultural practices and values.

In an effort to further examine preservice teachers' beliefs, I asked a group of preservice elementary school teachers to discuss stereotypes or other beliefs held by teachers or school administrators that might impede the mathematical empowerment of particular groups of students. Their responses were remarkably similar to those identified by Irvine and York (1993), Delpit (1992), and Paine (1989). These university students discussed how judgments about students' potential mathematics performance are often based on outward appearances, on experiences that teachers have had with students' siblings or with their race and ethnicity category, and on perceived socioeconomic status. These preservice teachers also noted that tracking and parental expectations seemed to impede students' mathematical potential.

Given the beliefs that teachers and administrators have about African American students and their parents, it is important for mathematics teacher educators to help teachers overcome these beliefs and to assist them in developing instructional strategies that will benefit all students. We need to help teachers realize the existence of their beliefs and how those beliefs determine how and what they teach. Each person has social identities that determine how people perceive and interact with each other (Lee 1985). Social identities include age, ethnic background, geographic origin, religious background, gender, ability, cultural influence, personal and family influences, economic class, and others. Teachers must first come to understand who they are as individuals and how their personal social identities influence other people. Then they must think about beliefs they have about students based on these social identities. After bringing these beliefs and stereotypes to the surface, teachers must examine which beliefs help or hinder their ability to provide students with an equitable education.

It is essential that teachers understand how they have been socially programmed in their attitudes toward various groups. Only then can teachers acknowledge their biases and work to diminish their effects as much as possible. This can be very stressful and painful for teachers, but it is necessary. Teacher-educators or in-service program presenters might profitably allow teachers to talk about beliefs and stereotypes. An effective prompt to stimulate this discussion is as follows: "Discuss stereotypes or other beliefs held by teachers or school administrators that impede the mathematical empowerment of particular groups of students."

This prompt is particularly effective because when teachers respond to this question, they do not feel that they are being put on the spot; they are answering the question on the basis of beliefs that others possess or that they have observed. Thus, they openly discuss the issues without feeling threatened. As a follow-up, the facilitator over the group can ask the following questions regarding the beliefs and stereotypes that are disclosed:

1. How would this belief affect instruction?
2. What are the consequences for students when teachers hold this particular belief?
3. How could you change the mind-set of someone who has this particular belief?
4. What if someone felt this way about you or your children? How would you react?

> **We need to help teachers realize the existence of their beliefs and how those beliefs determine how and what they teach.**

These questions will help teachers think about the consequences of holding such beliefs and why they must be actively challenged. The questions may also help teachers to think about how those belief systems can be changed.

Other approaches are also needed. For example, teachers might be asked to videotape a classroom lesson and then to analyze how they interacted with or questioned students from different cultural backgrounds. This type of analysis may well be very illuminating for the teacher who is not conscious of his or her differential treatment of certain groups of students. Another approach is to present different vignettes of classroom situations in which students were placed in inequitable situations. Teachers can discuss what happened in the vignettes, suggest alternative ways of handling the situations, and reflect on their own classroom behaviors.

Finally, in order to help preservice and in-service teachers provide equitable instruction to African American students, they must be exposed to other teachers who have positive beliefs about African American students and practice pedagogy that is encouraging and mathematically empowering. All too often we do not have access to classroom teachers who are both pedagogically and content sound, and so we place preservice teachers with cooperating teachers who use a pedagogy that is very directive, controlling, and debilitating. Thus, we end up reinforcing negative beliefs about how children learn. If we want to see preservice teachers develop equitable pedagogy, we must place them with teachers who model this approach. Preservice teachers operate more by the old adage of "seeing is believing" than by any words spoken during a college methods class.

It is equally important to expose preservice teachers to a diverse teaching faculty at the university level who are cognizant of issues related to culture and believe that the current structure of society can be changed. Preservice teachers should also have a variety of teaching and learning experiences in different settings with diverse student populations. They should especially work with African American students under competent supervision prior to being solely responsible for students. Furthermore, we must help in-service teachers form alliances with colleagues who believe that all students can learn mathematics and who teach in ways that build on students' strengths and move them forward. Through these alliances, teachers can help each other become more effective in the classroom.

EFFECTIVE STRATEGIES FOR TEACHING AFRICAN AMERICAN STUDENTS

It is not enough to simply challenge counterproductive beliefs and practices. Preservice and in-service teachers need to be exposed to positive practices that will enhance the learning of all students, including African Americans. As a teacher and a mathematics educator, I have taught African American students enrolled in grades K–12 and beyond. My experience is that most African American students like mathematics, and they want to learn mathematics. I have also found that there is no one set way to present lessons that will appeal to all African American students all the time. However, there are certain strategies that are more conducive to helping students reach their full mathematical potential.

Help students develop a relational understanding of concepts

Students who are able to associate an understood idea with many other existing ideas in a meaningful network of concepts and procedures have a relational understanding of the idea (Skemp 1987; Sleeter 1997; Van de Walle 1997). For example, one might initially help primary students develop an understanding of basic facts by beginning with real-world situations in which the students use objects to find solutions in order to help them connect their actions to mathematical symbols. Once students understand the arithmetic concept, instruction should address the development of strategies for deriving the facts, only using drill and practice to develop automatism.

Help students develop number sense

Number sense refers to an intuitive feel for numbers and their various uses and interpretations. Number sense also includes the ability to compute accurately and efficiently, to detect errors, and to recognize results as reasonable (Reys et al. 1998). Number-sense skills are becoming more and more important with increased use of calculators and computers. Moreover, helping students develop number-sense skills is mathematically empowering. Strategies that are used to help students learn basic facts can also be used to help students with mental-math skills that are useful in recognizing results as reasonable. For example, helping students develop strategies such as adding to ten can help them add larger numbers. Given the computation: $8 + 6 = $ ___, a child would say that $6 = 2 + 4$; so, I can add 2 to 8 and get 10 and then add 10 and 4 to get 14. The same process can be used when a child computes $48 + 5 = $___. The child would know that $2 + 3 = 5$, so he or she could add $48 + 2$ and get 50 and then add 50 and 3 to get 53.

Express a deep belief in the capabilities of your students

Expectations must be high and attainable if students are to develop their full mathematics potential (Ladson-Billings 1995; Sleeter 1997). Since students conform to teachers' expectations (Good 1987), it is important for teachers to expect that their students can learn and do challenging mathematics. I have often taught African American students who were pleasantly suprised at what they were able to accomplish. Some of the students have even said that no one had ever believed that they could do some of the mathematics that I required them to do.

Enable students to use mathematics as a tool for examining issues related to race, ethnicity, gender, and social class (Sleeter 1997; Tate 1995)

For example, Tate (1995) described a classroom in which middle-grades students were concerned about the number of liquor stores within the neighborhood surrounding the school. The students and the teacher discussed the problems of having the liquor stores within close proximity of their school. The situation with the liquor stores provided a rich context for the students to use mathematics as a tool. The students did research and found that the disproportionate number of liquor stores in their neighborhood was a function of a city code that relegated those establishments to their largely African American community. Consequently, the students reconstructed and proposed new tax incentives to get the liquor stores to move away from their neighborhood. Thus, the students simultaneously saw the power of mathematics and developed sensitivity toward critical issues of justice in their community.

Create a classroom environment where students are able to find and justify their solutions, as well as question other students about their responses to the same or different questions

Studies have shown that students from diverse backgrounds perform better when they are able to communicate effectively with other students about mathematical concepts. One example of a successful program based on this principle is Project IMPACT (Increasing the Mathematical Power of All Children and Teachers). This project addressed schoolwide reform in elementary school

It is not enough to simply challenge counterproductive beliefs and practices. Preservice and in-service teachers need to be exposed to positive practices that will enhance the learning of all students, including African Americans.

mathematics in predominantly minority urban schools where it had been established that black and Hispanic students were lagging significantly behind their white and Asian counterparts (Campbell 1996). As a result of the project, classrooms became places where thoughts were accepted, ideas were investigated, and meaningful problems were solved. Student achievement increased significantly.

QUASAR (Quantitative Understanding: Amplifying Student Achievement and Reasoning) was designed for middle schools (grades 6–8) in economically disadvantaged communities and has also been successful in increasing students' mathematical power. In QUASAR classrooms, teachers expected students to understand the mathematics they were asked to learn, the instructional practices supported the development of students' understanding, and the mathematical tasks used provided challenging settings in which students could apply and extend their developing understandings (Silver and Stein 1996).

Develop partnerships with African American students' parents

In order to insure that African American students are successful in school mathematics, teachers must develop meaningful partnerships with parents or other caregivers. Bennett (1986) stated that "parents are their children's first and most influential teachers" (p. 126). Parents can assist with the mathematics education of their children in many ways, such as helping their children with homework, discussing real-world situations that involve mathematics with their children, reinforcing mathematics concepts that are learned in school, and helping their children to develop critical-thinking skills.

The first step toward developing partnerships with African American parents is to believe that all parents are interested in their children's education. If teachers have this belief, then they will at least attempt to make some contact with their students' parents. Teachers must be creative in finding ways to involve parents and caregivers in their children's mathematics education.

Sending brief newsletters home that describe what mathematics is being taught is one way to involve the parents. In the letter, teachers can make suggestions about things adults can do at home to help reinforce concepts that children are learning in school. Teachers can also send home a letter that describes the mathematics topic taught in class on a given day. In the letter the teacher can include some problems for the parent and child to solve together.

Schools can host Family Math Nights. These are evenings where mathematical centers, games, and activities are taken from classrooms and set up in the cafeteria or all-purpose room. Students serve as tour guides for their families, parents, or adult guests, explaining the use and purpose of manipulative materials and engaging their guests in mathematical tasks. These evenings can be held once a month or once a semester. The goal is to orient parents to the methods of instruction used in the classroom. Family Math Nights can be held at all grade levels.

Schools can also set up programs, such as Family Math (Stenmark, Thompson, and Cossey 1986) and Multicultural Literature as a Context for Mathematical Problem Solving: Parents and Children Learning Together (Strutchens and Perkins 1994), where parents and their children come together to do mathematics once a week for four or more weeks. This can be done in the context of literature, science, or other subjects. The objective is to have parents and children working together to solve routine and nonroutine mathematical problems so that parents and children develop stronger mathematics skills. Programs like these also help parents and children communicate with each other better about mathematics. They assist parents in taking an active role in their children's mathematics education, and they help parents feel more welcome in the school.

The aforementioned strategies are not novel ideas. Indeed, many might consider them common practices used by effective teachers. However, many of these techniques are not implemented in mathematics classes that contain large numbers of African American students. In order to help teachers value the need for implementing such strategies, we must expose them to good methods of teaching mathematics and show them examples of successful mathematics students who are similar to their students.

CONCLUSION

In this chapter, I have discussed debilitating stereotypes and beliefs held by mathematics teachers of African American students and ways to counter those beliefs. I have also provided suggestions that might be shared with preservice and in-service teachers regarding effective mathematics instruction for African American students. I realize that it is not a small task to change habits of the mind, nor is it a small task to change how one provides instruction, but both are possible. We must help teachers see a need to change, provide them with evidence that the changes will make a difference, and then help them change if we want to see improvement in African American students' mathematics achievement.

REFERENCES

Bennett, William J. "First Lessons." *Phi Delta Kappan* 68 (October 1986): 125–29.

Bodmer, Walter F., and Luigi Luca Cavalli-Sforza. "Intelligence and Race." In *The Nature and Nuture of Behavior: Developmental Psychobiology*, edited by William T. Greenough, pp. 125–35. San Francisco, Calif.: W. H. Freeman Co., 1973.

Campbell, Patricia F. "Empowering Children and Teachers in the Elementary Mathematics Classrooms of Urban Schools." *Urban Education* 30 (January 1996): 449–75.

Chunn, Eva Wells. "Sorting Black Students for Success and Failure: The Inequality of Ability Grouping and Tracking." *Urban League Review* 11 (Summer-Winter 1987–88): 93–106.

Delpit, Lisa D. "Education in a Multicultural Society: Our Future's Greatest Challenge." *Journal of Negro Education* 61 (1992): 237–49.

Ginsburg, Herbert P., and Robert L. Russell. *Social Class and Racial Influences on Early Mathematical Thinking.* Monographs of the Society for Research in Child Development, vol. 46, no. 6 (serial 193). Chicago, University of Chicago Press, 1981.

Good, Thomas L. "Teacher Expectations." In *Talks to Teachers*, edited by David C. Berliner and Barak V. Rosenshine, pp. 159–200. New York: Random House, 1987.

Haberman, Martin. "The Pedagogy of Poverty versus Good Teaching." *Phi Delta Kappan* 73 (1991): 290–94.

Irvine, Jacqueline J. "Teacher Communication Patterns as Related to the Race and Sex of the Student." *Journal of Educational Research* 78 (August 1985): 338–45.

Irvine, Jacqueline J., and Darlene E. York. "Differences in Teacher Attributions of School Failure for African-American, Hispanic, and Vietnamese Students." Paper presented at the meeting of the American Educational Research Association, Atlanta, April 1993.

Jensen, Arthur R. "How Much Can We Boost IQ and Scholastic Achievement?" *Harvard Educational Review* 39 (Winter 1969): 1–123.

Ladson-Billings, Gloria. "Making Mathematics Meaningful in Multicultural Contexts." In *New Directions for Equity in Mathematics Education*, edited by Walter Secada, Elizabeth Fennema, and Lisa B. Adajian, pp. 126–45. New York: Cambridge University Press, 1995.

Lee, Enid. *Letters to Marcia: A Teacher's Guide to Anti-Racist Education.* Toronto, Ontario: Cross Cultural Communication Centre, 1985.

National Council of Teachers of Mathematics. *Curriculum and Evaluation Standards for School Mathematics.* Reston, Va.: National Council of Teachers of Mathematics, 1989.

Oakes, Jeannie. "Opportunities, Achievement, and Choice: Women and Minority Students in Science And Mathematics." In *Review of Research in Education*, Vol. 16, edited by Courtney B. Cazden, pp.152–222. Washington, D.C.: American Educational Research Association, 1990.

Ogbu, John, and Maria E. Matute-Bianchi. "Understanding Socio-Cultural Factors: Knowledge, Identity, and School Adjustment." In *Beyond Language: Social and Cultural Factors in Schooling Language Minority Students*, pp. 73–143. Los Angeles: Evaluation, Dissemination and Assessment Center, 1986.

Ornstein, Allan C., and Daniel U. Levine. "Social Class, Race, and School Achievement." In *An Introduction to Foundations of Education*, edited by Allan. C. Ornstein and Daniel U. Levine, pp. 363–96. Dallas, Tex.: Houghton Mifflin, 1984.

Owen, Steven V., Robin D. Froman, and Henry Moscow. *Educational Psychology: An Introduction*. 2nd ed. Boston, Mass.: Little, Brown & Co., 1981.

Paine, L. "Orientation towards Diversity: What Do Prospective Teachers Bring?" (Research Report 89-9). East Lansing, Mich.: Michigan State University, National Center for Research on Teacher Learning, 1989.

Reys, Robert E., Marilyn N. Suydam, Mary M. Lindquist, and Nancy Smith. *Helping Children Learn Mathematics*. 5th ed. Boston, Mass.: Allyn & Bacon, 1998.

Singham, Mano. "The Canary in the Mine: The Achievement Gap between Black and White Students." *Phi Delta Kappan* 80 (September 1998): 9–15.

Silver, Edward A., and Mary Kay Stein. "The QUASAR Project: The 'Revolution of the Possible' in Mathematics Instructional Reform in Urban Middle Schools." *Urban Education* 30 (January 1996): 476–521.

Silver, Edward A., Marilyn E. Strutchens, and Judith S. Zawojewski. "NAEP Findings Regarding Race/Ethnicity and Gender: Affective Issues, Mathematics Performance, and Instructional Context." In *Results from the Sixth Mathematics Assessment of the National Assessment of Educational Progress*, edited by Edward A. Silver and Patricia A. Kenney, pp. 33–59. Reston, Va.: National Council of Teachers of Mathematics, 1997.

Skemp, Richard. *The Psychology of Learning Mathematics*. Hillsdale, N.J.: Lawrence Erlbaum Associates, 1987.

Slavin, Robert E. "Ability Grouping and Its Alternatives: Must We Track?" *American Educator* (1987): 32–48.

Sleeter, Christine E. "Mathematics, Multicultural Education, and Professional Development." *Journal for Research in Mathematics Education* 28 (December 1997): 680–96.

Stenmark, Jean Kerr, Virginia Thompson, and Ruth Cossey. *Family Math*. Berkeley, Calif.: Lawrence Hall of Science, 1986.

Strutchens, Marilyn, and Fran Perkins. "Mathematically Empowering Parents and Children through Multicultural Literature." *Becoming: Georgia Middle School Association and Georgia Association of Middle School Principals Journal* 6 (1994): 13–15.

Tate, William. "Mathematics Communication: Creating Opportunities to Learn." *Teaching Children Mathematics* 1 (February 1995), 344–49, 369.

Weiss, Iris R. *A Profile of Science and Mathematics Education in the United States: 1993*. Chapel Hill, N.C.: Horizon Research, 1994.

Van de Walle, John. *Elementary and Middle School Mathematics: Teaching Developmentally*. 3rd ed. New York: Longman, 1997.

BIBLIOGRAPHY

Blank, Rolf K., and Doreen Langesen. *State Indicators of Science and Mathematics Education 1997: State-by-State Trends and New Indicators from the 1995–96 School Year*. Washington, D.C.: Council of Chief State School Officers, 1997.

Ingersoll, Richard M., and Kerry Gruber. *Out-of-Field Teaching and Educational Equality*. Washington, D.C.: U.S. Department of Education, National Center for Education Statistics, 1996.

Teacher Expectations and Their Effects on African American Students' Success in Mathematics

2

Kathy M. Cousins-Cooper

Evidence exists that indicates African American students are failing in school at disproportionately high rates compared to their white counterparts (Tribble 1992). Mathematics is a subject in which the performance of African American students has been continually below that of other ethnic groups (Secada 1989, 1992). This observation is manifested in the results of the Mathematics Assessment of the National Assessment of Educational Progress (NAEP) that indicate that African American students have consistently scored significantly lower on these standardized tests compared to white students. A recent report of the mathematics assessment of the NAEP indicated that even though the mathematics proficiency of the students has increased, the increases did little to alter the relative standings of the demographic groups (Mullis 1993). The underachievement of black students in mathematics may be one of the reasons for the underrepresentation of black students in advanced mathematics courses. Rowser and Koontz (1995) reported that even though African American students comprised 10 to 30 percent of enrollment at various schools, seldom was there more than one African American in the advanced mathematics classes. As a result, the majority of African American students will not be prepared to enter a technological, scientific career because of their low enrollments in higher-level secondary and postsecondary mathematics courses.

To understand the urgency of this problem, one could examine the projected demographic changes for the future. In 1976, 24 percent of the country's school population was nonwhite, and by 1984, the percentage of nonwhite students had increased to 29 percent. For the year 2000, the projected percentage of nonwhite students in the country's schools will be between 30 and 40 percent (Center for Education Statistics [CES] 1987; Hodgkinson 1985; Secada 1992; Veltman 1988). Also, by the year 2000, 85 percent of the new members of the U.S. workforce will be blacks, Latinos, and white women (Commission on Professionals in Science and Technology 1986; Rowser and Koontz 1995).

What are some of the factors that influence mathematics achievement? Oakes (1990) associates several societal factors with a student's performance in mathematics classes; they include socioeconomic status, which is defined by parents' educational levels, family income, the occupation of the head of the household, and the number of possessions; parents' involvement and expectations; and students' perceptions and expectations. Reyes and Stanic (1988) assert that when examining the performance of African American students in mathematics, a researcher cannot ignore the importance of socioeconomic status, because of the disproportionate percentage of African American students who are low in socioeconomic status and the disproportionate percentage of majority students who are high in socioeconomic status.

Although teachers need to be aware of the factors that affect mathematics achievement for African American students, it is essential to focus in particular on those factors that mathematics educators can alter, such as the teachers' expectations for their students' success in studying mathematics. The following areas will be discussed: (1) the teachers' expectations of African American students' achievement level in mathematics and (2) implications for practice.

TEACHER EXPECTATIONS

Ever since the Pygmalion experiment conducted by Rosenthal and Jacobsen (1968), much attention has been focused on how teachers' expectations affect students' academic performances. Rosenthal and Jacobsen provide evidence of the self-fulfilling prophecy of teacher expectations that implies that the existence of a teacher's expectation will increase the probability of the child's actual performance moving in the expected direction. More often than not, teachers expect that African American students will perform poorly on mathematical assessments; this means that the teacher has low expectations for the performance of African American students. In addition, teachers have negative attitudes about African American students, which may include a low expectation for academic success. Irvine (1985) refers to several studies that determined that teachers, particularly white teachers, have more negative attitudes and beliefs about black children than about white children. These negative attitudes occur most often in regard to such factors as potential for success in college, deviant behavior, ability, and certain personality characteristics.

To what extent are these attitudes and beliefs manifested in the social interaction of the classroom? Ladson-Billings (1994) describes the typical classroom as one in which students try to outdo one another academically and one where individual success, as opposed to collective success, is valued. This situation is a disadvantage for some African American students, because they may be oriented toward a cooperative-learning style (Grant 1989). In addition, Ladson-Billings (1994, p. 55) notes that in many classrooms "the teacher is viewed as all-knowing, and the students are viewed as know-nothings." For minority students, this situation is even worse. Low expectations for these students can take a variety of forms. For example, if a teacher is too critical or too complimentary about a minority student's action, then the remark may be taken negatively by the minority students. Other subtle behaviors, such as a teacher's avoiding calling on a minority student in class, will send a negative message to the student that may convey the idea that he or she does not have the academic ability to participate in the class discussion.

The difficulties African American students experience in the school system are not all caused by the students themselves; some are the result of negative interactions with teachers. Teachers must be made aware of their actions in the classroom and the effects these actions can have on the students' academic performances. With a deliberate effort for improvement, teachers can exert behaviors that convey to their students that all of them can be successful and are expected to be successful. For example, a teacher can assign a problem for the class to solve. As the students work the problem, the teacher may walk around the classroom from desk to desk to facilitate the students' problem-solving processes by asking probing questions that help the students organize their thoughts. By asking probing questions instead of solving the problem for the student, the teacher communicates to the student that he or she is capable of solving the problem. As an educator of African American students, I find that this approach allows the students to serve as the main problem solver instead of the teacher. The students work at solving the problem collaboratively, check

By asking probing questions instead of solving the problem for the student, the teacher communicates to the student that he or she is capable of solving the problem.

one another's processes and results, and become excited when they determine that their answers are correct. My role as a teacher is to guide them in the problem-solving process and to encourage them by conveying my expectations for their success. In summary, the interactions that occur in the classroom, such as the verbal and nonverbal communication, the inclusion of all students in class activities and discussions, the respect and inclusion of cultural differences, affect a student's academic experience.

Irvine (1992) indicates several characteristics of teachers who are effective in teaching minority students. Effective teachers are competent in their subject matter, hold high levels of expectation for their students' academic performances, and provide their students with high-level knowledge. Teachers that instruct African American students need to go beyond being effective (Malloy 1997). They must recognize the cultural experiences of their students and incorporate them in their teaching. To develop a classroom environment that is equitable for all students, teacher-student interactions should include teaching in a manner that acknowledges students' cultural backgrounds and making cultural referents an integral part of the curriculum.

Moreover, Ladson-Billings (1994, pp. 17–18) describes culturally relevant teaching as "a pedagogy that empowers students intellectually, socially, emotionally, and politically by using cultural referents to impart knowledge." Cultural referents are part of the curriculum in their own right. For example, a teacher attempting to make mathematics culturally relevant to African American students would incorporate problem-solving activities that connect to the lives and experiences of the African American student. In addition, teaching mathematics in a culturally relevant style to African Americans is not difficult to do given the rich history of mathematics in the countries of Africa. One could focus on the African origins of algebra to inform the students that "the first use of algebra appeared in the writings of Ahmes, an Egyptian mathematician who lived around 1700 B.C." (Ladson-Billings 1994, p. 118). In addition, teachers can use mathematics projects, presentations, or journals to allow African American students to disseminate the culturally relevant aspects of mathematics. For example, having students research an African American mathematician, African mathematician, or significant contributions of African Americans in mathematics can serve the dual purpose of increasing the awareness of the student and the teacher about the vital role African Americans and Africans played in the development of mathematics and of heightening the self-confidence of the student studying mathematics. Activities that focus on the cultural contributions of African Americans in mathematics will ultimately help to motivate more students to study and excel in mathematics.

In summary, teachers can increase the number of African Americans studying mathematics by modifying their classroom practices. Teachers should employ various teaching strategies that allow African American students to strengthen their methods of reasoning and help them develop new ones. Teachers must structure the content to be culturally diverse to reach students from the African American cultures and other cultures. In addition, teachers must ensure that they maintain high levels of expectation for African American students' success in studying mathematics.

IMPLICATIONS FOR PRACTICE

How can we improve the instruction we give African American students in mathematics to optimize their levels of achievement? Teachers should make sure that African American students are actually engaged in doing mathematics while they are in their classes. By encouraging them to participate in the class

Concerned educators will seek methods to improve their students' motivational level and their own expectations for their students' success in order to be more inclusive of all students regardless of the cultural differences.

and making their participation in class an integral part of each session, teachers can determine if their students have an understanding of the concept being taught. Methods of encouraging the students to participate include having them solve problems in class, asking them probing questions about the content, allowing enough wait time for them to respond to the question, providing them with acknowledgement and feedback, and allowing them to explain to their classmates how they solved a problem (Malloy 1997). All these methods convey the message to the student that the teacher expects them to attain and explain the concepts of mathematics.

The mathematics curriculum for African American students should be the same as that for other students (Ladson-Billings 1995). Some teachers of African American students have made the mistake of watering down the curriculum because they believe these students will not be able to grasp the concept being taught. For example, when they teach methods of solving quadratic equations, many teachers require their students to learn the quadratic formula in lieu of the completing-the-square method. However, I require my students to learn both of these methods because there will be other times when they have to complete the square to solve a problem (e.g., manipulating the equations for circles and the conic sections). As with other concepts in mathematics that have a number of viable methods for solutions, African American students should be presented with all methods for the solution of the problem, be required to learn them, and after they have learned them, be allowed to choose the method they prefer.

What we teach African American students needs to be the same as what we teach students with other ethnic backgrounds. It is how we teach it that needs to be modified. Teachers should provide a learning environment that is responsive to the cultural needs of African American students. Because African American students tend to learn in a relational style, concepts should be taught using a variety of strategies so that students who are relational in their learning, as well as those with an analytic learning style, may have an equal opportunity to learn (Banks 1988). In addition, because African American students excel in a cooperative learning environment (Grant 1989), teachers should encourage students to learn collaboratively and expect them to teach each other and take responsibility for each other (Ladson-Billings 1995). This practice means helping the students remove the notion of individualism and instead work for the group.

A colleague of mine uses cooperative learning to teach methods of differentiation in a calculus class. The class, which is predominantly African American, uses class time and time after class to work in their cooperative groups. Each student is made responsible for his or her classmates in the group because a quiz is given to each student based on the content the group reviewed, and the score for each student in the group is the average of the scores of the classmates in the cooperative group. The higher-achieving students work with the lower-achieving students to help them grasp the concepts so that everyone can learn the concepts and receive good quiz grades.

Most educators underestimate the intellectual capacities of their students and in particular those who have a previous record for failure (Hilliard 1995). However, teachers should prepare African American students for the future and give them the tools they need to experience a successful academic future. After all, the sequence of studying mathematics is similar to building a house in that you want your students to build their mathematical foundation on rock and not on sand. If students do not receive appropriate instruction and guidance at the beginning of studying mathematics, they will surely encounter problems ahead with future mathematics concepts and courses. It follows that teachers must maintain high expectations for African American students' success in studying mathematics. Teachers should treat all students as if they are intelligent and capable of learning mathematics.

African American students learn in an environment in which they believe the teacher cares about them and has a sincere interest in their welfare. Affective interaction between teachers and students is fundamental to the teaching and learning of African American students (Malloy 1997). Thus, it is imperative that teachers demonstrate a connectedness with each of the students (Ladson-Billings 1995) and that teachers establish good relationships with African American students. These relationships can be developed simply by being kind and courteous to students. Giving students a little recognition, listening to them, respecting them, and smiling can mean a lot to the students. To solidify these relationships, teachers can make arrangements to meet with their students in a setting other than the classroom. Perhaps, they might even volunteer to take small groups of students on mathematical field trips in an effort to discover the uses of mathematics in the community.

CONCLUSION

Educators, in particular mathematics educators, need to seek methods to improve their instruction so that they can optimize the mathematics achievement level of African American students. This paper focuses on a variable that affects mathematics achievement that educators can alter—teacher expectations. Concerned educators will seek methods to improve their students' motivational level and their own expectations for their students' success in order to be more inclusive of all students regardless of the cultural differences.

REFERENCES

Banks, James A. "Ethnicity, Class, Cognitive, and Motivational Styles: Research and Teaching Implications." *Journal of Negro Education* 57 (1988): 452–66.

Center for Education Statistics. *Condition of Education.* Washington, D.C.: Government Printing Office, 1987.

Commission on Professionals in Science and Technology. *Scientific Manpower, 1989 and Beyond: Today's Budget—Tomorrow's Workforce.* Washington, D.C.: Commission on Professionals in Science and Technology, 1986.

Grant, Carl A. "Equity, Equality, Teachers, and Classroom Life." In *Equity in Education,* edited by Walter G. Secada, pp. 89–102. London: Falmer Press, 1989.

Hilliard, Asa G. "Mathematics Excellence for Cultural 'Minority' Students: What Is the Problem?" In *Prospects for School Mathematics,* edited by Iris M. Carl, pp. 99–114. Reston, Va.: National Council of Teachers of Mathematics, 1995.

Hodgkinson, Harold L. *All One System: Demographics of Education, Kindergarten through Graduate School.* Washington, D.C.: Institute for Educational Leadership, 1985.

Irvine, Jacqueline J. "Making Teacher Education Culturally Responsive." In *Diversity in Teacher Education,* edited by Mary E. Dilworth, pp. 79–92. San Francisco: Jossey-Bass Publishers, 1992.

———. "Teacher Communication Patterns as Related to the Race and Sex of the Student." *Journal of Educational Research* 78, no. 6 (1985): 338–45.

Ladson-Billings, Gloria. "Making Mathematics Meaningful in Multicultural Contexts." In *New Directions for Equity in Mathematics Education,* edited by Walter G. Secada, Elizabeth Fennema, and Lisa B. Adajian, pp. 126–45, New York: Cambridge University Press, 1995.

———. *The Dreamkeepers: Successful Teachers of African American Children.* San Francisco: Jossey-Bass Publishers, 1994.

Malloy, Carol. "Including African American Students in the Mathematics Community." In *Multicultural and Gender Equity in the Mathematics Classroom*, 1997 Yearbook of the National Council of Teachers of Mathematics, edited by Janet Trentacosta, pp. 23–33. Reston, Va.: National Council of Teachers of Mathematics, 1997.

Mullis, Ina V. S. *NAEP 1992 Mathematics Report Card for the Nation and the States*. Washington, D.C.: National Center for Education Statistics, 1993.

Oakes, Jeannie. "Opportunities, Achievement, and Choice: Women and Minority Students in Science and Mathematics." In *Review of Research in Education*, 16, edited by C. B. Cazden, pp. 153–222. Washington, D.C.: American Educational Research Association, 1990.

Reyes, Laurie Hart, and George M. Stanic. "Race, Sex, Socioeconomic Status, and Mathematics. *Journal for Research in Mathematics Education* 19 (January 1988): 26–43.

Rosenthal, Robert, and Lenore Jacobsen. *Pygmalion in the Classroom: Teacher Expectation and Pupil's Intellectual Development*. New York: Holt, Rinehart & Winston, 1968.

Rowser, Jacqueline F., and Trish Y. Koontz. "Inclusion of African American Students in Mathematics Classrooms: Issues of Style, Curriculum, and Expectations." *Mathematics Teacher* 88 (September 1995): 448–53.

Secada, Walter G. "Educational Equity versus Equality of Education: An Alternative Conception." In *Equity in Education*, edited by Walter G. Secada, pp. 68–88. London: Falmer Press, 1989.

———. "Race, Ethnicity, Social Class, Language, and Achievement in Mathematics." In *Handbook of Research on Mathematics Teaching and Learning*, edited by Douglas A. Grouws, pp. 623–60. New York: Macmillan, 1992.

Tribble, Israel. *Making Their Mark: Educating African-American Children*. Silver Spring, Md.: Beckham, 1992.

Veltman, Calvin J. *The Future of the Spanish Language in the United States*. Washington, D.C.: Hispanic Policy Development Project, 1988.

Reaching All Students Mathematically through Questioning

3

Dorothy Y. White

The role of communication in developing children's mathematical thinking has gained considerable attention in recent years (National Council of Teachers of Mathematics [NCTM] 1996). Mathematics teachers have been encouraged to initiate and orchestrate discourse by posing questions that elicit, engage, and challenge students' thinking; listen carefully to students' ideas; and ask students to clarify and justify their ideas orally and in writing (NCTM 1991). The underlying assumption is that classroom discourse allows teachers to stimulate students' thinking and reflect on students' understanding. By actively listening to students' ideas and suggestions, teachers demonstrate the value they place on the students' contributions (Davis 1997; Pirie 1996). Mathematics educators argue that the focus of teachers' questions should center on mathematical sense making and reasoning. More important, teachers should engage all students in the discourse by monitoring their participation in discussions and valuing their contributions to the class's thinking.

Engaging all students in classroom discussions has direct implications for equity in mathematics education. For example, the nature of the teacher's questions, whom she or he selects to respond to these questions, and whose answers are valued enough to warrant further investigation can impact student participation and achievement. For African American students, a better understanding of the role of discourse is imperative, since numerous studies have reported their poor academic performance in mathematics (NCTM 1997). Furthermore, there is evidence of a disproportionate number of African American students placed in low-tracked mathematics classes that are largely taught by teachers who use direct instruction, rely heavily on worksheets, and cover less of the curriculum (Oakes 1990). In contrast, high-track classes include more problem-solving tasks, more-experienced teachers, and a greater emphasis on developing students' competence and autonomous thinking. An equitable learning environment is one where all students are afforded an opportunity to learn mathematics, participate in mathematics lessons and discussions, and have their ideas valued and respected. Thus, if communication is essential to the learning of mathematics and equity is a central focus of the current reform movement, then we need to examine the nature and type of communication involved in classrooms of diverse student populations.

Unfortunately, the literature on mathematics teaching offers few models of pedagogy built on successful practice with African American students. However, as Ladson-Billings (1992, p. 115) suggests,

> [by providing] more anecdotal and ethnographic evidence of teachers who are experiencing academic success with urban and minority students, ... [and by] carefully examin[ing] aspects of these classrooms ... to determine what specific factor(s) or combination of factors are important in producing these successes ...

Engaging all students in classroom discussions has direct implications for equity in mathematics education.

The research reported in this material was supported by the National Science Foundation under Grant numbers MDR 8954652 and ESI 9454187. The opinions, conclusions, or recommendations expressed in these materials are those of the author and do not necessarily reflect the views of the National Science Foundation.

theoreticians can begin to construct models of teacher education that can better serve the variety of students that more and more teachers are likely to meet in the classroom.

In this paper, I will attempt to describe how one teacher transformed her classroom practices in order to meet the mathematical needs of all her students. In particular, I will examine how the teacher, as a result of her involvement in a teacher-enhancement program, used questioning and listening techniques as a means of exploring her students' mathematical content knowledge and engaging them in mathematics lessons.

THE CONTEXT

Ms. Tyler was a white first-year teacher who taught third grade in a large, urban school district just outside of Washington, D.C. She and her students were participants in a longitudinal research study entitled Project IMPACT (Increasing the Mathematical Power of All Children and Teachers). As a participant in Project IMPACT, Ms. Tyler took part in a twenty-two–day summer in-service program where current mathematics reform documents, findings from recent research related to teaching and learning mathematics from a constructivist perspective, and issues relating to equity and cultural diversity were addressed. For ten mornings during the summer in-service program, Ms. Tyler taught a small group of four to five students who were enrolled in summer school and had just completed third grade. Morning teaching sessions were followed by discussions about her teaching with project staff and with other third-grade teachers in her school.

During the school year following the summer in-service program, Ms. Tyler received academic support from an on-site Project IMPACT mathematics specialist. She also participated in weekly planning sessions with the mathematics specialist and the other third-grade teachers at the school. For more information on Project IMPACT, see Campbell and White (1997) and White (1997).

Setting the Stage: Before Project IMPACT

Ms. Tyler used a hands-on approach to teaching mathematics. She began her lessons by giving directions on an assigned task, followed by having students work on problems. Most mathematical tasks were in the form of a worksheet, where students used manipulative materials to solve problems. Students worked on tasks either individually, in small groups, or in pairs. Groups were mixed both racially and across gender. As students worked, Ms. Tyler walked around the room to monitor their progress and to answer questions. Once the students had completed their task, the class assembled as a large group to share their answers.

On the surface, Ms. Tyler seemed to follow the recommendations of the NCTM *Curriculum and Evaluation Standards* (1989) and *Professional Teaching Standards* (1991). She used centers, journals, and children's literature books to provide various contexts for children to explore mathematical concepts. She occasionally included open-ended tasks that were motivating and had more than one correct answer, and she always had manipulatives available for the students' use. However, a further examination of Ms. Tyler's mathematics class found that she rarely engaged students in the problem-solving process. Communication was usually in the form of the teacher asking a question and a student giving an answer. The focus of her questions was on the correct answer, which she accepted without question. That is, she did not investigate further to understand how her students arrived at their answers. Instead she assumed the correct answer implied correct thinking.

When Ms. Tyler did ask students to elaborate on their answers, it was usually when an answer was incomplete or incorrect. She wanted to make sure that all the students had the same answer and understood the procedures they were to follow. Ms. Tyler also asked open-ended questions for which there was more than one correct answer. For these questions, the intent was not to have students explore the various ways mathematics problems can be thought about and solved but rather to reinforce a mathematical skill.

Consider the following example where students recited the fractional part of a bag of goodies (Campbell and White 1997, p. 340). In the lesson, each child was given a bag of twelve pieces of assorted "goodies": pretzels, M&Ms, and wrapped candy. The number of goodies varied from bag to bag. Ms. Tyler asked an open-ended question to have the selected students name fractional parts of their bags.

T: What fractional part of your bag is pretzels? Everybody's won't be the same. What fractional part of your bag is pretzels, Janice?

Janice: Four-twelfths.

T: Yours is four-twelfths [*writes 4/12*]. April?

April: Six-twelfths.

T: Yours is six-twelfths [*writes 6/12*]. Rudy?

Rudy: Uhm three-fourths.

T: Three-fourths [*writes 3/4*].

Rudy: I mean one-fourth.

T: One-fourth?

Rudy: [*Nods yes*].

T: OK. One-fourth [*crosses out 3/4 and writes 1/4*]. So Rudy grouped his into four parts. Julio?

Julio: Four-twelfths.

T: Four-twelfths. Just like this one. Mikal?

Mikal: Six-sixths.

T: Six-sixths, six-sixths. That means that all, your whole bag is pretzels. Is that right?

Mikal: No, I have six pretzels.

T: You have six pretzels. OK, so six out of how many in all, Mikal? How many parts in your bag in all?

Mikal: Sixteen.

T: Six are pretzels, that's the top number.

Mikal: Six out of twelve.

T: Good. So six-twelfths is pretzels.

Notice that Ms. Tyler did not ask students to explain their correct answers and, in some cases, would assume a student's thinking. For example, in the exchange with Rudy, Ms. Tyler interpreted the students' thinking. She did not ask Rudy to explain; instead, she explained how she wanted the class to think about the problem. When a student was incorrect, as in the case of Mikal, Ms. Tyler led him to the correct answer through her questioning. The example above was typical of the types of questions Ms. Tyler posed during mathematics instruction.

Eighty-five percent of Ms. Tyler's questions were answered by volunteers. Ms. Tyler was fair in her selection of students across both gender and race. There were twenty-two students enrolled in Ms. Tyler's mathematics class with the following racial composition: 55 percent African American, 18 percent Hispanic, and 27 percent white. With the exception of the one Hispanic female student,

Ms. Tyler made sure all students were selected to respond to her questions. However, all of Ms. Tyler's questions required students only to recall mathematical facts, procedures, or definitions or to count manipulative materials. None of the questions required the students to engage in independent thought or reflection. Thus, although all students were treated equally, no student was exposed to genuine mathematical problem solving and exploration.

Learning New Approaches: Project IMPACT Summer In-Service Program

Ms. Tyler welcomed the opportunity to learn and try out new approaches to teaching mathematics with children enrolled in summer school. She found that working with colleagues to solve adult mathematics problems gave her an insight into the many different ways to solve problems and an understanding of how the children in her class feel when they solve problems as a group. She also recognized the importance of the classroom climate in fostering students' participation and thinking.

The recommendations for teaching that were discussed from a constructivist perspective made a lot of sense to Ms. Tyler. She believed in the importance of viewing mathematics from various perspectives and the teacher's role in helping students construct their own mathematical knowledge. However, as Ms. Tyler attempted to implement the recommendations, she was faced with frustration. She began to realize there is a fine line between when to continue questioning and when to proceed with the lesson. However, by the end of the summer, Ms. Tyler realized that change takes time. "I can see that *over time* is when the good results will come next year. It's necessarily day-by-day successes. It's a process just as writing and reading is, and I can see that." More important, Ms. Tyler realized the importance of questioning not only in improving students' mathematical content knowledge but also in providing a classroom environment where children are comfortable to think and share their ideas and thoughts.

Implementing Change

The academic year following the summer in-service program found that Ms. Tyler had maintained several aspects of her former mathematics teaching. She continued to encourage students to use manipulative materials as they solved problems and explored mathematical concepts. She provided several contexts in which students might explore mathematical ideas and continued to mix students into groups across gender, race, and now across ability.

What did change, however, is how Ms. Tyler approached the teaching of mathematics. Rather than give students directions to follow, Ms. Tyler began her lessons by asking the class what they noticed about a particular problem and how they would solve it. During mathematics lessons, Ms. Tyler assumed the role of facilitator. She led the class in the problem-solving process but wanted students to solve problems in their own way. Once students were assigned to work on problems, Ms. Tyler walked around the room to monitor their progress and to answer questions. As in the previous year, student groups were mixed across gender and race; however, in this academic year, Ms. Tyler often changed the groupings of children depending on the mathematical topic. As she explains, "[The groups] are always different because, from the whole group, you really see what their strengths and weaknesses are on a given topic." Halfway through small-group work, Ms. Tyler stopped the class for students to share their solutions, strategies, and progress. Small-group work was then followed by whole-class sharing.

Rather than give students directions to follow, Ms. Tyler began her lessons by asking the class what they noticed about a particular problem and how they would solve it.

The most noticeable change was in the focus and content of Ms. Tyler's questions. The majority of her questions focused on the student's thinking process, not the correct answer. Most of her questions were open-ended and allowed for multiple answers and solution paths. She expected students to share their answers and how they arrived at them as well as to evaluate the answers of others. Moreover, she expected students to explain their answers and to listen to the ideas of others. In her words, "We need to listen and pay attention to each other so we can learn from each other."

Three vignettes are presented below to explore Ms. Tyler's change in questioning patterns. The vignettes are centered on three themes: (1) exploring students' answers, (2) incorporating students' background knowledge, and (3) encouraging student-student communication. For each vignette, a brief explanation of the question focus and the importance of the question with regard to the mathematical content and student learning are presented.

Exploring Students' Answers

Ms. Tyler's main focus in asking questions was to explore how students arrived at their answers. She focused more on students' thinking and their various solution strategies and less on the correct answer than she had in the previous year. She found that by asking students to explain their answers she not only learned how they thought about answers but also provided the other students with various ways to think about and solve problems. Consider the following example where students shared how they measured items in the classroom (Campbell and White 1997, p. 341). The question was open-ended, since students could use various ways to solve the problem. Here, Ms. Tyler was not concerned with the correct computational answer but rather with the different ways students went about the measurement process.

T: How did you do the measuring? People keep saying "I measured, I measured, I took it" and what's *it* and how did you actually do the measuring, Timothy?

Timothy: Uhm, me and Todd, uhm, put the rings, uhm, uhm, around one side, which was 23 for the short part.

T: So you put 23 links for the short part.

Timothy: And added 23 to 23, because it would be the same as the other side.

T: So this side's the same as this side [*points to long and short sides of desk*]?

Timothy: No, the other side.

T: You mean the opposite side over here? This side is the same as this over here [*points to two short sides*]?

Timothy: Uh huh.

T: Oh, so you didn't need to measure both sides, because you knew it was the same; how did you know it was exactly the same?

Timothy: Because it wouldn't be a rectangle if it was different.

T: Oh, so you knew that this is a rectangle. You looked to see that the top of my desk was a rectangle. You measured one side because you knew that the opposite sides were the same length?

Timothy: Uh huh. And the other one was, uhm, side was 44, and I added 44 to 44.

T: So you measured the short side and added two short sides together.

Timothy: I got 20, 46 for the short sides, and I got 88 for the other sides.

T: And then you added the two longer sides together. OK, so you have 88 and?

Timothy: Twenty-six, I mean 46.

T: And 46.

Timothy: Which was 154.

T: So then, how did you get 154?

Timothy: I added the 88 and 46 together.

T: And why did you add 88 and 46 together?

Timothy: Because it would be around, the top of the desk.

T: So you added all the sides together, to get 154. And that, that, that's how many links went across, around the top, of my desk, without measuring all around, so that's one way of doing the measuring. Really good thinking…. Uh hum. Did anyone else measure the desk in a different way? One person measured, took a whole chain and counted one by one. Other people added up sides, but only measured two sides, the long and the short side. Hilary?

Hilary: I measured around the sides but it wasn't quite even….

T: So you had one long chain around the top, and you were going to count by fives.

Hilary: We were going to break it up into fives, and then count each one, group of five.

T: Group of five, OK. Did you think, why were you going to count by fives?

Hilary: Uh, we, because we have, uhm, up to like, uhm, 100 to count very quickly. So counting by fives is quicker and we could count as much as we could five, and take it off and put it back.

T: So you thought it would be quicker, OK. And so, so did your partner?

Hilary: [*Nods yes*]

In the example above, Ms. Tyler wanted students to share the different ways they solved the problem. She intentionally asked follow-up questions to interpret students' understanding of mathematical concepts and to ascertain any misconceptions. This was illustrated in her response to Timothy when she pointed to the adjacent sides instead of the opposite sides of the desk. By asking such questions, Ms. Tyler made sure she understood the students' reasoning, and she had the opportunity to introduce and reinforce mathematical vocabulary. In addition, having students elaborate on their answers provided the other students with a clear interpretation of the solution as well as options for solving and thinking about mathematics problems.

Incorporating Students' Background Knowledge

Ms. Tyler wanted her students to make sense of mathematical ideas, so she included more cognitively demanding questions in her teaching. Questions where students had to analyze and interpret information on the basis of their prior knowledge and experiences or to make conjectures and predictions about new mathematical ideas by exploring the underlying concepts are considered cognitively demanding. The following example illustrates how Ms. Tyler wanted her students to use their background knowledge to solve a problem. In this example, she asked the class to think of a name for a shape made with five tiles known as a *pentomino*. Ms. Tyler had told the students the name *triominos* for three tiles, and the students had discussed how the "tri" stands for "three." Ms. Tyler asked them to use the information to help answer the question for five tiles and wanted the class to explain why their answers made sense.

T:	What might we call, what do you think we might call five squares together? [*Shows five squares in a row*] ... Tammy? Well, what do you think it will have in it? ... Hum?
Tammy:	(inaudible)
T:	Uh hum, so what does that tell you about this here?
Tammy:	Something that means the word *five.*
T:	Something that means the word five. Anything else?
Tammy:	*Nos* at the end.
T:	Nos at the end, OK.... OK. Dennis, what, give Tammy a hand. She thinks that it's gonna be a word that means *five,* and it's going to have *nos* at the end. What are you thinking? Tell us what you're thinking.
Dennis:	Fifthominos.
T:	Fifthominos. And tell me how you got that.
Dennis:	Well, the fifth is like, uhm, five, and the three was triominos, so the five would be fifthominos.
T:	Fifthominos, so you think that definitely, as with all the other words, there would be an *ominos*. And I like your idea about fifth. There is another word for five. Besides fifth, so that's a good clue. What would they call, if it were fifthominos, what would they call the one with four?
Dennis:	Fourthominos.
T:	Uh hum, and what would they call the one with three?
Dennis:	Thirdominos.
T:	Thirdominos. Would that be in the same pattern?
Dennis:	Yeah.
T:	It would be. Does fifth follow the pattern that they've started here?
Dennis:	[*Shakes head no*]
T:	No, it doesn't, but that's a good idea. Lucas, what's?
Hilary:	Maybe it begins with a *T.*
T:	Maybe it begins with a *T* like the other two. Lucas, what do you think?
Lucas:	Uhm, maybe it's like five, you know when you have five children.
T:	Uh hum.
Lucas:	Like quintuplets, yeah, so quintominos.
T:	Quintominos. It certainly could be. These are not called quintominos. Let me, they're actually *pent-ominos.* And "pent" means "five."

In the example above, Ms. Tyler's follow-up questions were asked to have a student extend his knowledge by making conjectures about a pattern. By asking Dennis to give the various names for other shapes according to his theory, she valued his line of thought and helped him see how his conjectures did not fit. For all the students' responses, Ms. Tyler respected the students' mathematical reasoning, although the answers were not correct. The example also illustrates the fine line between when to continue questioning and when to tell students the answer. In this example, Ms. Tyler opted to tell the answer after some students had shared. One could argue that she should have continued the same line of questioning with Lucas as she did with Dennis. However, in the interest of time, she opted to tell the answer in order to proceed with the lesson. Often teachers are faced with this dilemma; what is important is that the students' answers were valued for their mathematical soundness and not dismissed.

She expected students to explain their answers and suggestions.

Encouraging Student-Student Interactions

Ms. Tyler also wanted her students to judge the correctness of the different answers and strategies that were offered. Questions such as "How many people agree or disagree?" and "Why do you agree or disagree?" were indicative of the type of questions she posed to have students judge the correctness of answers. She wanted the students to be responsible for judging the answers and ideas of others and did not assume the role of mathematical judge and jury. At the same time, she expected students to explain their answers and suggestions. Consider the following example where the students worked on fact families. One student had just answered a story problem and arrived at the corresponding number sentence $18 - 8 = 10$. In this example, she wanted the students to name the different fact families for the initial equation.

T: Are there, is there another way to move around the numbers, and it'll still go with the story?... Tammy?

Tammy: Ten minus 8.

T: So if I'm using all ...

Tammy: No, no ...

T: I saw Dennis's hand go up and then come down. I saw Benita's hand go up and then come down. Tell me what you're thinking, Dennis.

Dennis: Uhm, there's, there's one more to do, 10 plus 8.

T: Oh, OK. If you want to switch around your, uhm, addition, 10 plus 8 equals 18 [*writes* $10 + 8 = 18$]. All right ...

.
.
.

Dennis: Eighteen equals 8 plus 10.

T: What was that? What was that?

Dennis: Eighteen equals 10 plus 8.

T: [*Writes* $18 = 10 + 8$.] Does that work?

Some: Yes.

T: All right. Sarah?

Sarah: Eighteen equals 8 plus 10.

T: [*Writes* $18 = 8 + 10$.] Eighteen equals 8 plus 10.... Mitch?

Mitch: Eight, uhm, equals 18 minus 10.

T: Eight equals 18 minus 10 [*writes* $8 = 18 - 10$]....

.
.
.

Sarah: I disagree with that answer [*points to* $8 = 18 - 10$].

T: What?

Sarah: You can't do that because you can't take, you can't take 18 away from 10.

T: Is he taking 18 away from 10?

Sarah: Uh huh.

Some: No.

Sarah: Yeah, cause it's backwards. He says, if you flip it over, you can't take 10 away from 18. I mean you can't take 18 away from 10. The 18 and the 10....

T: So you're saying this [*writes* $8 = 18 - 10$] is the same as this [*writes* $10 - 18 = 8$]?

Sarah: Uh huh.

T: What do you have to say, Mitch? Sarah is, Sarah is questioning your, your number sentence. Do you agree with her? Do you disagree? Do you have a reason why you say this does work?

Mitch: The answer is 18, but if you flip it over, it doesn't make sense. It just looks backwards, if the 18 is really behind the 10.

Some: I don't know what she's talking about.

T: Sarah's saying, uhm, this is saying 8 equals 18 minus 10. This is saying 8 equals 10 minus 18.

Mitch: It doesn't make sense. If, if you twist it around, then it, then it, if you turn it around, then it makes, doesn't make sense, because you can't take 18 away from 10.

T: Well, the trickiest thing about number sentences is that this is the part [*circles* 18 – 10 *and* 10 – 18] that we're really looking at. The answer actually can go on either side of the number sentence, even though we don't often see it this way, sometimes we will. This is, take a look at this, just this part, 18 minus 10, and the 10 minus 18. Do you think they are the same, or do you think they are different? Just, just this part, forgetting that the answer is there.

Mitch: They're the same, but they're different. And what we were talking about over here is that you can't take a bigger number away from a smaller number.

T: Is, are you subtracting a bigger number from a smaller number here?

Mitch: Yeah.

T: Philip, can you say what you're saying out loud, please?

Philip: Uhm, it, I know what, I think I know what Sarah is trying to say, uhm, the problem isn't totally turned around, it's just the answer is.

T: All right, so Sarah would be right if it was totally turned around. If all the number was the exact flip. So if it was 8 equals 10 minus 18, that's totally turned around and would not work, because then you would be taking a bigger number from a smaller number? Is that what you're saying? But here, it's just that the answer is moved around but, but the problem part is staying the same. Well, no, this one. So this [*points to* 8 = 18 – 10] is the same as this [*writes* 18 – 10 = 8], only the answer is moved? Is that what you're saying?

Philip: [*Nods yes.*]

T: Do you agree with that?

Sarah: Yes.

T: You have to look so carefully, always, because some things like that you have to say, wait a minute, is this not working, or is it just moved around in a different way?

A common misconception regarding the equal sign is that equations must be written on the left and answers on the right. In this example, Sarah's disagreement may be based on her misconception about the equal sign for subtraction problems. Ms. Tyler did not assume the role of authority in verifying students' answers; rather, she posed the problem back to Mitch to have him explain his answer and whether he agreed with Sarah's comment. When Mitch was unable to respond and seemed confused, Ms. Tyler noted Philip's comment and encouraged him to add to the discussion. Once Philip offered his explanation, Ms. Tyler returned to Sarah to see whether she agreed with Philip's assertion.

The importance of this exchange is Ms. Tyler valued the students' right to disagree and be confused and encouraged others to participate to form a consensus. She wanted her students to accept (reject) answers freely and talk to one another before accepting the correct answer.

Summary of Changes

The changes in Ms. Tyler's teaching were most evident in the questions she posed and the way she selected students. In the previous year, Ms. Tyler was more concerned that all students had the correct answer and followed along. She often assumed that the answer as well as the thinking was correct and rarely asked students to speak to one another. In contrast, during Project IMPACT, Ms. Tyler expected students to explain their answers and focused more on finding out what her students knew than on what she wanted them to know. She found that by asking more-challenging questions, she not only reinforced mathematical skills but extended the students' mathematical thinking.

Ms. Tyler's selection of students did not change; she continued to select the majority of her students from volunteers. What did change was an increase in the number of students who offered to answer. In Ms. Tyler's class, students of all racial, gender, and academic backgrounds were called on to answer questions. There were twenty-seven students enrolled in her mathematics class, 48 percent African American and 52 percent white. Again, Ms. Tyler made sure that all students participated in class discussions; however, during Project IMPACT she approached her selection of students differently. As she explains,

> I'm very methodical in my head, "OK, well, I've heard from this person." Sometimes, I call on children who, like if it's a general question, I'll call on children that would be most likely … like "what do you notice about this?" I call on the children first that would be most likely not to figure out the really in-depth things, so that they can offer something. Because it's … I found that if I wait, if I call on the children who are gonna pick up the really complicated things first, then the other kids won't say anything.

Ms. Tyler also recognized that all students needed an opportunity to share their thoughts and ideas, and by examining the students' strengths and weaknesses, she afforded more opportunities for her students to do so. By asking students to explain their answers, Ms. Tyler found that she needed to alternate her instructional grouping practices to meet the needs of her students.

CONCLUSION

The aim of this paper was to describe how Ms. Tyler changed her classroom practices to meet the needs of all her students. The examples presented are not all inclusive; rather, they highlight the change in the focus and type of questions Ms. Tyler posed during mathematics instruction. The examples were also presented to illustrate the power of questioning in understanding and extending students' mathematical thinking. By expecting all students to explain their answers and make sense of their ideas as well as the ideas of others, teachers communicate the idea that they value every student's mathematical thinking.

Developing good questioning techniques and reaching all students is by no means an easy task. The change in Ms. Tyler's questioning techniques were gradual and developed over time. She began by realizing the importance of questioning and making a commitment to follow each student's answer by asking him or her to explain his or her thinking. Once she felt comfortable accepting students' various answers and solution strategies, she was able to ask more-challenging questions and adjust her instruction accordingly.

The realities of many schools may make the changes in Ms. Tyler's teaching seem unrealistic for most mathematics teachers. However, there are some guiding principles that can be used by any teacher at any school:

1. *Become a reflective teacher.* Ms. Tyler made a conscious effort to reflect on her teaching and highlight areas of strength and weakness. By keeping a journal and taking note of students who participate in class discussions, teachers can begin to identify areas that need work and those areas that work well.

2. *Engage in active questioning and listening.* Ms. Tyler decided to first focus on asking students to explain their answers and solution strategies. In doing so, she realized areas of strength in her students. She also made decisions to include all students and to monitor their willingness to participate in lessons. As a result, she carefully selected the order in which students shared their thoughts and adjusted her groups and lessons accordingly. By striving for group consensus and participation, teachers can increase students' participation and feelings of success.

3. *Open the lines of communication.* The ability to share her frustrations, triumphs, and disappointments made change possible for Ms. Tyler. She found by sharing with her peers that she was not alone and that others were struggling with the same issues. Together she and her colleagues were able to devise solution paths. With today's technological advances, such as e-mail, teachers can open lines of communications with teachers in their own schools and in other schools. Most schools have interschool mailing systems at no cost. These vehicles should be used to help ease the stress and inevitable frustrations that accompany change.

Asking challenging questions and listening to students' answers and solution strategies are not enough to bring about change in students' mathematical content knowledge. It is also necessary to interpret students' responses as indicators of their levels of understanding and to adjust instructional practices accordingly. Reaching all students through communication requires that students' ideas be encouraged, valued, and used to shape instruction. All students, and African American students in particular, need opportunities to solve problems on their own and share their solutions with peers and teachers.

Developing good questioning techniques and reaching all students is by no means an easy task.

REFERENCES

Campbell, Patricia F., and Dorothy Y. White. "Project IMPACT: Influencing and Supporting Teacher Change in Predominately Minority Schools." In *Mathematics Teachers in Transistion*, edited by Elizabeth Fennema and Barbara Scott Nelson, pp. 309–55. Mahwah, N.J.: Lawrence Erlbaum, 1997.

Davis, Brent. "Listening for Differences: An Evolving Conception of Mathematics Teaching." *Journal for Research in Mathematics Education* 28 (May 1997): 355–76.

Ladson-Billings, Gloria. "Culturally Relevant Teaching: The Key to Making Multicultural Education Work." In *Research and Multicultural Education: From the Margins to the Mainstream*, edited by Carl A. Grant, pp. 106–21. Bristol, Pa.: Falmer Press, 1992.

National Council of Teachers of Mathematics. *Communication in Mathematics: K–12 and Beyond.* 1996 Yearbook of the National Council of Teachers of Mathematics, edited by Portia C. Elliott. Reston, Va.: National Council of Teachers of Mathematics, 1996.

———. *Curriculum and Evaluation Standards for School Mathematics.* Reston, Va.: National Council of Teachers of Mathematics, 1989.

———. *Multicultural and Gender Equity in the Mathematics Classroom: The Gift of Diversity.* 1997 Yearbook of the National Council of Teachers of Mathematics, edited by Janet Trentacosta. Reston, Va.: National Council of Teachers of Mathematics, 1997.

———. *Professional Standards for Teaching Mathematics.* Reston, Va.: National Council of Teachers of Mathematics, 1991.

Oakes, Jeannie. *Multiplying Inequities: The Effects of Race, Social Class, and Tracking on Opportunities to Learn Mathematics and Science.* Santa Monica, Calif.: Rand Corp., 1990.

Pirie, Susan E. B. "Is Anybody Listening?" In *Communication in Mathematics: K–12 and Beyond,* 1996 Yearbook of the National Council of Teachers of Mathematics, edited by Portia C. Elliott, pp. 105–15. Reston, Va.: National Council of Teachers of Mathematics, 1996.

White, Dorothy Y. "The Mathematics Classroom Question and Response Patterns of Third-Grade Teachers in High-Minority Population Schools." Doctoral diss., University of Maryland at College Park, 1997, *Dissertation Abstracts International* 58-09A (1997): 3451.

A High Level of Challenge in a Collaborative Setting

Enhancing the Chance of Success for African American Students in Mathematics

4

Rosalie A. Dance
Karen H. Wingfield
Neil Davidson

... the mathematics classroom is one of the most segregated places in America.
—Lee Stiff
"African-American Students and the Promise of
the *Curriculum and Evaluation Standards*"

Only those who have already experienced a revolution within themselves can reach out effectively to help others.

—Malcolm X

A revolution in the mathematics classrooms of this nation has the potential to right inequities in American society that have stood for generations. Knowledge of mathematics is empowering. It gives access to mathematically dependent professions and provides a theoretical foundation for other professions; furthermore, the status accorded to those who know mathematics is empowering. Inequity in the mathematics classrooms of this nation is a pervasive problem. A high school we visited in a suburb of Washington, D.C., offered an illustrative example: with an almost 1:1:1:1 mix of black, white, Hispanic, and Asian students, not one black or Hispanic student was enrolled in precalculus or calculus. Our schools have changed since 1954 and *Brown v. Board of Education of Topeka;* generally, our mathematics classrooms have not.

In this article, we describe a classroom of predominantly African American students in an inner-city public high school that might provide a model for change to increase the participation of African American students in advanced mathematics. This classroom example suggests that implementing reform based on the vision of the *Curriculum and Evaluation Standards for School Mathematics* (NCTM 1989) and building on that vision to create challenging collaborative learning environments where students learn real mathematics and solve real problems in the context of issues that matter creates an environment in which African American students can thrive mathematically. A key factor in the culture of the observed classroom corroborates Davidson's (1990a) suggestion that fostering students' ability and talent for communication in mathematics classrooms can enhance mathematics achievement.

> **Knowledge of mathematics is empowering. It gives access to mathematically dependent professions and provides a theoretical foundation for other professions; furthermore, the status accorded to those who know mathematics is empowering.**

The authors would like to thank the students who participated in this study for the superb assistance they gave us. We would also like to acknowledge and thank Olivia Saracho for her guidance and support in the methodology and technology for the conduct of the study.

Challenge in a Collaborative Setting at the University Level

One of the most pertinent educational experiments of our time was Uri Treisman's project at Berkeley (Treisman 1992; Fullilove and Treisman 1990), now being emulated in university mathematics departments across the country. The University of California at Berkeley had a history like that of so many colleges and universities; black and Hispanic students entered the university, enrolled in calculus, and failed it in much higher proportions than other students. The mathematics faculty initially hypothesized that minority students' failure was due to the following factors: low income, low motivation, poor academic preparation, and lack of family support. A similar list might have been generated by well-intentioned mathematics educators around this nation. But note: *these are all factors over which educators have no control.* If these are causal factors, then we are relieved of responsibility; there is very little we can do.

Treisman gathered evidence that contradicted the initial hypotheses. He found that Berkeley's black calculus students had *high* motivation, strong family support, and excellent high school academic preparation. And he found that these students spent a *lot* of time alone in their rooms studying calculus.

Seeking understanding, Treisman also studied Berkeley's Chinese students, who, as a group, had the lowest failure rate among the university's freshman calculus students. The significant difference Treisman found between the two groups lay in the way they studied, not in their level of income, motivation, academic preparation, or family support. The Chinese students organized "study gangs" for collaborative problem solving. Their private study was intended to prepare them for their collaborative sessions. These study gangs became the model for the Honors Workshops at Berkeley.

The Honors Workshop model for minority students in elementary calculus has now been successfully replicated on many campuses. The Honors Workshops look like experiments in collaborative learning, and indeed they are; but the nonstandard problems that are used in the workshops, more challenging than problems given in a standard course, are a critical factor. Students in the workshops demonstrate an intensity and an enthusiasm that would warm the heart of any mathematics teacher. Treisman attributed the enthusiastic interchange that takes place in the workshops to students' real interest in the problems. The model of students working together on challenging calculus problems at universities informed our work at the secondary level in a public high school.

Participation in Mathematics at the Precollege Level

Susan Gross (1988) studied the participation and performance of women and minorities in mathematics in a large public school system in an affluent county in which student academic success is above average. She found the following:

1. No evidence of racial or ethnic difference in mathematics achievement appeared in kindergarten or grade 1. Differences emerged by second grade and widened thereafter.
2. Black parents expressed the strongest desire of any parent group for students to study mathematics. They sensed a lack of support from school and teachers. Black students who took advanced mathematics courses credited their parents, not their teachers, with giving them the support they needed. Teachers thought that one of the black students' weaknesses was a lack of family support!

3. Black students in advanced mathematics courses felt isolated and "token." Only 3 percent of eligible black or Hispanic students enrolled in advanced mathematics in spite of their eligibility; counselors and teachers persuaded them they would have difficulty. Teacher responses to the researcher's questions corroborated students' beliefs; they *did* see the students as tokens and as having low ability.

4. Secondary school mathematics teachers demonstrated inadequate nurturance of minority students.

5. Secondary school teachers demonstrated insensitivity to racial stereotyping with regard to mathematical ability.

Ramifications of the Treisman and Gross Studies

Gross's findings suggest that we need to effect changes within us, changes in our way of seeing and in our expectations. Treisman's model and the subsequent work in university calculus courses have illustrated the potential of a high level of challenge in a collaborative environment; the success of cooperative learning environments in mathematics at the precollege level has also been well documented (Davidson 1990b). As teachers observe their students in intense and enthusiastic interaction solving challenging problems, respect for the process grows and nurturance of students' ways of learning becomes a priority. A high level of mathematical challenge in a cooperative and collaborative environment can provide a foundation for a solution to inequity in mathematics education at the secondary school level.

IN A MATHEMATICS CLASSROOM: CHALLENGE AND A SENSE OF COMMUNITY

We studied the culture of one mathematics classroom in a predominantly African American inner-city public high school, seeking patterns that might indicate ways to build an educational environment to support African American students in their mathematics learning (Dance 1997). We call the school-within-a-school where the classroom was located "Drew High School," which is not its name. Data were collected through the observation and videotaping of class sessions approximately once a week for most of an academic year and through interviews with the teacher and several students.

The students were ninth and tenth graders in an integrated mathematics course. The mathematics program at Drew had a history of student persistence in the study of mathematics through high school and beyond. Most of the students in the school were African American. The teacher was experienced and respected; she had taught in the program for several years. Were there influential factors within the culture of the mathematics classrooms in this program that differed from mathematics classrooms elsewhere? We found two significant factors that we believe merit further study. The first factor we term a *sense of community* within the classroom; the second, an *atmosphere of challenge*. The bridge between these two factors was composed of the patterns of interaction among members of the classroom community and the quality of communication among them.

A Sense of Community

The sense of community within the mathematics classroom that was the focus of our study was characterized by mutual respect among members of the community (teacher and students) and by a pleasure in one another's successes. Students helped each other as they worked in small groups, and their interactions were supported by the teacher's clear respect for students' mathematical ideas. In whole-class discussion, students' contributions were highly valued.

Students helped each other as they worked in small groups, and their interactions were supported by the teacher's clear respect for students' mathematical ideas.

35

The interaction patterns during whole-class discussion were nontraditional. In most traditional classroom discussions, both turns and topics are carefully controlled by the teacher; furthermore, students' remarks are nearly always addressed to the teacher with the teacher's response serving as an evaluation of the student's contribution (Edwards and Westgate 1987). In the mathematics classroom we studied, the topics of discussion focused on the activities provided by the teacher, but the teacher did not appear to try to control the direction of active discussion. Students' remarks were frequently addressed to other students, and responses to their remarks came from students without first being evaluated by the teacher. This mode of interaction placed some control in the hands of the students. The teacher was an active participant in the class discussions; she knew what she wanted the students to learn and made sure that they got from the discussion what they needed, but it was not important to her that the information should come from her. Students' mutual respect for one another's mathematical thinking allowed this process to work.

The following is taken from a transcript of the class in mid-September during an activity to develop students' understanding of algebraic structures. This whole-class discussion illustrates the teacher's practice leading to an early development of a sense of community and an atmosphere of challenge.

A student has just stated the associative law of addition symbolically, and the teacher has written it on the board.

T: [*Pointing*] What are these symbols?

S1:   Parentheses.

S2:   Grouping symbols.

S3:   They tell you what to do first.

S1:   You work inside the parentheses first.

T: [*After a pause*] What do a, b, and c stand for?

S4:   Numbers.

S3:   They are variables, like x.

S5:   They can be anything you need.

T: They represent any numbers *in the set you are working with.* What if we had … instead of …? [*She wrote "×" and "+" on the transparency.*]

S2:   It would still work.

Several students: It would be right.

S6:   Even for subtraction....

S6:   [*After a pause during which she has been writing*] Oh, no! Sorry.

S5:   Isn't it?

T: [*As she writes this example on the board*] What is $3 - (5 - 4)$?

S6:   Three minus one.

S8:   Now try bracket 3 minus 5 bracket take away 4.

T: [*Writing what student said*]: What is $(3 - 5) - 4$?

S7:   Negative two take away four.

S1:   One equals ...

S6:   Negative six.

S5:   Do another one.

S2 gets up and writes on the board: $(9 - 8) - 7 \neq 9 - (8 - 7)$ [*students did not need permission to go to the board*].

The students talk in small groups as they calculate. There are nonverbal expressions of satisfaction; some students look surprised.

T: Are there other operations that associativity works for?

Many students say "no"; some say nothing. One student, J, says it works for division and restates this opinion with conviction when others say division is not associative. For about four minutes, students show him and one another numerical evidence, communicating within groups. Eventually, most students seem to agree that division is not associative; the teacher is aware that J, at least, remains unconvinced.

T: J is not convinced it won't work for division. Let's try some examples.

She writes, representing the majority view: $12 \div (8 \div 2) \neq (12 \div 8) \div 2$.

J: Twelve divided by four …
S4:   Is not equal.… Hmm.
S1:   Three over two divided by two. (Right side.)
S8:   What is that?
S9:   Three.
S10:   Three-fourths.
S3:   [*Showing puzzlement*] Three equals three. Three is not equal to three.
S1:   [*After a pause*] Three-fourths. Three doesn't equal to three-fourths.

The teacher has written results as students have stated them. Now she writes: $3 \neq 3/4$. She discusses the process errors that led some students to get 3 on the right-hand side. Students who had made errors in the division reworked their calculation.

S11:   I got it.
S3:   Okay.

J looks comfortable.

T: [*Concludes*] So we don't expect associativity to work for division. [*She looks at J, who nods agreement.*] Now are you also going to be able to convince yourself that associativity doesn't hold for subtraction?

[*Students say they have examples.*]

The teacher's self-restraint in this discussion was characteristic. She did not exhibit a need to do all the teaching. Students developed the meaning of the parentheses. She extended students' concept of the use of variables a little. She took advantage of a student's comment about subtraction and offered an example; her example included practice with signed numbers. She was pleased to let a student provide the next example and did not contribute to the discussion of it. She let students develop the division result. She recognized that at least one student was unconvinced by his group's work, and she provided an example, including practice with fractions, for all to work together. She let students work through it and announce results without speaking herself. The arithmetic processes were clarified without any overtones of "remediation." She accepted students' contributions to the discussion with an air of respect for their ability to think mathematically.

Indicators of a sense of community

As an aid to studying the presence of a sense of community in the classroom, we used a modified version of Scott Peck's (1987) descriptive indicators of community. We looked for, and found, indications of (1) inclusivity and commitment to membership; (2) consensus based on mutual respect; (3) respect for and encouragement of individuality; (4) realistic expectation of more than one "right" way to do things; (5) awareness of the community; (6) safety—a safe place to learn and to try out ideas; (7) ability to disagree gracefully; (8) leadership open to all members; and (9) a spirit of love and peace.

The transcript above offers an illustration of the spirit in this classroom community. *Mutual respect* for one another's mathematical thinking was apparent in this early discussion and was able to grow because of discussions like this. It was *safe* to disagree and *safe* to make an error. It was also safe to make an intelligent contribution to the discussion without fear of opprobrium. More than one student took *leadership* roles for short periods in this discussion; leadership was not "owned" by anyone.

There were many indications that students felt *committed to membership* in this community. Nevertheless, outside pressure sometimes resulted in a student's gradual disappearance from class. Other students' concern demonstrated the sense of *inclusivity* and the *spirit of love* in the community. The following passage from the transcript of an interview with Tamika illustrates one student's thoughts and feelings about this sensitive issue.

Interviewer: Among Drew students, when someone is not doing well, for instance, not coming to school or hanging out in the halls, is there a feeling among the rest of you that you should try to do something about that?

Tamika: We might have a person like that in Drew. And there are times like that. And if a teacher sees that, they'll want to conversate with them, see if they're having any family problems or whatever. And you know, when you see that, you feel a little empty place or something because the person is not in the class.... And then it goes on, day after day. You'll start to worry about that person. That does happen.... Students usually know about it before the teachers. Everybody notices, and everybody cares. If you see the person, you say, "Oh, you decided to come to school today." They might just come a certain part of the day, usually in the evening. And you tell them they need to come to school. They say, "Oh, I'll be there, I'm coming." But they don't, and that's even worse; you not telling the truth.

The safety issue. The mathematics teacher in this classroom recognized that it was difficult for students to ask for help when they failed to understand something. To build a sense of safety and mutual respect in the community, she made a conscious effort to model appropriate behavior in this regard. She openly acknowledged errors she made and corrected them. If a student pointed out an error or asked a question that brought an error to her attention, she was sincere in her thanks. She believed that students could be persuaded to feel as proud of asking a question as of providing an answer, and she endeavored to make it so.

Students received useful rewards for good work (new pencils and "late tickets" for a homework assignment were favorites) and expressed pride when they received these rewards. We have been told of students who try to hide their academic successes, in some cases to avoid the epithet of "acting white" (see Fordham and Ogbu [1986]). We did not see such secretiveness in the classroom we studied. Students shared their successes exuberantly, and the response from classmates was positive. This may have resulted from the strong sense of community that evolved in this classroom. Any suggestion that the students were not acting black would surely have been erroneous; no such suggestion was ever made in this classroom.

Respect for individuality. When students worked on group assignments, they effectively reached consensus on the presentation of their group results. However, much of their work was to be seen as the individual's accomplishment, not the group's; thus, they worked together and discussed the problems, but they handed in their own individual solutions. In spite of this collaboration, there was a surprising diversity of methods within small groups. The teacher's demonstrated interest in student approaches to problems that differed from her own encouraged students' individuality. Students demonstrated interest in others' approaches to a problem, but they did not give up their individual ideas as a result of the exchange. Tamika commented on this in an interview:

Interviewer: Now, in class most of the time you are working in a group together. Tell me how that works for you.

Tamika: Probably you learn to work better with others. Being cooperative. And maybe you can help other people with something they don't understand. Or maybe they'll help *you* with a problem you don't understand. You learn their point of view about how to do the problem, not just this is right, this is wrong; you might learn another way of solving the problem.

Interviewer: So you see it that way? That sometimes there is more than one right way?

Tamika: Yes. There might be an easier way, or maybe a longer method, or … or just different.

Interviewer: When your group does something like that, do you try to determine which way of doing the problem is better?

Tamika: If I'm not sure about the problem, if I get it right my way, maybe a group member in my group might say, "You coulda did it this way." Or I might say to somebody else, how did you do this problem?

Interviewer: Even though you have it right?

Tamika: Yes.

Interviewer: And you might do that for someone else, too? You might look at their paper and say, "Look, here's another way you could do that"?

Tamika: Yes. But we don't usually change our way of doing it. I mean, we might be able to do it better after we talk, but we don't usually pick one person's way to go.

Awareness of community. The sense of community within this classroom and the school-within-the-school was strong enough to be an object of contemplation by students. The following comments were made in separate interviews.

Hawa: My class? Well, it's basically like a little community....

Tamika: In my homeroom, we all talk about (math) class. We check to see what the other class is doing, and they check to see what we're doing. We always talk about that. And you talk to *other* people, you'll say, "I'm in Drew," and they'll say, "Ain't that hard? Never would I be in Drew!" (Recall that Drew is the school-within-the-school.)

Dion: Yeah, everybody's proud to be in Drew, and our math class!

Jeremy: I know here I really belong. Being a Drew student, everybody makes me feel like I really fit in. Even though I'm a ninth grader. It's like everybody looks out for you when you're in the ninth; so we can make it to where they are. The older students kind of show you how to be.

All leaders. On leadership, Tamika commented, "It's nice in math, that way. Sometimes I'm helping, and sometimes I'm getting helped."

The student whom the teacher thought to be the most mathematically talented in the class said, "I like this class. I can be a leader when I want to, and when I want to be quiet, I can be quiet. Anybody can move our group along, anybody can take charge. Or everybody sometimes."

The teacher's demonstrated interest in student approaches to problems that differed from her own encouraged students' individuality.

The building of a sense of community

The teacher was intentional in her efforts to help students develop a sense of community. A significant factor in her teaching grew out of her sincere interest in students' developing a relationship with one another. She considered conversations and help sessions that they had with each other to be at least as important as those in which she played a part. The teacher said of this first course in a three-year integrated mathematics program, "This is where you learn to work with others and where you see the need to work with others."

Only during quizzes or tests were students in this class expected to work in isolation. In all learning activities, students worked *collaboratively* (or *cooperatively;* we are not making distinctions here between these terms). They were seated in small groups, making effective cooperation easy; they also developed ideas through whole-class discussion, usually after small-group work, in a cooperative style. Students interacted freely in whole-class discussion to develop mathematical ideas. Every student felt free to contribute; discussions were not limited to a few "star" students. The teacher listened actively but spoke only when she felt she needed to contribute. The teacher provided experiences early in the year to help students learn to value one another's ideas, but on the whole, students' response to the collaborative mode of working was natural and positive. It seems more accurate to say they were *freed* to work cooperatively than to say they were taught to do so. The freedom to collaborate and to communicate with each other on their own terms was a foundation of the community that was built in this classroom.

An Atmosphere of Challenge

An atmosphere of challenge was the essential companion to the sense of community in the classroom. The community spirit grew out of the common challenge its members faced in learning mathematical concepts by investigating and solving real problems. An atmosphere of challenge is built in a classroom from the first day of class and is carried from one day to the next. It is more than the level of difficulty of problems and investigations; it has much to do with the manner in which activities are presented and engaged.

The term *challenging* can usefully be understood to include the concept of "interesting." A problem may be difficult; however, if a student has no interest in it, the student will not truly be challenged by it. Thus, an atmosphere of challenge can be enhanced by mathematics problems that are set in contexts of interest and concern to students. These may be real-world contexts, such as social issues, economic issues, or environmental issues. With mathematics, students can explore more deeply issues and topics they have learned from other school subjects, such as history, geography, biology, chemistry, physics, art, or music.

If remediation or the review of essential skills and concepts can be integrated into new and challenging investigations and problems, the atmosphere of challenge is enhanced. Conversely, an atmosphere of challenge can be damaged by time set aside from more-stimulating activities for remediation in isolation.

What makes an activity challenging?

To determine whether an activity was challenging, in our study we examined (*a*) the activity itself and (*b*) the teacher's actions. A one-step problem, especially a problem that can be solved by a direct appeal to a recently learned theorem or concept, could provide valuable practice, but such problems were seen as "practice" and not as challenges. Both during investigations to develop new concepts and after they have mastered the essentials of an idea, students need the opportunity to use the concept in a challenging context where they can

The teacher provided experiences early in the year to help students learn to value one another's ideas, but on the whole, students' response to the collaborative mode of working was natural and positive.

integrate it with other mathematical knowledge to solve a new problem. Problems and investigations that provided opportunities to view acquired knowledge from a new perspective or to begin to construct new knowledge were often classified as *challenging*.

No matter how difficult a problem appeared to be, it could not be seen as challenging if it was similar to another problem students had already done or had seen their teacher do. An atmosphere of challenge would not develop in a classroom if students were given opportunities only to mimic problems and not to solve them.

In several classrooms we observed during this study, when students received too much assistance from the teacher, the atmosphere of challenge was seen to be diminished. If the teacher prepared the students for a problem by providing a model to mimic, the problem was not seen as challenging by the researcher. Similarly, if the teacher walked students through a problem, the problem could not be seen as a challenge to students. Only if the teacher refrained from both of these actions was a problem considered challenging.

In an interview, a student commented that it was good to have "a problem where you gotta ask the teacher. That's where you see that challenge!" But when asked if the teacher should answer the question that "you gotta ask," he said, "Sometimes, if you really can't get it. But if you *can* get it, she should just clue you in on some point and let *you* get it." When asked how this class measured up, he said, "This is how I *like* the class!"

The teacher's manner contributed to an atmosphere of challenge; her apparent interest in the problems, her interest in multiple solutions, and her demonstrated respect for students' solutions different from her own enhanced an atmosphere of challenge. She made it clear that she had a high regard for her students' mathematical thinking, and she maintained high expectations for their ability to solve problems. The atmosphere thus created was both comfortable and energizing for this class of African American students.

The researcher in this study determined whether an activity was challenging on the basis of two criteria: when the mathematical requirements of the activity could be classified as challenging *and* the teacher's actions and manner permitted the challenge and did not detract from it. We observed and assessed thirty hours of mathematics activity in the classroom that was the focus of our study. About twenty hours of activity (1206 minutes; 67 percent of the time) was assessed as challenging by a consensus of students, teacher, and observer-researcher. This compared with an average of about 4 percent in other classrooms we observed at a similar level in the same school district.

In the assessment of students in this classroom, somewhat more of the classroom activity was challenging. There were two kinds of activities that students considered challenging that did not fully meet the researcher's criteria for challenge.

1. Students almost always considered investigations challenging if they did not know what the outcome would be when they began, received no hints of what to expect from their teacher, and if several students might follow the same guidelines and get different results from which generalizations were to be drawn. The researcher agreed that these were valuable attributes of an activity but did not consider the investigation to be challenging if students had step-by-step instructions, did not have to determine what to do themselves, and if it was relatively easy to draw conclusions.

2. Activity assessed by the researcher as drill and practice often took on a challenging character, in the assessment of students, because of the words and actions of the teacher. If the teacher used the time students were

engaged in "drill and practice" to help students learn metacognition or to place the skill they were practicing in the context of their knowledge of mathematical structure, such sessions were not viewed as drill by the students, even though they agreed that they already knew how to do the problems.

It is significant that more than two-thirds of the classroom activity was assessed as challenging by the researcher on the basis of both its content and the "atmosphere." It is also worth noting that students often felt that an atmosphere of challenge was maintained even when the mathematical activity was not very difficult.

Response to varying levels of challenge

There was a distinct difference apparent in the demeanor and level of engagement of the students on days when the activity was challenging and days when the activity was repetitious drill or remediation that was not embedded in something new and challenging. A high level of challenge was accompanied by a high level of involvement, animated discussion, and evident pleasure. Drill and practice, especially if it was seen as remedial, was accompanied by silence and boredom; students worked on the activity but without their characteristic excitement and pleasure.

When asking students about their enjoyment of challenging mathematics problems, the researcher inquired particularly about a challenging investigation they had done to determine the number of moves required to complete the Tower of Hanoi puzzle. The following comments were made in separate interviews.

Interviewer:	Do you like interesting, difficult math problems?
Amina:	Yes. It depends how difficult they are, but I usually like problems that make me think.
Interviewer:	... Do you remember the Tower of Hanoi problem?
Amina:	Oh yeah! I liked it! ... At first it didn't seem like anybody would ever get it.
Leda:	Is that where you had the three pegs and the disks? Yes, that was interesting. It took a long time! ... The class was fun.
Andrew:	Most of the time I don't even like to come to school. But when Ms. W comes up with problems like that, it's worth the trip.
Hawa:	That was terrible! And then all of a sudden I saw it!

Preference for an atmosphere of challenge does not guarantee that students will act responsibly in meeting such challenge. However, if we are to improve the likelihood that African American students are to continue to study mathematics, to enroll in further courses, mathematics must continue to appeal to them and to seem to them worth doing. The teacher in our study believed her students preferred a challenge. She believed they thought the work in Mathematics 1 was more challenging than the work in other math classes elsewhere; she believed, too, that they were proud of being a part of this more challenging environment and would not want it to appear easier. Students unanimously confirmed that perception.

Leda:	I like to work. I like havin' a good problem that's difficult, that can get me thinking.... Some other people would rather do times tables all day.... But I want something to work at.
Jeremy:	Even if you don't get good grades, you really learn stuff.... It's a whole lot of work. I'm trying new depths, and I really want to get into it.

Implications

A high proportion of students who have been enrolled in the course these students were taking, from the same teacher, have historically continued their study of mathematics beyond high school. For that reason, the culture of this classroom (the practices of the teacher and the students within the classroom) may offer guidance that will help other teachers in other schools design an environment in which African American students who have not traditionally persisted in the study of mathematics may do so. We view the sense of community and the atmosphere of challenge that were characteristic of this classroom as key elements of the culture. We suspect that the nurturance of challenge and community in mathematics classrooms would enhance the success of other students like those in this classroom, African American students from an inner-city neighborhood with a multitude of urban problems. It is important to note that both the sense of community and the atmosphere of challenge were built on cooperation and communication.

We believe that every mathematics classroom's culture could develop the key characteristics that we have studied. The building of a sense of community and an atmosphere of challenge does not depend on personality characteristics of the teacher or special circumstances. Such work does require a deep sense of commitment to the task, openness to students, and flexibility. A community of teachers committed to the task should be more effective than single teachers working in isolation, but even an isolated teacher can influence the culture within his or her own classroom.

The atmosphere of challenge and sense of community built in the school's mathematics program

Although this teacher played a key role in the development of a sense of community in her classroom, it is important to note that her classroom was part of a larger community. The establishment of both a sense of community and an atmosphere of challenge in the school program was a long-term process that included the participation of many caring teachers over the years. Students worked collaboratively in all mathematics classes, strengthening the social support network for learning year after year. The older students in the school, themselves beneficiaries of the community spirit, played an important role in making these students in grades 9 and 10 feel that they were part of an established, caring community by offering guidance and counsel. Teachers in a school program working together to establish a sense of community will surely be more effective than one working alone.

None of the teachers in the program received special training relating to issues of classroom culture. This teacher, and others, maintained an attitude of awareness to students' responses to pedagogical practices. She modified her practice after reflecting on her observations, treating teaching as an interactive, evolutionary process. She and other mathematics teachers constituted a community for sharing thoughts about working with students and developing the curriculum and materials. The teaching of mathematics is a continuing revolutionary art; it cannot be perfected because the circumstances of teaching and of mathematics are always evolving. This teacher had been part of the school program for more than ten years. The program itself, and the community of teachers in it, was in existence when she came. A sense of community for students in the program emerged after perhaps three or four years of the program's existence; an atmosphere of challenge was probably there from the start. This teacher's contribution to the level 1 mathematics course *enhanced* the school's sense of community and the mathematics program immeasurably.

Summary of the teacher's behavior in fostering respect and community

The mid-September episode recorded in this article demonstrates some of the ways the teacher worked to create an appropriate classroom environment. In particular, her clear respect for students' ability to develop the mathematics together with just a little guidance from her helped to promote the atmosphere of mutual respect that was a significant factor in the sense of community as it contributed to the atmosphere of challenge attained in this classroom. The transcript of this episode illustrates the manner in which classroom dialogue proceeded. Students made contributions to the discussion without using the teacher as a conduit. The teacher's willingness to participate in the discussion on those terms served as a demonstration of respect for students' mathematical thinking. Such respect was further demonstrated in her verbal responses and in body language suggesting active listening and strong interest. The respect she demonstrated for each student's intellectual process served as a model for students to respect each other and strengthened each student's belief in himself or herself.

The teacher made a conscious effort to create the environment that proved so conducive to a positive attitude toward mathematics in her students. She perceived her role as the teacher of the school's level 1 mathematics course to include a role of building community; in her view, this was a highly significant role, essential to the success of the school. She focused many intentional acts on strengthening students' relationships to one another throughout the year, with special vigilance in the first six weeks.

1. She counseled students working together cooperatively to notice and respect each other's thinking.

2. She responded to students' work and to students' interactions in a manner that bespoke her respect and her caring for each student, expecting that this attitude would be emulated by students.

3. She demonstrated her trust in students by allowing them to move about the room as they worked without having to ask permission and by listening to them carefully without an attitude of judgment as they discussed mathematics.

4. She strengthened students' trust in one another and the safety of the classroom environment by nurturing students' positive interactions, including mathematical disagreement, and by speaking quietly, directly, and personally to any student whose words or acts were hurtful or belittling to another.

5. She encouraged individuality by honoring unusual approaches; she praised intelligent thinking even when her praise could be applied to only a part of a piece of work. This seemed to enhance her students' ability to receive instruction on incorrect portions.

6. Through her words and actions, she cast herself as an intellectual equal of her students without minimizing her role as caring adult.

7. She shared her leadership role in the classroom community by her acceptance and positive response to initiatives from any student in both whole-class discussion and small-group work.

Summary of the teacher's behavior in fostering an atmosphere of challenge

As this teacher worked to establish a sense of community in her classroom, she also worked intentionally to establish an atmosphere of challenge because she believed that students preferred to view themselves as meeting a challenge rather than accomplishing routine tasks. Mathematics activities that might be perceived as routine in another classroom were often presented in this classroom in a manner that enhanced the atmosphere of challenge. This was achieved by the following:

1. Minimizing the assignment of problems too similar to problems students had already seen. Each problem included a little bit of new thinking or integration of prior knowledge even while providing practice in a new skill.

2. Directing students' questions to others in their small group and helping students learn to value what they received from other members of the group

3. When a group of students encountered difficulties, asking questions that focused their thinking and turned their attention toward knowledge they had already acquired that might bear on the current problem

4. Demonstrating new methods and good techniques by the teacher but not demonstrating solutions to prototype problems

5. If students used approaches different from those she expected, helping them improve their argument or understand the flaws in it, as needed, but not requiring that they follow a prescribed approach. When an atypical and correct approach was offered, she celebrated it.

6. Maintaining an attitude of real interest in the mathematics, the problems, and the students' mathematical thinking that seemed to influence students' attitude toward mathematics

7. Seeking nonroutine mathematics activities that would teach students the skills and concepts needed to build mathematical strength while demonstrating the power of mathematics to investigate the real world. Although the real-world issues were not the focus of discussion in the mathematics classroom, the effect of working on mathematics in real-world contexts was to build students' belief that mathematics was about issues that mattered.

One of the challenging real-world problem situations that was used was adapted from Landwehr and Watkins (1986). To review the concept of linear functions and the skill of writing the equation of a line, students fit lines to data on life expectancy at birth of various populations. Studying the equations that show, for example, the increase in life expectancy since 1960 of white males and black females, respectively, gives significance to the concept of slope. (In 1960, black female life expectancy was about one year less than that for white males; by 1980, black female life expectancy was about four years longer than that of white males.) Data sets by race and gender in the United States are available from the National Center for Health Statistics. Life expectancy data from every country in the world are available from the United Nations Population Fund's *World Population Prospects*. Carefully chosen sets of life expectancy data permit students to compare wealthy nations with poor nations, for example, and thus to learn one of the most dire consequences of poverty. It is also possible to see the devastating effects of war on a population by observing changes in life expectancy where a lengthy war has been fought.

Problems that demonstrate the power of mathematics to model the real world help students who want to change their world see the value of acquiring this great tool. Such problems have the additional advantage of appealing to the learning style of a broader range of learners. Traditional mathematics instruction has not proved effective for many holistic learners, whose intellectual process moves most effectively from a concern with the larger world and its problems to mathematics for methods of solution.

THOUGHTS FOR THE TEACHING COMMUNITY

In formulating recommendations for the teaching community, let us begin by linking the experience in this classroom to a larger perspective on reconstructing our national mathematics classroom culture. During the 1990s, the mathematics education community has been moving toward the changes prescribed by the three *Standards* documents published by the National Council of Teachers of Mathematics (1989, 1991, 1995). These documents call for classroom practices that teach students to investigate, to construct their own knowledge, to work together, and to learn from one another and from their own experiences. They also call for a strong core curriculum that will assure that everyone learns appropriate mathematics. The changes prescribed by the *Standards* are slowly becoming part of the culture and, in some instances, creating backlash.

Traditionally, large numbers of American students have been effectively barred from the learning of mathematics through relegation to "remedial" classrooms (Rosenbaum 1980; Simmons and Grady 1990; National Center for Educational Statistics 1985). However, teachers like Orr (1987) observed that for her students who were speakers of black English vernacular to succeed, their work in mathematics must be made *harder* "so that it captures students' minds." The traditional response to low achievement in the routine tasks of our mathematics classrooms was to make the tasks even lower level, more routine, less interesting, less challenging. The *Curriculum and Evaluation Standards* suggests that there is little value in accomplishing the lower-level, rote, computational tasks if they are not integrated with problem solving, communication, reasoning, and connections. A small body of research suggests that students from societal groups who have disproportionate numbers of low achievers in mathematics (and thus students likeliest to be assigned the most routine and least challenging mathematics tasks) have a high probability of being holistic learners, kinesthetic learners, and social learners—learners unlikely to gain from the traditional remedial classroom and not necessarily students with less potential ability (see Boykin [1986]; Stiff [1990]; Kagan [1980]; Sharan and Shaulo [1990]; Papert [1984]). The classroom in this study provides an outstanding example of the vision many mathematics educators have for broadening participation in mathematics.

Figure 4.1 summarizes aspects of the culture of the classroom that we believe influenced students' decisions to continue their study of mathematics. A sense of community and an atmosphere of challenge, the two constructs of such importance to students' attitudes, interact and enhance each other. These are conditions and practices that can be emulated in other classrooms.

We can achieve a sense of community in the mathematics classroom

We have endeavored to provide a picture of how one teacher's beliefs and practices influenced the culture of a classroom from which students tended to persist in the study of mathematics. The cooperative learning movement, with the support of segments of the mathematics education community and the National Council of Teachers of Mathematics, has moved mathematics education along the path away from teacher lecture and away from students working in isolation. This is a big step away from the traditional classroom. In the context of a classroom where students work together cooperatively, the concept of community becomes viable. If teachers envision the development of a sense of community in their classrooms, if the development of community becomes a goal, we may effect radical change in classroom culture.

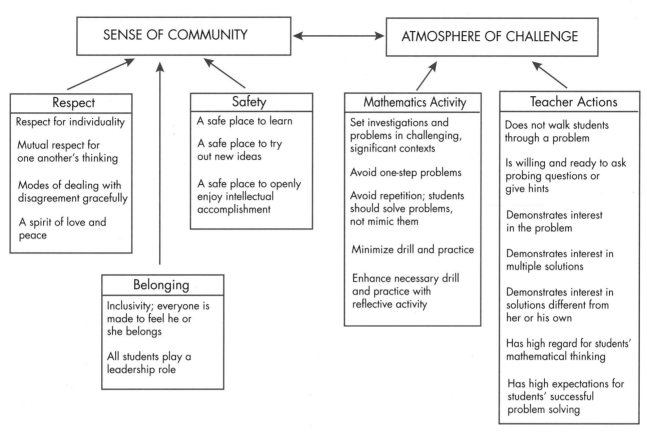

Fig. 4.1. Factors that influence students continuing the study of mathematics

We must provide challenging experiences and an environment that supports students' success in meeting the challenge

If the goal is to prepare students to choose to persist in the study of mathematics, then the focus of the community will be on meeting the challenge of learning and enjoying mathematics together. For some students, the need to grapple with challenging problems and to meet with success in doing so is exceedingly strong; we must offer classroom experiences that can meet that need so that students do not have to look beyond the school for the fulfillment of it.

Each teacher's approach to the development of a sense of community and an atmosphere of challenge may differ

The culture of each classroom is very much influenced by the personality and practices of its teacher. The teacher in the classroom we studied is a unique person; other teachers will develop their own special approaches to the development of the culture of their classrooms. The aim of this study was to contribute to the development of an understanding among educators of how to provide a classroom environment that enhances a positive attitude toward the study of mathematics and increases the likelihood that members of a group that has been underserved by mathematics education will persist in the study of mathematics. The findings indicate that a sense of community and an atmosphere of challenge are highly desirable aspects of the classroom culture, possibly crucial for some students.

A cautionary word on the subject of challenge

Preference for an atmosphere of challenge does not guarantee that students will act responsibly in meeting such challenge. However, if we are to improve the likelihood that students are to continue their study of mathematics and enroll in further courses, those courses must continue to appeal to them and to seem to them worth doing. This teacher believed students preferred a challenge. She knew that they thought the work in Mathematics 1 was more challenging than the work in other mathematics classes elsewhere; she believed, too, that they were proud of being a part of this more challenging environment and would not want it to appear easier. Students unanimously confirmed that perception. The mathematics teaching community might capitalize on that attitude.

IN CONCLUSION

We have focused attention on the *atmosphere of challenge* and the *sense of community* in the classroom we studied. There were three other factors present that might also influence students' decisions to continue studying mathematics:

1. The course these students were taking was the first course in a mathematics program that offered a solid foundation for further study at the college level. We cannot expect students to succeed in a university mathematics program if we do not provide a strong foundation at the secondary school level.

2. The students had African American role models. These included some of the teachers in the program (and the teacher in this classroom), but perhaps most important, it included older students in the program. The ninth- and tenth-grade students in this classroom spoke appreciatively of the assistance given to them by older students "to help us get where they are." It is important to have a core of students who can look to one another for models of success and persistence.

3. Both black and nonblack mathematics teachers in the program of which this classroom was a part have contributed effectively to students' success. It is important that teachers of all races learn to recognize and respect the particular qualities and talents of all their students.

We can create classroom environments where a culture can develop that inspires joy and pride in success, a culture that may influence African American students to continue their study of mathematics who in other circumstances might end it early. Such an outcome would enrich mathematics and enrich our society. At Drew High School, we have seen such a culture develop in a classroom where students were freed to work together and to interact and communicate as leaders and thinkers, where a sense of community among the students was an explicit goal of the teacher, and where an atmosphere of challenge was valued and maintained.

REFERENCES

Boykin, A. Wade. "The Triple Quandary and the Schooling of African-American Children." In *The School Achievement of Minority Children: New Perspectives*, edited by Ulric Neisser, pp. 56–88. Hillsdale, N.J.: Lawrence Erlbaum Associates, 1986.

Dance, Rosalie A. "A Characterization of Aspects of the Culture of a Successful Mathematics Classroom in an Inner City School." Doctoral diss., University of Maryland, 1997.

Davidson, Neil. *Cooperative Learning in Mathematics: A Handbook for Teachers.* Reading, Mass.: Addison Wesley, 1990a.

————. "Small-Group Cooperative Learning in Mathematics." In *Teaching and Learning Mathematics in the 1990s*, 1990 Yearbook of the National Council of Teachers of Mathematics, edited by Thomas J. Cooney, pp. 52–61. Reston, Va.: National Council of Teachers of Mathematics, 1990b.

Edwards, Anthony D., and D. P. G. Westgate. *Investigating Classroom Talk.* Philadelphia: Falmer Press, 1987.

Fordham, Signithia, and John Ogbu. "Black Students' School Success: Coping with the 'Burden of Acting White.'" *Urban Review* 18 (1986): 76–206.

Fullilove, R. E., and Philip Uri Treisman. "Mathematics Achievement among African-American Undergraduates at the University of California, Berkeley: An Evaluation of the Math Workshop Program." *Journal of Negro Education* 59, no. 3 (1990): 463–78.

Gross, Susan. *Participation and Performance of Women and Minorities in Mathematics*, 1988. (ERIC Document Reproduction no. ED 304 515)

Kagan, Spencer. "Cooperation—Competition, Culture, and Structural Bias in Classrooms." In *Cooperation in Education*, edited by S. Sharan, P. Hare, C. D. Webb, and R. Hertz-Lazarowitz . Provo, Utah: Brigham Young University Press, 1980.

Landwehr, James M., and Ann E. Watkins. *Exploring Data: Quantitative Literacy Series.* Palo Alto, Calif.: Dale Seymour Publications, 1986.

National Center for Educational Statistics. T*he Condition of Education.* Washington, D.C.: U.S. Department of Education, 1985.

National Council of Teachers of Mathematics. *Assessment Standards for School Mathematics.* Reston, Va.: National Council of Teachers of Mathematics, 1995.

————. *Curriculum and Evaluation Standards for School Mathematics.* Reston, Va.: National Council of Teachers of Mathematics,1989.

————. *Professional Standards for Teaching Mathematics.* Reston, Va.: National Council of Teachers of Mathematics, 1991.

Orr, Evelyn W. *Twice as Less: Black English and the Performance of Black Students in Mathematics and Science.* New York: W. W. Norton & Co., 1987.

Papert, Seymour. *Mindstorms: Children, Computers, and Powerful Ideas.* New York: Basic Books, 1984.

Peck, M. Scott. *The Different Drum: Community-Making and Peace.* New York: Simon & Schuster, 1987.

Rosenbaum, James E. "Social Implications of Educational Grouping." In *Review of Research in Education*, edited by D. C. Berliner. Washington, D.C.: American Educational Research Association, 1980.

Sharan, Shlomo, and A. Shaulov. "Cooperative Learning, Motivation, and Achievement." In *Cooperative Learning: Theory and Research*, edited by Shlomo Sharan. New York: Praeger, 1990.

Simmons, W., and M. Grady. *Black Male Achievement: From Peril to Promise.* Report of the Superintendent's Advisory Committee on Black Male Achievement. Upper Marlboro, Md.: Prince Georges County Public Schools, 1990.

Stiff, Lee. "African-American Students and the Promise of the *Curriculum and Evaluation Standards.*" In *Teaching and Learning Mathematics in the 1990s*, 1990 Yearbook of the National Council of Teachers of Mathematics, edited by Thomas J. Cooney, pp. 152–58. Reston, Va.: National Council of Teachers of Mathematics, 1990.

Treisman, Uri. "Studying Students Studying Calculus: A Look at the Lives of Minority Mathematics Students in College." *College Mathematics Journal* 23 (November 1992).

United Nations Population Fund. *World Population Prospects.* New York: United Nations, 1995.

African American Students' Success with School Mathematics

5

Vivian R. Moody

A proliferation of research documents the underachievement and underparticipation of African Americans in mathematics. Although we have some conceptions about why African American students do not fare well with school mathematics because of this research, consistent documentation of low mathematics achievement places an emphasis on unsuccessful African American students. Focusing on unsuccessful students has the propensity to lead to stereotypes or generalizations (Matthews 1984). The formation of these generalizations and stereotypes leads to the assumption that the problem lies with African American students. Some research programs have sought to discover what the problem is with African Americans rather than what the problem is with the schooling and mathematical experiences of African Americans (Boykin 1986; Neisser 1986). These research programs seem to follow the same basic principle: "If African Americans do badly in school, we must discover what is wrong with them!" Seeking to discover what the problem is with African American students, some scholars have proposed deficits or deficiencies in African Americans themselves or in African American culture. I contend that deficits and deficiencies lie in particular schooling practices rather than in African American students themselves or in African American culture.

It is important that we reframe our research efforts away from studies of African American student failure in mathematics. Much can be learned from those African American students who have been successful with school mathematics. Listening to success stories has the potential to create a dialogue among mathematics educators about particular factors and schooling practices that contribute to the success of African American mathematics students. Success stories enable us as mathematics educators to create a discourse that goes beyond merely exposing problems that exist in the mathematics education of African American students. Such discourse can help us explore ways to improve the mathematics education and ultimately the mathematical experiences of African American students. The purpose of this article is to describe the success stories of two African American mathematics students—Ashley and Sheilah.

> **Much can be learned from those African American students who have been successful with school mathematics.**

ASHLEY'S SUCCESS STORY

Ashley was a junior attending a predominantly black university and majoring in mathematics and political science. Ashley had a 4.0 grade point average at this university. She attended a predominantly white middle and high school. In high school, Ashley was a member of the mathematics and science magnet program. She made A's in all her high school mathematics courses and graduated from high school with honors. Ashley's plan was to serve as a role model for other African American youths. She believed that her mathematics degree

The research presented in this article was conducted as a dissertation study at the University of Georgia under the direction of Patricia S. Wilson.

51

would start her on the path toward finding her special place in mathematics history, a place that would contribute to the success of other African American youths.

Parental Support

Ashley's parents divorced during her early childhood. Ashley and her mother moved from Denver, Colorado, to the Southeast when she was in third grade. Although Ashley spent some of her early years living with her grandmother, for the most part, she grew up in a single-parent home with her mother as the dominant figure in the household.

Ashley's earliest mathematical experiences began long before she started school. She stated, "As far back as I can remember, I always had a problem to solve" (Ashley's autobiography, 11 July 1996). Ashley's mother gave her problems involving addition and subtraction to solve while her mother did housework. Ashley commented that her mother would say, "Do this problem for Mommy while I wash dishes" (Ashley's autobiography). Ashley stated that she did not realize then that solving these problems for her mother was mathematics. Because of this early childhood experience with mathematics, Ashley developed positive attitudes toward mathematics and liked mathematics very much before attending school.

However, Ashley's mathematical experiences in the context of schooling, for the most part, can be denoted as a "struggle." She struggled with becoming successful in school and maintaining a sense of identity. Ashley believed that as an African American, she had to acquiesce to the ideologies of school culture to become successful. Consequently, her conformity to school culture sometimes resulted in peer criticism. Her African American peers accused her of acting white.

> **Because of this early childhood experience with mathematics, Ashley developed positive attitudes toward mathematics and liked mathematics very much before attending school.**

Ashley said that her mother and grandmother played a significant role in helping her contend with the struggle of being successful in school and with school mathematics. Ashley's mother took a vested interest in Ashley's education. She communicated to Ashley that education was valuable by attending school functions such as Parent Night, Honors Day, and PTA meetings. Moreover, Ashley said that she often became weary of studying and working hard in her mathematics classes and opted to "hang out" with her friends and attend parties. She said her mother told her that she had ample time to be with friends and that it was important for her to work hard in order to succeed in school.

Ashley stated that her grandmother constantly reminded her that she could become anything she wanted. Ashley said that her grandmother told her that "she could succeed in school just like anyone else." This seemed to have had an impact on Ashley's desire to be successful in mathematics.

Ashley stated that she sometimes had difficulty in mathematics when she was first introduced to new concepts. She stated that her approach was to "keep trying." Ashley did not elaborate further on how she dealt with the difficulty of grasping new concepts beyond working hard. However, when asked if she received help during any difficult times in her schooling in general or with mathematics in particular, she stated, "My mom more than anything and my grandmother" (Interview 1 with Ashley, 27 June 1996). Ashley further stated,

> My mom is a strong-willed woman. She is very intelligent and she just tells me things to let me know that, hey, you are just as good as anybody else and I am very proud of you, you know, and she has expectations that I have to meet.

From Ashley's comments, it seems that Ashley recognized that her mother not only supported her but set high expectations for her. Ashley seemed to have appreciated her mother's role rather than feeling pushed or controlled by her mother. Ashley commented several times that she studied really hard, and this in part may have stemmed from her mother's expecting the best from her. It is unclear exactly what role her mother's expectations played in Ashley's success, since she did not elaborate on the high expectations her mother set for her, but it seems that her mother's doing so was a factor in Ashley's success.

Some research (Kibler 1995) has indicated that strong mothers who expect their children to do well in school and encourage them to do well have an impact on their children's success in school. Kibler (1995) studied seven poor African American high school graduates. She found that a strong mother was a significant factor that fostered the high school graduation of the African American students. Kibler found that the mother was the dominant authority in the family, and there were strong home-school relationships because of the mother's involvement in the graduate's education.

Ashley's mother also served as a role model in Ashley's mathematics education. Ashley stated (Interview 2 with Ashley, 17 July 1996),

> [My] mother … is my main role model. She has come a long way herself. She went back to school and everything and tried giving me a role model to look up to. She also has encouraged me a lot and math used to be her favorite subject in school, and she's the one who started me off in math.… I guess too … she could find love there for me and encouragement, too, because you need that.

Ashley said that her mother exemplified a strong African American woman. Ashley asserted that although the odds were stacked against her mother because she was a single-parent and was African American, her mother superseded struggles of oppression and poverty. Her mother's returning to school suggested to Ashley that education, particularly mathematics education, was vital in dealing with life's challenges and struggles.

Some scholars (Johnson 1984; Kibler 1995) believe that parental support and role models are important factors contributing to African American students' success in mathematics. Johnson (1984) argued that African American students tend not to be successful with school mathematics because of an absence of role models and a lack of significant others, such as parents, who have an interest in mathematics achievement.

Caring Educators

Ashley's first experience with a caring educator who she believed contributed to her success with school mathematics was in third grade. Ashley was placed in a higher-level class in third grade when she moved from Denver to the Southeast. Ashley believed that students were placed in particular classes on the basis of their ability and that their ability was determined by standardized tests. After about a week of being in the higher-level class, Ashley was given a placement test to determine if her class placement was on target. Ashley did poorly on the placement test and was then placed in a lower-level class. She stated, "I know I was just a scary little girl. I am not good at taking standardized tests at all. I cannot take them. I don't know why.… I have to learn how to take them, I think.… I froze up" (Interview 2 with Ashley). As Ashley talked more about her experience of moving to the Southeast, it becomes evident that her class placement after taking the standardized test may have been *off* target. Ashley stated (Interview 2 with Ashley),

> I had only been there [Southeast] a couple of weeks, and I had to take all my shots over because they had lost my shot record. So, I was going through a lot of bad

stuff and then I wasn't with my mom at the time. I went to live with my grandma. So, I was trying to get, you know, get used to being away from my mom.

It is unclear whether these circumstances were taken into consideration when Ashley was given the placement test. Although there is little information about exactly what determined Ashley's placement in the lower-level class, it is evident that Ashley perceived her placement as resulting from the placement test. As such, Ashley believed that her academic abilities were determined by this placement test.

This experience seemed to have had adverse effects on Ashley's self-concept. In some sense Ashley was labeled as not being as smart as other children when she was taken out of a classroom environment that was deemed "too hard" for her. Ashley stated, "I guess they [school administrators] thought I was kind of retarded. I felt bad because I knew it was the lowest class. Everybody used to say, that's the lowest class and Ms. [Carter] teaches the lowest class" (Interview 2 with Ashley).

Fortunately for Ashley, the African American teacher, Ms. Carter, who taught the lower-level third-grade class believed that Ashley was good in mathematics. Ashley said, "She noticed something in me and she began to talk to me" (Interview 2 with Ashley). Ashley stated that Ms. Carter seemed to have noticed that she had substantial potential in mathematics. She said that Ms. Carter began to give her extra help and more attention in class. Ashley stated that Ms. Carter's being attentive to her helped her become confident in doing mathematics. Consequently, Ashley made all A's in mathematics the remainder of the year.

Ashley had two African American female mathematics teachers in sixth and seventh grade who were also significant others in her mathematics education. Ashley stated that her sixth-grade mathematics teacher "was amazing to me because she was the first black woman mathematician I had ever seen" (Ashley's autobiography). Ashley said that since her sixth-grade mathematics teacher was African American, this reinforced her belief that African Americans could excel in mathematics. She said that she seemed to have formed a bond with this teacher and noted that this teacher cared about her doing well in mathematics. Perhaps the bond Ashley mentioned was fueled by their sharing a common cultural frame of reference.

Ashley's seventh-grade mathematics teacher encouraged her to take an algebra placement test. The results of this particular test determined whether or not students would take general mathematics or algebra 1 in eighth grade. From Ashley's perspective, this placement test "would determine if I knew enough to get into algebra early" (Ashley's autobiography). This test was not required for all students, but it was mandatory for those students who wanted to take algebra 1 in eighth grade. Ashley did not want to take this test because of her fear of standardized tests (perhaps stemming from her third-grade experience) but did so because her seventh-grade mathematics teacher believed in her ability to do mathematics. Ashley's seventh-grade teacher told her that she needed to get an early start in higher mathematics. At the time, Ashley did not know what her teacher meant by that or what a difference getting an early start in higher mathematics would make in her mathematical experiences. However, Ashley did take the test and stated, "I am awful at taking placement tests, but I succeeded" (Ashley's autobiography). Ashley perceived her seventh-grade mathematics teacher's act of encouraging her to take the algebra placement test as reaching out to her and attributes her *jump start* in higher mathematics to her seventh-grade teacher.

At the time of the study, Sheilah was a graduate student pursuing a master's degree in mathematics education at a predominantly white university. Sheilah attended a fundamental magnet middle school and a predominantly black high school, where she graduated as valedictorian of her class with a 4.0 grade point average. She obtained a bachelor's degree in mathematics from a predominantly black university and completed her undergraduate studies with honors with a 3.97 cumulative grade point average. Sheilah's plan was to serve as a role model for other African American youths by teaching high school mathematics. She believed that teaching mathematics would allow her to make a difference in the lives of African American students.

Parental Support

Sheilah's mother received a master's degree in mathematics and had taught collegiate mathematics for several years. Sheilah stated (Interview 1 with Sheilah, 3 July 1996),

> I really, really, really have grown to respect her because she got her master's in math, not math education, you know, where you can balance the two, but just pure math, and her comprehensive exam was an oral exam in front of professors, and I can't imagine even doing that.

Some research (King 1995) has found a relationship between the mother's level of education and African American students' mathematics self-efficacy—students' self-concept of their ability to do mathematics. King found that African American students whose mothers had graduated from college had a significantly higher mathematics self-efficacy than those African American students whose mothers did not complete a college degree. For Sheilah, her mother's ability to do mathematics seemed to have been an important constituent in her own ability to do mathematics. In this sense, Sheilah seemed to have embraced the cliché "seeing is believing." Sheilah said that her mother's receiving a master's degree in mathematics was important in her own success with mathematics. In other words, *seeing* her mother succeed in mathematics helped her *believe* that she too could succeed in mathematics. Sheilah asserted that her mother had "traveled the road that she was now traveling" and consequently understood the challenges she was faced with in endeavoring to succeed in mathematics. Sheilah stated (Interview 1 with Sheilah),

> If it had been somebody else telling me, you can do it and had not gone to where I'm trying to go, I would be like, what do you know, but I know that my mom knew what she was talking about because she had been through this. She's had to have those abstract math courses and then to be tested orally, I knew she understood. Knowing that she understood and she cared, that helped me out a whole lot.

Sheilah said that when she was faced with difficulty in mathematics, her mother encouraged her to "stick with it" and not quit. During her graduate studies, Sheilah contemplated dropping her real analysis class but did not, because her mother encouraged her to "tough it out." Sheilah said (Interview 1 with Sheilah),

> My mom was really strong because I think she could really empathize with me and she was like, well [Sheilah], you know, God's not going to put more on you than you can handle, and you can do this. You are not a quitter, because I was thinking about dropping real analysis. I was just thinking really hard. She's [her mother] like if you do drop it now, when are you going to take it again, you know, you are not a quitter.

Seeing her mother succeed in mathematics helped her believe that she too could succeed in mathematics.

Sheilah in some sense began to question her ability to do mathematics because of her difficulty in her real analysis class. However, her mother's intervention seemed to have helped Sheilah maintain a positive mathematics self-efficacy and confidence about doing mathematics. Although her mother's words of "you are not a quitter" sound forceful, Sheilah indicated that she felt she was not being controlled or pushed by her mother. She said that her mother told her she could succeed in mathematics, and she believed her.

Sheilah's father also contributed to her success with school mathematics. Sheilah's father taught middle school mathematics. Sheilah stated that her family sometimes engaged in mathematics meetings at home where she and her parents traded teaching strategies.

The role of Sheilah's father in her success was somewhat different from her mother's role. Sheilah stated that her father told her to do her best when she had difficulty in her mathematics courses. Sheilah stated (Interview 3 with Sheilah, 13 August 1996),

> My father was there [for me] in that he would say, whatever you do, I only want the best because he is the kind that he never pushed me too hard. He always expected the best from me, but if my best was, you know, failure sometimes, he was always understanding, and knowing he understood in saying that, all your dad asks for is the best, it was a real comfort, you know, and that really helped me.

Sheilah said that her father's role in her success was significant because he supported her endeavors in a way that helped relieved the pressure and the challenges that were involved in becoming successful with school mathematics. Being told by her father that doing her best was enough comforted Sheilah when she was faced with difficulty in her mathematics courses.

Caring Educators

For Sheilah, it seems that the often-held view of mathematics that only a select few can learn or do mathematics, which Anderson (1990) refers to as an elitist view, was eradicated by her African American female mathematics educators' ability to do mathematics. Sheilah stated, "I had several good black female mathematics instructors, so I knew that *we* [emphasis hers] could handle mathematics" (Sheilah's autobiography, 9 July 1996). These educators seemed to have served as role models and perhaps *evidence* that African Americans can become successful with school mathematics.

Besides giving Sheilah role models for doing mathematics, African American mathematics teachers served as supporters and nurturers for Sheilah. Sheilah stated in reference to one of her African American mathematics teachers (Interview 2 with Sheilah, 17 July 1996),

> She's the only black female teacher that taught me at [this black university] and I often compare her to my mother because they are so much alike. She would always be there to just encourage me. When I had a class I just didn't think I could make it, I would just go sit in her office and say look, this is what's going on, tell me what to do and she was always there. She was good support in undergraduate [school], really good support.

Some scholars (Irvine 1990; Kibler 1995; Ladson-Billings 1995) have indicated that caring educators are significant others in the success of African American students. According to Irvine (1990), teachers do make a difference in the achievement of African American students (pp. 46–47):

> The role that teachers play in the school performance of black children is central and critical. Teachers' personal and cultural attributes as well as their attitudes

and behaviors are important. However, the organizational and environmental context in which teachers perform their role and duties is an important feature that explicates teachers' essential influence and potency.

Teachers' attributes such as warmth, affect, and enthusiasm have been found to be highly correlated with student achievement (Irvine 1990). Irvine reported that 813 minority, low-income adults, aged 18 to 34, were asked to describe teachers who had influenced them the most. Their descriptors included approachable, pleasant, easy to relate to, accepting, tolerant, helpful, concerned, caring, thoughtful, and perceptive of and sensitive to the needs of students. These attributes were also evident in Sheilah's description of some of her caring teachers. Sheilah described her fifth-grade teacher as follows (Interview 2 with Sheilah):

> She cared and she didn't just let us do whatever. I mean, she really cared about the students and she knew her stuff.... She cared and she wouldn't accept less than the best of us. She was the first black teacher I had and she really took me to the side and worked with me.

It seems that Sheilah's fifth-grade teacher not only cared for her students but also set high expectations for them as indicated by Sheilah's statement, "She wouldn't accept less than the best of us." A proliferation of research documents the notion that teachers' expectations affect students' achievement. Some research (Brophy and Good 1970; Cooper 1979; Good 1980) indicates that teachers who communicate to their students positive expectations about their performance influence their students' success in school. Moreover, "students treated as competent are likely to demonstrate competence" (Ladson-Billings 1995, p. 137).

LEARNING FROM ASHLEY'S AND SHEILAH'S STORIES

Ashley's and Sheilah's stories give us insight into elements that fostered or contributed to their success with school mathematics. Their stories suggest that African American teachers serving as role models, caring educators, and parental support all played a significant role in their becoming successful with school mathematics.

The Need for Role Models

Ashley's and Sheilah's stories indicate that African American mathematics teachers were significant others in their mathematical experiences. These teachers communicated high expectations to Ashley and Sheilah and also supported and nurtured them when they were faced with difficulty in their mathematical experiences.

Although Ashley and Sheilah both commented that caring educators were important and alluded to caring educators as not necessarily being African American, they specifically referred to African American teachers who they believed played a vital role in fostering their success with school mathematics. For Ashley, African American mathematics teachers helped her become successful by giving her "somebody to look at, somebody who is real." Particularly, these teachers represented models of persons who had become successful with school mathematics and reminded Ashley that she could also become successful. Further, Ashley was faced with the dilemma of selling out or acting white when she endeavored to become successful with school mathematics. African American mathematics teachers, serving as role models and supporters, helped Ashley deal with this dilemma by communicating to her that being successful with school mathematics was not a tactic for rejecting African American culture.

For Sheilah, African American mathematics teachers served as evidence that mathematics is not limited to certain groups. She stated that since she had several good African American female mathematics teachers, she knew African American females could "handle" mathematics. From Sheilah's perspective, African American mathematics teachers, serving as role models, seemed to have eradicated the notion that mathematics is too rigorous for African American women.

Ashley's and Sheilah's stories suggest a need for more African American mathematics teachers in schools, which in turn suggests a need to recruit more African American mathematics teachers. Perhaps having role models for doing mathematics will help those African American students who face the dilemma of acting white or those African American students who need *reinforcing agents* to remind them that mathematics is not limited to whites. Moreover, "the presence of African American mathematics teachers in classrooms helps to formulate students' ideas about who excels in mathematics" (Stiff 1990, p. 153). The notion of African American students *seeing* African American mathematics teachers may help African American students become confident in doing mathematics. African American mathematics teachers can also stimulate in African American students a sense of belonging in mathematics classrooms and ultimately in the field of mathematics. African American students' beliefs about who can learn or do mathematics is influenced by who they have seen learning or doing mathematics. African American role models play a significant role in shaping how African American students see themselves as learners and doers of mathematics.

The Role of Teachers

Ashley and Sheilah both purported that teachers contributed to their success with school mathematics.

Ashley and Sheilah both purported that teachers contributed to their success with school mathematics. As Ashley and Sheilah talked about the characteristics of teachers who were influential in their schooling and mathematical experiences, they both emphasized nurturing and caring as key constructs in teaching mathematics. How can teachers become caring and nurturing educators? Ashley and Sheilah both viewed caring educators as persons who believed in their ability to do mathematics. Ashley stated that her sixth- and seventh-grade mathematics teachers contributed to her success because they encouraged her in mathematics. For Ashley, encouragement took the form of someone saying, "You can do it!" This meant that someone else who was perhaps an authority on mathematics believed that she could do mathematics. Encouragement also entailed someone "looking out for her" and making special efforts to help her succeed in mathematics. For instance, Ashley believed that her seventh-grade mathematics teacher made special efforts to help her succeed in mathematics by pushing her to take the algebra placement test to get into the algebra 1 class in eighth grade.

For Sheilah, caring took the form of teachers being approachable and willing to give extra help. Sheilah accentuated that she was able to approach caring teachers outside of class and ask them to explain concepts further. Sheilah alluded to teachers whom she could "go to" and ask for extra help as "good teachers." Further, these teachers took time to assist her when she had questions or difficulty in mathematics.

The Role of Parents

Both Ashley and Sheilah indicated that parental support was vital in their becoming successful with school mathematics. What seems to have been important for both Ashley and Sheilah is that their parents were supportive, caring, and nurturing. It is evident that Ashley and Sheilah had very different home-life situations. However, parental support for both of them took much the same form. Although neither Ashley nor Sheilah reported that their parents were instrumental in sitting down with them each night to do mathematics homework, they both placed an emphasis on their parents setting high expectations for them and encouraging them to do well in mathematics. When Ashley encountered difficulty in mathematics, her mother and grandmother encouraged her by telling her to "keep trying." Similarly, Sheilah's mother encouraged her by telling her "don't quit!" It seems that both of these phrases are couched in the context of expectations. Ashley's and Sheilah's stories both suggest that their parents encouraged them to do well in mathematics because their parents believed they *could* do well in mathematics.

CONCLUDING REMARKS

Ashley's and Sheilah's stories give us knowledge about their lives in school as successful African American mathematics students. Understanding their lives opens up other avenues of inquiry that will give us more insightful stories. The more we know about different African American students' success stories, the better equipped we will become to improve the mathematics education of African American students and help foster successful African American students.

REFERENCES

Anderson, S. E. "Worldmath Curriculum: Fighting Eurocentrism in Mathematics." *Journal of Negro Education* 59 (Summer 1990): 348–59.

Boykin, A. Wade. "The Triple Quandary and the Schooling of Afro-American Children." In *The School Achievement of Minority Children: New Perspectives*, edited by Ulric Neisser, pp. 57–92. Hillsdale, N.J.: Lawrence Erlbaum Associates, 1986.

Brophy, Jere E., and Thomas L. Good. "Teachers' Communication of Differential Expectations for Children's Classroom Performance: Some Behavioral Data." *Journal of Educational Psychology* 61 (October 1970): 365–74.

Cooper, Harris M. "Pygmalion Grows Up: A Model for Teacher Expectation, Communication, and Performance Influence." *Review of Educational Research* 49 (Summer 1979): 389–410.

Good, Thomas L. "Classroom Expectations: Teacher-Pupil Interactions." In *The Social Psychology of School Learning*, edited by James H. McMillan, pp. 378–85. New York: Academic Press, 1980.

Irvine, Jacqueline J. *Black Students and School Failure: Policies, Practices, and Prescriptions.*. New York: Greenwood Press, 1990.

Johnson, Martin L. "Blacks in Mathematics: A Status Report." *Journal for Research in Mathematics Education* 15 (March 1984): 145–53.

Kibler, Madge H. "Raising High School Graduates in Public Housing: Perceptions of Parents and the Graduates." Doctoral diss., University of Georgia, 1995.

King, John D. "Investigating the General and Mathematics Efficacy and Attributions of African American Students, as Predictors of Pursuit of Mathematics-Related Careers." Doctoral diss., University of Georgia, 1995.

Ladson-Billings, Gloria. "Making Mathematics Meaningful in Multicultural Contexts." In *New Directions for Equity in Mathematics Education*, edited by Walter G. Secada, Elizabeth Fennema, and Lisa B. Adajian, pp. 126–45. New York: Cambridge University Press, 1995.

Matthews, Westina. "Influences on the Learning and Participation of Minorities in Mathematics." *Journal for Research in Mathematics Education* 15 (March 1984): 84–95.

Neisser, Ulric. "New Answers to an Old Question." In *The School Achievement of Minority Children: New Perspectives*, edited by Ulric Neisser, pp. 1–17. Hillsdale, N.J.: Lawrence Erlbaum Associates, 1986.

Stiff, Lee. "African-American Students and the Promise of the *Curriculum and Evaluation Standards*." In *Teaching and Learning Mathematics in the 1990s*, 1990 Yearbook of the National Council of Teachers of Mathematics, edited by Thomas J. Cooney, pp. 152–58. Reston, Va.: National Council of Teachers of Mathematics, 1990.

Race Consciousness, Identity, and Affect in Learning Mathematics

The Case of Four African American Prospective Teachers

6

Norma C. Presmeg

What are the strengths that help African American prospective mathematics teachers cope with the stresses they frequently encounter in predominantly white universities? "It seems like black students have a harder time than any of the other students," said Dany (pseudonym) in an interview. Hall and Allen (1989) quote studies that point to the "isolation and alienation, as well as depressed academic aspirations and achievement expressed by Afro-Americans on white campuses," and also to the "high physical and emotional stress that the students undergo in trying to sustain themselves in such hostile, alien environments" (p. 176). There is an interplay of sociocultural and psychological processes as students learn to cope with the stresses (Prillerman, Myers, and Smedley 1989). An enhanced understanding of some of the factors that aid prospective mathematics teachers in this coping was the aim of the study described in this chapter. Such an understanding is important because encouraging such students to finish their programs successfully helps to alleviate the shortage of African American teachers to serve as role models in mathematics classrooms (Mathematical Sciences Education Board 1990).

Although it is acknowledged that diversity also exists within ethnic groups (Cushner, McClelland, and Safford 1996), it appears that identification with a minority ethnic group and commitment to racial group objectives—what Hall and Allen (1989) called "race consciousness"—can be a powerful source of strength that facilitates coping when students of color are enrolled in predominantly white universities. In the "high-demand and often nonsupportive environments" of predominantly white universities, "noncognitive, personal and contextual factors such as positive self-concept, an understanding of racism, and the availability of supportive people at the university were more predictive of black student retention than academic ability" (Hall and Allen, p. 200). The three elements mentioned, namely, positive self-concept, an understanding of racism, and the availability of supportive people at the university, were aspects of the coping exhibited by students in the present study too. Prillerman, Myers, and Smedley (1989) reported that in coping, adjustment styles that combined a commitment to both personal and racial group objectives were most adaptive. These styles are elements of race consciousness.

In what follows, the actual words of four African American students on such a campus illustrate these issues as they pertain to their experiences in learning mathematics and their reasons for wanting to become teachers. These students coped and, in spite of setbacks, fulfilled their dream of teaching, for the purpose of "making a difference" in the communities from which they came.

> **Although it is acknowledged that diversity also exists within ethnic groups, ... it appears that identification with a minority ethnic group and commitment to racial group objectives—what Hall and Allen ... called "race consciousness"—can be a powerful source of strength that facilitates coping when students of color are enrolled in predominantly white universities.**

METHODOLOGY

Since the aim of the study was an open exploration of the nature of the difficulties, and the coping factors, experienced by African American prospective mathematics teachers on a predominantly white campus, a case study methodology was employed (Merriam 1988). Such a methodology allows the flexibility to pursue issues as they arise. The four students, Cord, Jane, Jinny, and Dany (pseudonyms), were each interviewed four times in the course of this qualitative research. The audiotaped interviews ranged in duration from twenty to fifty-five minutes and were semistructured around five themes that were designed to approach the students' difficulties and coping from several different angles, thus providing a form of data triangulation (Stake 1995) for validation. The five themes were as follows:

1. How the problem appeared to the students (and home and educational background)

2. Specific examples "worked aloud" from college mathematics textbooks. (The aim of this theme was to investigate students' feelings about, and memory of, mathematical content that they had studied.)

3. Six word problems from a cognitive preference measure (Presmeg's 1985 Mathematical Visuality instrument). (This instrument yields scores for *mathematical visuality*—that is, preference for using visual methods such as diagrams or imagery when solving mathematical problems—and for mathematical accuracy, the correctness of solutions.)

4. "Matchsticks," a nonverbal sequence of mathematical tasks involving arrays of squares outlined with matchsticks, leading to a generalized principle. (These tasks have the diagnostic purpose of investigating aspects of generalization from concrete instances illustrated by matchstick squares.)

5. Beliefs—"What is mathematics?" and follow-up themes in final interviews

Full transcripts of all interviews were analysed for recurrent issues that related to the difficulties experienced by the students and for factors that aided their coping. The results of third and fourth interview themes (mathematical visuality and matchstick squares) will not be reported in this chapter. The cognitive style measure of mathematical visuality and the matchstick tasks, although interesting in themselves, had little or no bearing on the fact that these were African American students. Their varied problem-solving styles, according to these interviews, reflected those of the general population and were not directly germane to the themes that emerged in the other interviews.

THE STUDENTS

The students were chosen on the basis of their having experienced difficulty with one or more of the required content mathematics courses. Three of the students, Jane, Jinny, and Dany, were prospective elementary school teachers. Cord, the only male, was enrolled in the program for prospective secondary school mathematics teachers. Three of the four students (Jane, Dany, and Cord) had completed one or more mathematics education courses taught by the author, whom they knew and trusted. Thus empathy was established quickly, and all the students appeared to see value in the study, the insights from which they hoped might help their successors even if the project was too late to spare them some hard experiences. All four students spoke with passion about their experiences, their beliefs, and the sense of mission that they entertained. From the wealth of data produced, protocols have been selected that illustrate these aspects.

Students were encouraged to talk freely about their home and educational backgrounds, from childhood onward, particularly as these affected their learning of mathematics. They were also questioned in detail about the university mathematics courses that they had taken. They shared impressions and beliefs, anecdotes, and above all, feelings about these courses. The main impression was the emotional impact of these courses on the student. Whereas the content was in large measure lost (Interview 2), the feelings remained and influenced the students' subsequent belief and value systems concerning mathematics and education (final interview). Although it is artificial to separate influences that interweave in their impact on the students' psychological functioning (Berry and Asamen 1989), for convenience of reporting, emergent themes will be grouped around the home, the school, and the university mathematics courses.

The Home

The literature concurs in stressing the importance of a supportive home environment for the academic success of minority students, irrespective of socioeconomic status, female-headed households, or other factors (Jenkins 1989; Lomotey 1990; Mathematical Sciences Education Board 1990; Banks and Banks 1995). Learning and academic achievement were valued in the homes from which these four students came. Jane spoke as follows:

Jane: The families [in elementary school], as a matter of fact, were very, very different from mine. Because my parents, I was raised, my parents were married, and I ... many of the kids that were my age, their parents were either divorced or they weren't married at all. And, um, they'd tell me, "You're different! You're different!" and I didn't know what they were seeing, what it is that's different, you know. And I found that they were much more streetwise. I was raised on a farm, I was raised out of the city, so it took some adjusting. I found it very strange, the way they act, at times. But eventually I had friends, you know, like, with everyone. You know, it's just, I could not, I've never been a person to stay in one clique. You know, I've always had to interact with everyone.

What Jane is describing here also suggests the incipient acceptance of the values of the school and teachers rather than those of any particular peer group or gang (Berry and Asamen 1989). It is likely that the values of the teachers were not incompatible with her home background values. She elaborated as follows:

Jane: I've always been a child to, um, and I guess most children do now, observe the adults; I read expressions. I still do. But as a child, I know, more so. And I just pick up, I guess subconsciously; it really mattered to me what the teacher thought about me. It really mattered to me. That depended on my performance, at one point. I mean, if the teacher had a bad day, perhaps it wasn't my fault, maybe she came in like that. It affected my performance. And I remember being very scared, you know, if she was in a bad mood, the whole day.... I was always concerned about my fellow classmates. You know, I'd finish my work and then help with their work, if that was permissible.

The caring for classmates that Jane expressed was also part of the genesis of her decision to choose a career in elementary school teaching, in spite of her parents' desire that she should take up a medical career. "I finally accepted the way that I felt, what I wanted to do," she said. She also described teaching her younger brother and sister their "time tables," that is, the multiplication tables. Like Jane, Jinny also described a "big sister" role in her volunteer work with African American children in a school in "a project area, well, *very* low economic area."

All four students gave the impression of self-awareness, strength, and commitment, as well as easy emotionality. Dany spoke as follows:

Dany: I always wanted to work with children, from really young. First I think I wanted to be a pediatrician. And then I worked with my godfather at his practice, and I am too emotional for it. I cry when the kids from preschool [where she works] leave to go to kindergarden. There is no way that I could … [*laughs*].

Later she considered physical therapy as a career before deciding on teaching. Her sense of mission in her career is clear in the following statement:

Dany: Now, there's a lot of goals that I have, you know, to becoming a teacher. That's why, y'know, trying to give kids morals and values, you know. And not imposing mine but letting them find morals and values for themselves because, nowadays, it's coming to, like, especially, we're talking about places where blacks are shooting blacks, you know, and it's all in, that inner-city thing. And so, somebody has to begin breaking the cycle for anything to start working.

This introduction to the circumstances of learning for some of the students sets the scene for the influences that they described in their schooling.

The School

There were two overriding themes in the students' descriptions of their schooling. First, there was the part played by role models in their decision to become teachers. Second, this decision was influenced by experiences, both positive and negative, from the classroom. These incidents, which the students had experienced or witnessed, sometimes seemed trivial in themselves, but their impact on the lives of the students was far-reaching.

Cord came from a middle-class home, but the predominantly African American elementary school he attended (a forty-five-minute walk from home) was in "a poor kind of neighborhood" in a large city. The junior high school he attended was "all black," and at that time he had decided he wanted to teach business education. But in the predominantly Hispanic and white senior high school he attended, there was a [white] teacher, Mrs. M., of whom he said, "She is the one that really inspired me in mathematics." Along with a detailed description of how she taught particular mathematical topics, he remembered, "She would always make it so much *fun* to learn all of these kind of little acronyms there." For his five senior high school mathematics courses, Cord's grades were a B, two A's and two C's. As a result of Mrs. M.'s teaching, he decided to become a mathematics teacher. The other three prospective teachers all described African American mathematics teachers who had been role models at one or another period of their education. These teachers were described as "mean" (Jinny), "demanding respect" (Jinny), "a friend" (Dany), "there for me—I'll never forget her name!" (Jane). Dany reported, "She was also a friend, she wasn't just my teacher. She was a very, she was a very strong person. I mean, face it, like you know people would say 'She is so ugly!' because facially, people thought she was, but her personality came off as beautiful."

In all the descriptions of teachers who were influential, an element of *caring* is central to the impact made by the teacher in stark contrast to the impersonality of some of the university mathematics courses with which these students struggled. In speaking of role models throughout her learning of mathematics, Dany commented, "I had more bad than good."

With regard to their schooling, Cord and Dany both had negative experiences that left deep imprints on their minds and about which they spoke with passion:

In all the descriptions of teachers who were influential, an element of *caring* is central to the impact made by the teacher in stark contrast to the impersonality of some of the university mathematics courses with which these students struggled.

Cord: My elementary experience was very bad, and that's why I decided to become a teacher. I had some good teachers, and a lot of 'em were not! It was a negative thing that happened [in fifth grade] that inspired me to become a teacher. One of my friends had asked the teacher to explain the lesson because he did not understand where she was going or how she was explaining it. And she said, "You know, I've explained it one time, and I'm not going to explain it again, whether you all learn or not! You have to realize, I wanna get my paycheck!" And, er, when she made that comment, I thought, you know, to myself, from that day on I just, you know, I was like, *God*, I wanna be a teacher, I wanna be a *good* teacher! So, y'know, from that day I wanted to be a teacher.

And from the interview with Dany:

Interviewer: And how did you feel about the mathematics? In elementary school?

Dany: I don't remember much of it [*laughing*]. I mean, I must have done it somehow, but … I remember third grade really well, and that was because we had one boy that could never do it, and, um, he would stand to the board and, and cry! And I would be so upset, and I would like, I would start screamin' the answers, and my teacher would be like, "Dany, be quiet then!" Like he'd be doin' ten plus seven, and, I would go [*loudly*] "It's seventeen!" And I would start after, he start, he's cryin' now. You know, you turn around, y'know, cause we're looking at the back of him. And we just, we waited! So long, so much! I guess cause I didn't want to wait any more. I would just say, "It's seventeen," and I always said that. And every time she would send him to the board I'd go "Not again!" But you know, now that you think about it, if you, if you did it, y'know if you had—if you didn't know, you didn't know! You know, you didn't have anyone to say, "Well, let's take out some beans and count ten of 'em, and let's count seven more and let's put them …" you know, we had no one, you know.

Dany's passionate description leads in to the students' reports of their perceptions of the university mathematics courses.

University Mathematics Courses

The students described nine courses ranging from college prep algebra through college algebra, college geometry, and trigonometry, to calculus. Cord's case is particularly serious. In school, as he said, "I took tests and everything and they found that I was very exceptional in mathematics." Yet in the university mathematics courses, his grades were as follows:

Trigonometry	D, A– (course repeated)
Precalculus	C
Calculus 1	F, D (course repeated)
College Geometry	F

He was repeating calculus yet again and would repeat geometry. (The other three students, who were prospective elementary school teachers, had taken other courses, that is, college prep algebra, college algebra, and logic and reasoning, and Jane had taken precalculus.)

Cord: Well, right now, I'm just debating my major. I'm debating whether I want to teach any more or go to another field. [*He was considering another service field, namely, public administration.*]

Interviewer: Why? Because of the math?

Cord: Yeah! It's just because I still have to take linear algebra, and, um, statistics, and what's the other one? And calc. 2. So I'm like, y'know, I dunno if I wanna go through that.

Interviewer: All this heavy math in order to be a high school teacher.

Cord: Exactly! That's where the problem comes in. I don't see the relevance for a lot of the math, but, y'know, I see it as, this department has been here for a long time, they're professionals, so apparently there's some relevancy to all this that I can't see because I'm not in the classroom. So that's how I think about it.

When questioned, Cord explained that he had taken some content mathematics courses concurrently with mathematics education courses that were taught according to a constructivist paradigm. He found a large discrepancy in the teaching methods employed. He spoke as follows:

Cord: We sat there for two and a half hours, no, two hours [in college geometry], listening to him lecture. It killed us! And when you take classes together, like doing, when I was doing college geometry, I was taking [the constructivist] course, Introduction to Applications for Mathematics Teachers, so it would be like, we came from [the constructivist] course, where we interacted and we just had fun, and we could apply our learning, and then we'd go to this course where we sit there for two hours and listen to this man lecture. And, y'know, we had to go through that all the time we were in [the constructivist] class, and it was just terrible! It was just, made me *miserable!*

Cord could not see why the course, college geometry, was required if the students were also required to take the education course, Teaching Algebra and Geometry in the High School, which was another constructivist course. He said, "Y'know, so to me that is two courses that are knocking each other." He continued as follows:

Cord: I didn't see any relevance for college geometry. And, with talking with people in the department, you know, math education students even, nobody could remember. I, when I was in the course, I tried to get help, and the people that took it before couldn't remember what it was about. Because, you take it and you get a grade, and you just do it!

Interviewer: So it's for the sake of the grade?

Cord: Yeah! Just because it's required.

Although the comments of Cord and the other students regarding pedagogy are not particular to the fact that they are African American, they are included to illustrate the strong passions that these experiences elicited in these students. These strong feelings were characteristic of all four students. Jinny was another student who spoke eloquently and repeatedly about the irrelevance of higher mathematics courses, most of which she had found "boring." She was fully convinced that higher mathematics was an instrumental subject in which rote memorization was the predominant mode of learning. Students were also eloquent in reporting the following further constraints:

- Fast pace of pure mathematics courses (Jinny, Dany, and especially Jane, for whom lack of time was often a problem)
- Large classes that made learning impersonal (Jane and Dany)
- Quantity of content matter (Jinny and Dany)
- Students' excessive workload (Jinny)

In the second interview, each student (1) selected examples from a college textbook appropriate to a content mathematics course they had completed and (2) worked out these mathematical tasks, explaining aloud how they were thinking, what they could remember, what their impressions and feelings were. Reactions of Jinny and Dany were typical. Both of these students appeared to recognize the material as they paged through the book, but when they came to do examples, in detail, it was apparent, first, that the mathematics had been learned in a very instrumental or procedural way, without real understanding of the concepts (Hiebert 1986) or of why certain procedures worked. Second, it was apparent that much even of this procedural learning had been forgotten. What remained was the affect or emotion that they associated with the experience of having done the course.

Cord made strong comments regarding the negative effects of a restrictive mathematics syllabus, particularly, in this case, at the university level. "A lot of teachers in the math department just follow syllabus. See, I *hate* syllabus! I hate syllabus with passion! Because syllabus confines you, to so much. And it limits, you know, what the class can do. So, in all the classes that I've had before, we had a syllabus and it limits you. Like, the teacher will say, 'Well, we gotta get past this, you know, we gotta get to this point, we gotta keep going.'"

The passion Cord referred to in his comments, typical of the articulations of all the students in this study at times, suggests that feelings and values may assume greater importance in mathematics education than cognitive aspects. The impression given was of the overriding importance of affective issues in the students' learning of mathematics at all levels, but particularly in higher education. When students learn university mathematics instrumentally (Jinny, Dany), just for the grade (Cord), and then forget the course contents after the final examination (all four students), it is not just that they might as well not have taken the course. It is worse than that because the negative affect that they associate with the experience of having taken the course, "successfully" or otherwise, remains after the course contents are forgotten. "God, I hated all of this stuff!" said Jinny, as she paged through a college algebra textbook the contents of which she had largely forgotten.

In the second part of the fourth interview, the students were asked about their beliefs about mathematics by means of the question "What is mathematics?" Cord had given this question much thought and had previously written an essay that addressed the subject. In contrast, Dany, Jane, and Jinny found the question a difficult one: Dany and Jinny had similar conceptions of mathematics as "a bunch of numbers," which also used formulas but was not particularly relevant to the real world "unless it's money or something" (Dany). The beliefs expressed here mirrored comments in other interviews concerning the way mathematics had been taught to these students. However, Dany reported that she would teach mathematics "hands on" and not as it was taught to her.

In contrast to the beliefs of Jinny and Dany, Jane saw mathematics as much more relevant to life:

Jane: To me, mathematics is a creative way of thinking. It's a creative way of solving problems that we have to deal with every day. It involves expanding the mind, for one thing; they are complex and simple at the same time, if I can use that together. I'm looking at it more so in a geometrical sense. Like, I'm always referring back to geometry: it seems like I can apply geometry to everything.

Even more than Jane, Cord saw mathematics as relevant to all of life and to every other subject of the school curriculum:

Cord: I think of mathematics as the infinite subject; it is the subject that governs all other subjects. And when I say govern, I mean, the world cannot revolve, or the world cannot exist, without mathematics.

With understanding and eloquence, he proceeded to give examples. With regard to how he hoped to teach mathematics, *understanding* was an essential ingredient, as it was also for Jane:

Jane: I want my students to understand *why* the answer is the answer. And I want them to, er, construct the answer in their mind; I want them to think about it.... I want them to express themselves, I want to know what's going on up here, in their mind. And, I don't want to necessarily tell them, even though, I do like to give information.... I must, that's one thing I want my students to see, if nothing else. "How is this going to affect my life? Why should I learn this? How will it affect the world that I'm gonna live in?" Because I believe that if they don't understand that, they will see it as useless, absolutely useless. There must be some type of connection there, some type of application, to their daily lives.

Cord commented further:

Cord: I don't see myself as a teacher. I see myself as an educator. You can't teach anyone, you can only educate them.... That while the students are learning from me, I'm also learning from them. And we can, you know, learn from each other. I see myself, when we're doing small groups and things, me getting into small groups, actually participating, helping, you know, exploring, and showing my students that I, too, learn new things everyday. Because a lot of times, students get a teacher and he'll know it all, the person with all of the knowledge, and they forget that they, too, can make knowledge and they just don't know how to, express it or unleash it.

CONCLUSIONS

This chapter can do no more than scratch the surface of the complex issues that have an impact on minority achievement and coping in university mathematics courses. In this exploratory study, four articulate African American students described issues and constraints that appeared to lie in the organization and teaching of the courses themselves, in psychological factors that influenced the feelings and beliefs of the students, and in background issues relating to the whole experience of being black in the United States. Chester M. Pierce (1989), who described himself as "a black psychiatrist living in the USA seeking to find unity and reduce stress," wrote as follows: "Since it is usually impossible for me to be conscious more than 30 minutes without thinking of my race, all of my professional life can be described as an effort to live as a black in the USA" (p. 299). Thus, although many of the themes in these interviews are not specific to the fact that the students in the study were African American, in a sense their ethnicity was implicit in their whole university experience.

More specifically, although the students interviewed in this study were not all explicit on the subject of *role models* with regard to their university mathematics courses, the importance of having good role models and mentors, preferably African American, in their learning of mathematics emerged in the students' descriptions of their school experiences. The need to recruit more minority faculty members as role models, for improved recruitment and retention of minority students, has been well documented in the literature (Mathematical Sciences Education Board 1990). Jinny described an African American role model in her college prep algebra course (Mrs. P.), who together with a white instructor in a later course (Mrs. G.), had influenced the way she wanted to teach: "I know I can be Mrs. G. and Mrs. P. ... because I'm gonna be mean, but I'm also gonna laugh with my kids!" Mrs. G. was described as "fun and understanding and kind," whereas the "mean" quality is one that Mrs. P. shared with role models Jinny found in school. "And they were, they're black women, and they demanded respect all the time; I mean, my fifth-grade teacher was the meanest woman in the world," Jinny added. But caring is important too (Dany), and the combination of strength of character and caring emerged frequently in all four students' descriptions of their role models.

Further psychological issues were related to the students' own perceptions of themselves as learners, which often appeared to be linked to teacher expectations (Jinny and Jane), illustrating a phenomenon often mentioned in the literature (Berry and Asamen 1989): "A person in our society often validates his identity through the evaluations of significant others" (p. 126). Parham and Parham (1989, p. 127) described a study that concluded that four factors were necessary for the development of positive self-concepts in African American children, namely, (*a*) maximum participation by parents and teachers; (*b*) mores and values of the home reinforced in the immediate community and school; (*c*) African American culture and lifestyles reflected in the educational curriculum; and (*d*) academic achievement being encouraged regardless of social class.

The comments of the students in the present study and their descriptions of early mathematics learning experiences provide some confirmation of the importance of these factors for later mathematics achievement. Reference to curriculum in point (*c*) is germane to comments made by Jane and Jinny, and by Dany particularly, who wherever possible introduced African American culture and music into her teaching, even in her part-time job at that time, teaching mathematics at the preschool level.

From the students' comments, it seems that the self-participation involved in a participatory mode of teaching and learning mathematics generates far more positive affect than does the traditional instructor-dominated mode that is apparently still the norm in university mathematics courses. All four students were eloquent in their descriptions of reasons why they aspired to teach mathematics in a participatory mode in their own classrooms one day (final interview). It is ironic that what these students aspired to in their visions of their own teaching is in many ways a reaction to what they experienced as learners of mathematics and later described with passion. The words of the students illustrate clearly how important affective issues and the phenomenon of *negative role models* are in the learning of mathematics. A traumatically experienced incident in a mathematics classroom could, in fact, inspire these African American students with a strong sense of purpose that causes them to aspire to teach in ways *opposite* to the negative pedagogy that they experienced.

In the sense of mission expressed by all the students in this study, their race consciousness was apparent. As he described in an essay written in his freshman year, Cord had been inspired by Martin Luther King, Jr. As he expressed it in this essay, Cord's ability to dream of making a difference was intact. Like Cord, Jinny, Jane, and Dany wanted to be teachers who would make a difference in the lives of African American children. Dany explained, "I need to focus on, where I come from also, and the people that, you know, I ... I dunno. The people that *I* come from, I need to focus with them, and make sure they understand, so, you know, we as a race can progress, instead of being stagnant, as we are, or have been." The impression was strong that this sense of race consciousness was a tremendous source of strength in the adaptations and coping required of these students in dealing with the stresses of their campus lives. Identification with an ethnic group can provide a sense of mission in the aspiration to become a mathematics teacher who makes a difference in the lives of students of that group. This sense of mission is a primary source of coping and strength that needs to be acknowledged and encouraged by educators of all prospective mathematics teachers. Particularly for African Americans, the sense of mission may be bound up with race consciousness, which may make all the difference in coping with the added stresses of their keenly felt campus experiences. Race consciousness was certainly a factor for the students in this study, who continued and achieved success in completing the mathematics education program.

REFERENCES

Banks, James A., and Cherry A. M. Banks. *Handbook of Research on Multicultural Education.* New York: Macmillan, 1995.

Berry, Gordon L., and Joy K. Asamen, eds. *Black Students: Psychosocial Issues and Academic Achievement.* Newbury Park, Calif.: Sage Publications, 1989.

Cushner, Kenneth, Averil McClelland, and Philip Safford. *Human Diversity in Education: An Integrative Approach.* New York: McGraw-Hill, 1996.

Hall, Marcia L., and Walter R. Allen. "Race Consciousness among African-American College Students." In *Black Students: Psychosocial Issues and Academic Achievement,* edited by Gordon Berry and Joy Asamen, pp. 172–97. Newbury Park, Calif.: Sage Publications, 1989.

Hiebert, James, ed. *Conceptual and Procedural Knowledge: The Case of Mathematics.* Hillsdale, N.J.: Lawrence Erlbaum Associates, 1986.

Jenkins, Louis E. "The Black Family and Academic Achievement." In *Black Students: Psychosocial Issues and Academic Achievement,* edited by Gordon Berry and Joy Asamen, pp. 138–52. Newbury Park, Calif.: Sage Publications, 1989.

Lomotey, Kofi, ed. *Going to School: The African American Experience.* Albany, N.Y.: State University of New York Press, 1990.

Mathematical Sciences Education Board. *Making Mathematics Work for Minorities: Framework for a National Action Plan, 1990–2000.* Washington, D.C.: National Research Council, 1990.

Merriam, Sharan B. *Case Study Research in Education: A Qualitative Approach.* San Francisco: Jossey-Bass, 1988.

Parham, William D., and Thomas A. Parham. "The Community and Academic Achievement." In *Black Students: Psychosocial Issues and Academic Achievement,* edited by Gordon Berry and Joy Asamen, pp. 120–37. Newbury Park, Calif.: Sage Publications, 1989.

Pierce, Chester M. "Unity in Diversity: Thirty-three Years of Stress." In *Black Students: Psychosocial Issues and Academic Achievement,* edited by Gordon Berry and Joy Asamen, pp. 296–312 . Newbury Park, Calif.: Sage Publications, 1989.

Presmeg, Norma C. "The Role of Visually Mediated Processes in High School Mathematics: A Classroom Investigation." Doctoral diss., University of Cambridge (England), 1985.

Prillerman, Shelly L., Hector F. Myers, and Brian D. Smedley. "Stress, Well-Being and Academic Achievement in College." In *Black Students: Psychosocial Issues and Academic Achievement,* edited by Gordon Berry and Joy Asamen, pp. 198–217. Newbury Park, Calif.: Sage Publications, 1989.

Stake, Robert E. *The Art of Case Study Research.* Thousand Oaks, Calif.: Sage Publications, 1995.

Focus on Instructional and Curricular Modifications Aimed at African American Students

The Use of "Call and Response" Pedagogy to Reinforce Mathematics Concepts and Skills Taught to African American Kindergartners

7

Maurice M. Martinez

The purpose of this discussion is to present one form of African American culture used successfully in reinforcing basic skills in mathematics with African American kindergartners. Cultural experiences enhance learning, especially when these experiences are highly valued and frequently used by members of a group. One such experience among African Americans is the use of the *call-and-response* mode in sacred and pleasurable interactions. This paper will discuss a successful use of call-and-response pedagogy in teaching mathematics to African American prekindergartners (three- and four-year-olds) and kindergartners (five-year-olds). The pedagogy is grounded in aural and oral communication, cultural patterns of religious and secular social group behavior, the use of hands, fingers, and rhythmic "tapping" to reinforce previously learned number sequences and relationships.

PRE-KINDERGARTEN PREPARATION

Nearly all the African American children enrolled in the Martinez School entered at age three. They came from every socioeconomic background and from all parts of New Orleans, including surrounding suburbs and distant locations such as Kenner and Gretna. Children were provided with bus and van transportation to and from school. The school day lasted four hours, starting at nine in the morning and ending at one in the afternoon. Specific goals and objectives were formulated for each age group. By the end of the school year they were taught:

Three-year-olds	Four-year-olds	Five-year-olds
1. Number recognition	1. Number sequences	1. The concept of *one more*
2. To count up to 20	2. To count to 50	2. To count forward and backward up to 100
3. To write each number from 1 to 20	3. To write each number from 1 to 50	3. Double-digit addition (without carrying)
4. To write each letter of the alphabet, upper and lower case	4. Single-digit addition	4. Subtraction
5. Word recognition and decoding	5. Individualized reading	5. Reading and writing
6. To write their names	6. To write words and sentences	

SMART HANDS

Mildred Bernard Martinez used an approach that empowered prekindergarten and kindergarten children to take control of their learning. The children gained—in Piaget's ([1932] 1965) terms—*autonomy* by viewing their hands as extensions of their thoughts and mental processes. In her approach, hands and fingers belonged to each person and could do things, could fulfill the wishes of each person on command. This sent a powerful message to the young children, transferring action and inaction from the person to the person's hands. Children were taught that they had *smart* hands that could do most anything. No longer could one place blame for failure on the inability of the mind to solve a problem. Perhaps, it was suggested, you were not using your hands in the best possible ways to help you solve the problem. In this approach, the blame now is transferred from the delicate and sensitive affective domain with accompanying feelings of incompetence and lack of self-confidence to an extension of one's *appendage outer self*—the hands and fingers. This notion seems to have something in common with Kamii's (1985) discussion of autonomy, that to the extent that the child becomes able to govern himself, he or she is less governed by other people. This allowed teachers to exercise high expectations, a correlate of an effective school (Edmonds 1979). It also placed the responsibility on each individual pupil to perform, with very little tolerance for excuses. In the course of the day, this was often challenged and tested by pupils.

One typical example of testing this approach was made by a four-year-old who refused to engage in the writing assignment during class time. The teacher walked over and quietly asked, "Why aren't you using your hands to write the number?" The boy replied, "Aww, my hands are lazy today and don't feel like writing. They're tired and need to take a rest." "OK," replied the teacher, "but when we go outside for recess, you will have to wake up your hands and stay with them in the room to exercise your hands and make them smart and strong." After a few minutes, the boy yelled out, "Look, look, my hands woke up. They're being smart hands now!" as he returned on task.

The use of hands and fingers in teaching mathematics to kindergartners has been well documented in studies by Ginsburg (1977), Jensen and Spector (1984), Baratta-Lorton (1976), and Ford (1987). The Martinez approach seems to have something in common with other techniques involving finger-counting systems from African and American Indian communities and the medieval system catalogued by the Venerable Bede. Zaslavsky (1979, 1994) presented a rationale for allowing—even encouraging—children to count on their fingers, citing number words from many languages that derive from names for gestures. Classrooms in the Martinez School were often filled with the voices of children engaged in the task, reinforcing one another in the search for solutions and sharing knowledge verbally.

In call-and-response teaching, nonverbal communication and other gestures were used to help clarify abstract forms of mathematical reasoning. This helped children to conceptualize, to form mental images in counting and addition. Mildred Martinez postulated that children between the ages of three and five years have a higher tolerance for the reteaching of concepts or the retelling of a story. She referred to this characteristic as *delight in repetition*. Studies have long shown that children when told a story—such as "Goldilocks and the Three Bears"—*remembered* every scene, situation, and character in the story. If the story was retold omitting any part of the original *first telling* of the story, the three-to-five-year-old was quick to respond to the storyteller by correcting the change from the original version. Kindergartners, she concluded, had more resilience for repetitive learning—condemned by many educators as *drill*. Beyond the age of six years, she found this criticism for the most part to be valid. As children grow older, there seems to be less tolerance for repetitive

Classrooms in the Martinez School were often filled with the voices of children engaged in the task, reinforcing one another in the search for solutions and sharing knowledge verbally.

learning. The call for mathematical reasoning that is purely analytical by many educators often fails to account for age and developmental differences, especially the willingness of three-to-five-year-olds to accept repetition of tasks and to feel secure in the imprint of acquired knowledge and their unwillingness to deviate from that learned imprint.

What follows is a specific example of the procedure used in the Martinez School. The teacher (M) pointed out to the children that they were given a pair of *smart hands* that do many things. In an aural and oral approach, a typical dialogue with the entire class would be something like the following:

Dialogue and Discussion

M: Your hands are going to help you to learn. These hands will help you to understand, to do things in school. Did you know that your hands can talk?

Class: Noooooo! [*Nearly all respond in disbelief.*]

M: Yes! You have talking hands!

Class: Ohhh, noooo! [*Giggling to one another, while looking at their hands.*] My hands can't talk!

M: What does this mean?" [*Making a number of different gestures, e.g., waving a pointed index finger … meaning no; waving hello and goodbye; "come here" gesture; palm out … meaning "stop"; thumbs up gesture of approval; clapping hands to praise, etc.…*]

Class: Ooooooh! Yes.

M: Your hands can do many things. Your hands can help you to dress. They can feed you when you are hungry. They help you to bathe. Your hands can make a person feel good when you give someone a great big hug. In school, your hands are going to help you to write.

Call-and-Response Technique

M: Open your hand. Look at it. Do you have anything in your hand?

Class: No!

M: Your hand is empty!

Class: Yes.

M: When your hand is empty, you have nothing in your hand! What do you have in your hand?

Class: Nothing!

M: What do you have in your hand?

Class: Nothing!

M: Another way of saying nothing is zero! What do you have in your hand?

Class: Zero!

(Repeat a few times until all children are responding verbally.)

M: Now, let's put one finger in your hand. What do you have in your hand?

Class: One!

The teacher explained that when we place one finger in the hand, we add one to zero. Children were able to build connections between the concrete use of one finger and the abstract symbol 1 or number one. They responded in a chorus: "One and zero are one." The concept was repeated in a call-and-response format several times until each child was responding. The teacher wrote the numeral 1 on the chalkboard, then zero under it with a plus sign, then an under-line ("are"), followed by the sum, 1:

```
  1      one
+ 0      and (+) zero
——       are
  1      one
```

This exercise was repeated in call-and-response format several times until all had mastered the concept. The new lesson uses the same pattern above, but with two fingers. The class responds: "Two plus zero are two." The same pattern is used for the numbers 3, 4, 5, 6, 7, 8, 9, 10.

THE TAPPING TECHNIQUE IN ADDITION

The *tapping* technique, used by four- and five-year-olds in the Martinez kindergarten, is a rhythmic approach in both problem solving and retention of skills needed to obtain the correct answer. The child is taught when working independently on an addition problem such as 4 + 2, to say: "Four and two are …" (then tap twice using the index finger or pencil [or pointer at the chalkboard] while counting "5, 6," the correct sum being 6). Another example is 4 + 3, where the child would say, "Four and three are …" (then tap three times while counting "5, 6, 7," the correct sum being 7). The tapping technique is also kinesthetic and produces a rhythmic sound that helps the child learn and retain the process of obtaining the correct answer. This is an interim technique that is used only until the child has memorized the addition facts and no longer needs to engage in tapping.

This Martinez School technique seems to be supported in the research of Groen and Resnick (1977), Ginsburg and Russell (1981), and in subsequent discussions on *counting all* and *counting on* strategies used by four-year-old children to combine and count separate sets in order to get a new set. Given, for example, the addition problem above, 4 + 2, a counting-all strategy would involve the child's counting both sets from the beginning, "One, two, three, four—five, six," whereas counting on, as Ginsburg described, is a more advanced and easier approach in that the child counts as follows: "Four—five, six." Tapping reinforces a counting-on approach.

WORD PROBLEMS

In a whole-class follow-up activity at their seats, pupils copy and solve on their tablets addition problems written on the chalkboard. They also learn to write the *word names* (one, two, three, …, seven, eight, …, etc.) of each number. While this is taking place, children are called in small groups to a table in the room. Additional reinforcement to ensure understanding is taught in small groups using manipulatives such as small cubes, wood blocks, and a large (two feet by three feet with two- and three-inch wooden beads in different colors) abacus. Each individual child in the group is required to solve an addition word problem as the other children in the group listen and observe. For example, the teacher takes six blocks and divides them into two sets of four and two, with a fun story: "I want to make a choo-choo train. If I take these four cars and add two more cars, how many cars will there be in the train?" The child is allowed to handle the blocks and to discover the answer. Different word problems are presented at the small-group table to each child. All the children gain a knowledge of formal addition by watching and participating. The abacus is used later in an entire class call-and-response review of the concepts *one more than* and *one less than* and in counting backward. Throughout the day, verbal interaction that focused on learning specific concepts was emphasized both in reading and in mathematics.

SUBTRACTION

In regard to children's learning of the basic arithmetic facts, Cobb and Merkel (1989) emphasized that *thinking strategies*—the child's use of a known sum or difference to find an unknown sum or difference—are crucial in a problem-centered approach. Their experiments in the second-grade curriculum point to the conclusion that in the early grades thinking strategies are compatible with mental computation. Children use mental computation strategies in their thinking strategies and computational algorithms.

In the Martinez School, instructional activities applied the call-and-response method to connect kindergartners' informal thinking strategies with formal mathematics skills through the use of concrete examples that were both enjoyable and reinforcing. In teaching subtraction, Mildred Martinez (M) used the call-and-response method in the following way. She held up a marshmallow to the entire class:

M: Look what I have. What is this?

Class: A candy … nooo … a marshmallow!

M: [*Placing the marshmallow in her open left hand*] "What do I have in my hand?"

Class: A marshmallow.

M: How many marshmallows do I have in my hand?

Class: One!

M: How many?

Class: One!

M: Now, I'm going to take away this one marshmallow from my hand. [*She put the marshmallow in her mouth and ate it as the children watched in astonishment.*]

M: [*Opened her empty left hand*] "How many marshmallows do I have in my hand now?"

Class: None!

M: What's in my hand?

Class: Nothing!

M: And what is another way to say "nothing"?

Class: Zero.

M: [*Writing on the chalkboard*] One take away one is zero.

$$\begin{array}{r} 1 \\ -\,1 \\ \hline 0 \end{array}\quad\begin{array}{l} \text{One} \\ \text{take away one} \\ \text{is zero} \end{array}$$

The teacher then produces a large bag of marshmallows and walks around the room placing one marshmallow on a napkin in front of each pupil, with instructions not to touch it until told to do so. When each pupil has one marshmallow, the teacher repeats the call-and-response lesson:

M: Everyone, put the marshmallow in your left hand. [*Each pupil does this.*] How many marshmallows do you have in your hand?

Class: One!

M: How many?

Class: One!

M: Now, take away the marshmallow and eat it. [*Smiles abound; pupils giggle in delight.*] Look at your left hand. What do you have in your left hand?

Class: Nothing.

M: And what is another way of saying "nothing"?

> **In the Martinez School, instructional activities applied the call-and-response method to connect kindergartners' informal thinking strategies with formal mathematics skills through the use of concrete examples that were both enjoyable and reinforcing.**

Class: Zero!

> *M:*   OK. Let's all say ... [*everyone repeats in unison*]: One take away one is zero.

The math fact is written on the chalkboard, and all the pupils copy it onto their tablets.

The next lesson involves two marshmallows. Two marshmallows are placed in the hand. One is taken away and eaten. What is left is one marshmallow. Children respond in a call-and-response chorus: "Two take away one is one!" This math fact is written formally on the chalkboard. The remaining one marshmallow is used to repeat the first lesson: "One take away one is zero." Children were taught two very important concepts in a short time. (Note that this was the last "eating-a-marshmallow" lesson for the day.) Subsequent "take away one" concepts using numbers 3, 4, 5, 6, ..., 10 were taught using concrete objects and the abacus. Each time, the formal subtraction example was written on the chalkboard and pupils copied it on their tablets.

CONCLUSION

The Martinez School approach seems to demonstrate that African American primary school students perform at higher levels when they are taught—

1. in a holistic social climate, that is, one that clarifies the meanings and connections between the following: informal and formal thinking, home language and school language, memory facts and standardized tests, relational learning styles and analytical learning styles, and verbal and nonverbal communication. This notion seems to share some of the findings in studies by Ginsburg and Baron (1993), Gay and Abrahams (1973), Good and Salvia (1988), Williams and Rivers (1972), Heath (1982), Hilliard (1976), Hale (1981), and Hall (1976).

2. in a school climate that is supportive and caring.

3. in a learning environment that provides opportunities for frequent and consistent monitoring of explicit curricula content to be learned with teachers or tutors present to help small study groups understand solutions to problems. In the Martinez School, small-group instruction follows each whole-class call-and-response lesson.

Small-group activity took place throughout the day. Individualized instruction and one-on-one review of new concepts were addressed in small groups in a nurturing climate of daily feedback and assessment. Students were made to feel comfortable in the group, to acknowledge that "I know this ... but I don't know that!" Peer support and reteaching, coupled with entire class call-and-response learning, provided each individual child with mastery levels of mathematics concepts. Such techniques worked successfully with African American children in New Orleans.

SUMMARY

This case study highlights the need for mathematics educators to find alternative ways to transmit computational skills to African American children. The use of pedagogy and techniques that recognize cultural patterns embedded in the African American experience can go far in facilitating the teaching of mathematics skills.

It is emphasized here that children, aged three to five years, enjoy *repetition.* Mildred Martinez felt that age six was too late to implement the same intensity of repetition exercises used with kindergartners. She believed that at age six and beyond students needed more developmentally appropriate strategies that move in the direction of current mathematics reforms. Her goals were to equip preschoolers with functional skills in basic math, and she did this quite well.

Postscript: The late Mildred Bernard Martinez was my mother.

REFERENCES

Baratta-Lorton, Mary. *Mathematics Their Way.* Menlo Park, Calif.: Addison-Wesley Publishing Co., 1976.

Cobb, Paul., and Graceann Merkel. "Thinking Strategies: Teaching Arithmetic through Problem Solving." In *New Directions for Elementary School Mathematics*, 1989 Yearbook of the National Council of Teachers of Mathematics, edited by Paul R. Trafton, pp. 70–81. Reston, Va.: National Council of Teachers of Mathematics, 1989.

Edmonds, Ron R. "Some Schools Work and More Can." *Social Policy* (March/April 1979): 28–32.

Ford, Phyllis. *Learning through Play: A Guide for Parents of 3-, 4-, or 5-Year-Olds.* Columbia, S.C.: South Carolina State Department of Education, 1987.

Gay, Geneva, and Roger D. Abrahams. "Does the Pot Melt, Boil, or Brew? Black Children and White Assessment Procedures." *Journal of School Psychology* 11, no. 4 (1973): 330–40.

Ginsburg, Herbert P. *Children's Arithmetic: The Learning Process.* New York: D. Van Nostrand Co., 1977.

Ginsburg, Herbert P., and Robert. L. Russell. *Social Class and Racial Influences on Early Mathematical Thinking.* Monographs of the Society for Research in Child Development, vol. 46, no. 6 (serial 193). Chicago: University of Chicago Press, 1981.

Ginsburg, Herbert P., and Joyce Baron. "Cognition: Young Children's Construction of Mathematics." In *Research Ideas for the Classroom: Early Childhood Mathematics*, edited by Robert J. Jensen, pp. 3–21. New York: Macmillan Publishing Co., 1993.

Good, Roland H. III, and John Salvia. "Curriculum Bias in Published Norm-Referenced Reading Tests: Demonstrable Effects." *School Psychology Review* 17, no. 1 (1988): 51–60.

Groen, Guy, and Lauren B. Resnick. "Can Preschool Children Invent Addition Algorithms?" *Journal of Educational Psychology* 69 (December 1977): 645–52.

Hale, Janice. "Black Children: Their Roots, Culture, and Learning Styles." *Young Children* 36 (January 1981): 37–50.

Hall, Edward T. *Beyond Culture.* Garden City, N.Y.: Anchor Press, 1976.

Heath, Shirley B. "Questioning at Home and at School: A Comparative Study." In *Doing the Ethnography of Schooling: Educational Anthropology in Action*, edited by George Spindler, pp. 102–31. New York: Holt, Rinehart, & Winston, 1982.

Hilliard, Asa G. III. *Alternative to IQ Testing: An Approach to the Identification of Gifted "Minority" Children.* San Francisco: San Francisco State University, 1976. (ERIC Document reproduction no. ED 148 038).

Jensen, Rosalie S., and Deborah C. Spector. *Teaching Mathematics to Young Children: A Basic Guide.* Englewood Cliffs, N.J.: Prentice-Hall, 1984.

Kamii, Constance. *Young Children Reinvent Arithmetic.* New York: Teachers College Press, 1985.

Piaget, Jean. *The Moral Judgement of the Child.* 1932. Reprint, New York: Free Press, 1965.

Williams, Robert L., and L. Wendell Rivers. "The Use of Standard versus Non-Standard English in the Administration of Group Tests to Black Children." Paper presented at the annual meeting of the American Psychological Association, Honolulu, 1972.

Zaslavsky, Claudia. "Africa Counts and Ethnomathematics." *For the Learning of Mathematics* 14, no. 2 (1994): 3–8.

———. "It's OK to Count on Your Fingers." *Teacher* 96 (February 1979): 54–56.

Lessons Learned from the "Five Men Crew"

Teaching Culturally Relevant Mathematics

8

Lillie R. Albert

> [C]ulturally relevant teaching is a pedagogy that empowers students intellectually, socially, emotionally, and politically by using cultural referents to impart knowledge, skills, and attitudes.
>
> —Gloria Ladson-Billings, *The Dreamkeepers*.

During the past ten years, several professional organizations have published documents advocating changes in mathematics education at all levels of instruction (National Council of Teachers of Mathematics [NCTM] 1989a, 1991; National Research Council [NRC] 1990, 1991). The fundamental assumption of these publications is that the mathematics curriculum needs restructuring, with consideration for what is taught and how it is taught. Recommendations for reform include having more student-centered activities, hands-on tasks, and problem-centered instruction. There also appears to be a common agreement that mathematics needs to be taught in a context that is relevant to students. It should not be unrelated to problems or situations that occur in the real world. These situations should include both the relevant mathematical and cultural experiences that students bring to school. In the mathematics classroom, "students should also be taught how to create their own interpretations of the past and present, as well as how to identify their own positions, interests, ideologies, and assumptions" (Banks 1993, p. 6).

The overall purpose of this paper is to discuss how critical reflection on my teaching led to changes in my curricular and pedagogical practices. These changes included taking into consideration more of the relevant cultural ideas, interests, and experiences of my students. This occurred after I engaged a class of diverse seventh-grade students (i.e., African Americans, Latinos, and Vietnamese) in an open discussion about a mathematics research project. The changes that we negotiated as a class motivated students to take pride in their work and to view mathematics as an activity that is meaningfully connected to everyday interests and experiences.

I begin my discussion of these changes with a brief summary of some of the misconceptions I had about students' ideas, interests, and experiences. Next, I review and highlight how the students and I revised the project to include some of their ideas and cultural experiences. This section is followed by a discussion of some of the lessons I learned from five African American male students. Finally, I discuss some pedagogical insights that emerged from both the revised assignment and from critical self-reflections.

MISCONCEPTIONS

Immediately after the publication of the *Curriculum and Evaluation Standards for School Mathematics* (NCTM 1989a) and after attending a "Writing to Learn Workshop" sponsored by my school district, I developed several mathematics projects for my seventh-grade mathematics classes that included a writing component. One of the five goals articulated by the *Standards* is that students must learn to communicate mathematically through writing as well as through reading and in conversation. This goal is important because as students learn to "communicate their ideas, they learn to clarify, refine, and consolidate their thinking" (NCTM 1989, p. 6).

Several of the projects focused on the history of mathematics, including one that culminated in an essay about a mathematician. Students were instructed to choose one mathematician from a prepared list, to research information about that person, and to write an essay about the most important contributions that person made to the field of mathematics.

After discussing the assignment with students, I gave them a few minutes to study it and ask questions about what they thought needed to be explained further. At that particular time, only one student had a question about the assignment—the length of the essay. We continued with our regular class activities. Several minutes into a group activity, a group of five African American male students approached me. The following exchange took place:

Students: Ms. A, could we talk to you for a few minutes about the research project?

Ms. A: Sure. What can I do for you?

Pat: Well, we were wondering (pause). Fred, you tell her. It's your idea.

Fred: Why do we have to write an essay?

I thought that Fred was going to continue with, "Hey, this isn't an English class." This had been one of the objections expressed by my first-hour class, and I felt well prepared to respond to this concern. However, I was surprised by Fred's and Pat's next questions.

Fred: Why can't we write a rap instead of the essay?

Pat: Well (pause), why aren't there only one black person on the list?

I had not anticipated that students would voice these concerns, and I could not immediately respond to them. I realized the message I was sending to my students with this assignment as it was designed was limited and dividing. The intent of the research project had been to involve students in a long-term writing project. Through such a project, students would ideally develop an appreciation of the history of mathematics and its place in the mathematics curriculum. I saw the project as a way for my students to learn about the contributions of different people to the field of mathematics. They would also learn about the development of mathematics from ancient time to the present. They would learn about the mathematicians' lives and their diverse backgrounds.

I had foreseen the advantages of having students involved in a substantial writing activity, but I had committed an error. I failed to include a sense of purpose for *all* my students by communicating to them that people of color—African Americans in particular—contributed limited ideas and knowledge to the field of mathematics. Because the assignment sheet listed only one person of color (i.e., Benjamin Banneker), students did not see themselves represented in the assignment. The most important oversight was embedded in the instructional approach I applied to the assignment: I had selected the topic and had specified the manner in which it was to be carried out by students. I assumed that because I left the decision up to students regarding which mathematician they would write essays about, I was accounting for differences in learning styles and interests. Simply offering a choice of subject does not necessarily accommodate learning styles or provide an engaging context in which students can view themselves and appreciate or value the relevance of mathematics. This

> **Simply offering a choice of subject does not necessarily accommodate learning styles or provide an engaging context in which students can value themselves and appreciate or value the relevance of mathematics.**

assignment did not reflect the interests and the cultural backgrounds of my students.

Students have always felt comfortable enough in my classes to ask questions, but usually their questions are about mathematics content or rudimentary procedures. However, the expectation of the extended writing project provoked questions apart from these contexts. These students were really asking: Where do I fit in? Do I have a place in this classroom? Do my background and experiences count? Accommodating these differences was more complex than I originally anticipated.

In the instructional approach that I used for this writing project, I had done what Frankenstein (1990) suggested we should not do. I developed an assignment that resulted in censorship and the silencing of voices. In other words, there was little, if any, cultural relevance embedded in the assignment. There were also larger issues of student engagement to consider. Providing relevant mathematical experiences for students is a start; however, we should also take the time to listen to students' ideas and to provide activities that include their interests. The discussion with the five African American students challenged me to make this assignment relevant for my students and to determine what I could do to make all learning experiences in mathematics relevant on a regular basis.

THE REVISED INCLUSIVE ASSIGNMENT

I had mixed reactions to the discussion I had with the five African-American male students that day, but it was immediately clear to me what I needed to do. I realized that if my students did not feel comfortable and confident in the situations that I had set up for them, it would be more difficult for them to be committed to the completion of the assignment. Considering the information I gathered from these students, I decided to restructure the assignment on the basis of the interests, ideas, and experiences the students brought to school by seeking information from the entire class.

Working very closely with one another, we decided that those students who felt more comfortable and confident writing raps or poems could approach the assignment in that manner. One student stated, "As long as we write about that person's contribution, it should not matter." Some students wanted to work in collaborative groups to complete the revised assignment, so they were given that option. It was also decided to include not only more mathematicians of color but more female mathematicians as well. The students and I agreed to do this together. The students would add mathematicians' names to the list as they discovered additional possibilities through their research at either the school library or the nearby public library. Complementing the students' research, I would visit several of the libraries at local universities to do research and find more names in order to make the list more diverse. I felt better about this particular assignment because its revisions were negotiated by the students rather than planned exclusively by me, as the original assignment had been. I also thought that this collaborative effort changed my students' dispositions toward the assignment.

LESSONS LEARNED

In our search to include more mathematicians from diverse cultural backgrounds, my students and I discovered some interesting and exciting information about the history of mathematics. For example, neither I nor my students had heard of Thomas Fuller, a slave brought to Virginia in 1724. Thomas Fuller could calculate the number of grains of corn in a given mass, even though he did not know how to read or write (NCTM 1989b, p. 160). Fuller became known as the "African Calculator" (Zaslavsky 1987). We also learned that the Pythagorean theorem had been used by the Egyptians as early as 2000 B.C. (Kline 1990). To be more inclusive, we expanded our list to include both gender and color. We added the female mathematicians Maria Agnesi, Hypatia, Mary Somerville, Sophie Germain, Ada Lovelace, Evelyn Boyd Granville, and several others, and so our revised list of mathematicians offered students a wide variety of choices.

The five African American male students who served as a catalyst for changing the original assignment enthusiastically embraced the revised assignment. Providing the students opportunities to make decisions based on their interests and experiences increased their level of involvement with the assignment. To my surprise, these five students did not select a person of color to complete the assignment. Instead, they chose to write a rap about the Englishman, Thomas Harriot. His contributions to the field of mathematics dealt with modern symbolism for the minus and plus signs and for the introduction of the symbols that represented less than and greater than (Groza 1968; Shirley 1991). Below is an excerpt from the rap these students wrote about Harriot.

> Right about now while I got the microphone in my hand,
> I'm going to tell you about this great man.
> He made the minus and plus signs, yes that's true.
> This is a message from the "Five Men Crew."
> Inventions and inventions and many of times,
> This is the man that gave us the minus and plus signs.
> This man had brain power, and right about now he's the man of the hour.

I noted, after the students had completed this rap, that it did not provide much historical information about Thomas Harriot. But the important, and perhaps crucial, point about this assignment was that it was initiated by the students themselves, thus giving them ownership of the activity. Connecting the mathematics to the students' experiences motivated them to take pride in their accomplishments. For the students, the rap was culturally relevant because the presentational context emerged from their interests and cultural experiences and so gave them voice in an informal, but constructive way. Students extended their thinking by engaging in an activity that they developed and structured. They did this in contrast to the original assignment (essay), which called for a more formal and abstract presentation.

Ladson-Billings (1994) suggests that "culturally relevant teaching uses student culture in order to maintain it and to transcend the negative effects of that culture" (p. 17). In confronting my own bias about rap, I acknowledged that I viewed it as highly overrated entertainment, and so I had never considered teaching mathematics through this medium. This assignment brought learning to new levels for me. Instead of being hesitant about my students' interests and experiences, I learned to accept and appreciate them.

Another group, consisting of three students, developed a play around the contributions of Harriot. The students used their own words to express and acquire understanding about Harriot's mathematical contributions, as illustrated in figure 8.1. This group of students completed the assignment by drawing on previous school drama experiences and by reconstructing those experiences into a context that mattered to them. In this instance, the students engaged in an intellectually challenging activity from which they expressed their understanding of division of whole numbers as an operation that requires the use of multiplication and subtraction. They extended the concept of the symbols by carrying out the familiar long-division procedure for a division algorithm.

Narrator:	One day Multiplication and Subtraction were having a fight. They each thought that their mathematical functions were better than the other. Subtraction felt this way because her job meant that she would get less than the original number when performing a subtraction problem. However, Multiplication felt that her job was better because she gets more than Subtraction had before when performing a multiplication problem. As you can see, they were getting nowhere. What they need is a mediator, or referee. I think that it will have to be me. But to get into Mathland, you have to become a math symbol, so I will become the "Equal Sign."
Equal Sign:	What seems to be the problem? I could hear the two of you fighting from miles away!
Subtraction:	Multiplication just waltzed up to me and said that she was better than me. I told her that she wasn't, and now she's angry with me.
Multiplication:	I am angry, too. If you can make bigger numbers, then you're better. Besides, who wants little, itsy-bitsy numbers, anyway?
Equal Sign:	Well, I think that you're both acting extremely childish. Little numbers add up to bigger numbers, and sometimes big numbers go [decrease] to little numbers. Hey! I have a great idea! Let's put both of you together, and make something that will make both of you equal, if your pardon the pun.
Multiplication and *Subtraction:*	What!?!?
Equal Sign:	I know! We'll call it *Division!* It will use both of you! You will take a number and see how many times it will go into another number. We can start with a problem such as 673 ÷ 11.
Subtraction:	For that you have to use Multiplication!
Equal Sign:	That's right! Then something is leftover; so we'll take what we got from multiplying 11 times 6 and take it away from the number we're dividing into!
Multiplication:	For that we use Subtraction!
Equal Sign:	Yeah! See, when you work together and don't argue, it's easy to find …
All:	The Solution!!!!!
Equal Sign:	Let's work another problem!

Fig. 8.1. Student example—"The Solution"

The students' completion of the assignment took on many forms as they searched for relevant contexts in which to present their understanding of the mathematical concepts or skills they learned through their study of the history of mathematics. Some students wrote short, informal poems and plays, whereas others wrote long, fluent essays or creative stories. For example, one student wrote a very elaborate essay about the story of pi after reading several historical books that told of an ancient Babylonian tablet that contained information about various geometrical figures regarding "the circumference of [a] circumscribed circle" (Beckmann 1971, p. 21). In her essay, the student created a coherent and meaningful explanation of pi by putting it into her own words. The following is excerpted from the student's essay:

Pi, (π), is the ratio of the circumference of a circle to its diameter that also crops up in many math situations, often quite unexpectedly. Pi is a mathematical constant value, that is, a number that has a constant value. When written as a decimal, Pi has no pattern that repeats, as does, for example, the decimal representation of

1/3. In fact, although Pi is an infinite decimal like 0.33333…, the calculation of the digits from various formulas is more trouble than it is worth. Pi to the hundredths—3.14— is sufficient.

Working with students to construct the activity or assignment was a very valuable experience for me. The assignment we created collaboratively was better and more successful than the assignment I had originally presented to the students because it was the synthesis of all our ideas. Most important, the students had developed their perceptions of the assignment, made it their own, and consequently felt themselves empowered by it. The new assignment changed students' dispositions toward mathematics because it provided a context for creative insights. One student included this footnote to her essay: "The responsibilities that a mathematician has require much accuracy and ability which I consider to be one of my strong points. Although a career as a mathematician may prove to be challenging, I rather picture myself doing the thing I love the most, writing a book." This quotation expresses the value of relevant teaching because it illustrates how the context of the new assignment was appropriate for this student. The student used her strength as a writer to complete her essay about Sophie Germain's contributions in the area of number theory. Appropriate learning contexts for the expression of mathematical understanding engage students in experiences that are rewarding and challenging and help them individualize instruction and construct personal meaning with their own ideas and interests.

PEDAGOGICAL INSIGHTS

Although students were engaged in redesigning the assignment, the focus on mathematical contributions was unevenly distributed in the essays, stories, plays, poems, and raps they constructed. It is very important for the teacher to articulate expectations for processes and products regarding the mathematical contributions of the selected mathematicians. First, teachers can strengthen the link to mathematical content by stating policies clearly when first assigning the project or assignment. Second, they should discuss with the students their obligations regarding the thoroughness required for an adequate presentation of mathematical contributions. Next, they should develop and share with students a scoring guide that outlines clear assessment guidelines for the assignment and then give a similar checklist to students for assessing their progress along the way. Finally, teachers should require a draft of the assignment from each student or student group and offer feedback to their students about the mathematical contributions and about the clarity of the presentation. Connecting these suggestions with students' ideas, interests, and cultural experiences will provide a relevant vehicle that encourages students to express and reflect their understanding of mathematical content and ideas.

As I attempted to find an answer to my own pedagogical concern and issues, I learned that "we need to be more aware of the hidden social messages in what we do and the power of their influences on the young people we teach" (Nickson 1992, p. 111). Although I thought I had indicated in my original assignment that I respected the interests and cultural backgrounds of my students, this assumption was not true because the lessons, activities, and materials I used regularly reflected Eurocentric perspectives. In subtle ways, the message I sent to students was that their cultural heritage was not worthy of being included. Proponents of multicultural education suggest that students need to see themselves in, and to learn about themselves from, deferential and authentic curriculum materials (Brook 1987).

This class of diverse students (i.e., African Americans, Latinos, and Vietnamese) taught me that I could take their experiences and build on them. Beyond the assignment, I realized the value of teaching mathematical concepts in a context students can identify, understand, and value. For example, when we study geometry, we can ground our understanding of it by looking more closely at its history, relating it to other cultures. Geometry was used by ancient Egyptians in developing their river systems (Groza 1968). There is also evidence that the Indus and Ganges of South Central Asia used scientific geometry in the construction of river basins and in developing irrigation systems (Li and Shiran 1987).

Uniting the history of mathematics with curriculum content and culturally relevant teaching is a pedagogical technique that supports and authenticates the understanding of mathematical concepts and ideas. Jones (1989) suggests that the history of mathematics, coupled with a current knowledge of mathematics and its real-world uses, helps students "see and appreciate the nature, role, and fascination of mathematics and that they too may have the thrill of discovery and invention" (p. 1). In other words, when teachers link the history of mathematics to culturally relevant teaching, they are setting the stage on which students learn to appreciate what mathematicians refer to as the *beauty and elegance of mathematics*. Students learn about the structure of mathematics and that its history extends across time and diverse cultures. Including the history of mathematics as part of the regular mathematics curriculum provides teachers and their students with new critical perspectives regarding mathematics as a continuous body of knowledge (Grugnetti and Jaquet 1996). Overall, connecting the history of mathematics to culturally relevant teaching can help students feel empowered when constructing and co-constructing mathematical knowledge in learning contexts that matter to them.

> **Uniting the history of mathematics with curriculum content and culturally relevant teaching is a pedagogical technique that supports and authenticates the understanding of mathematical concepts and ideas.**

CONCLUSION

The changes suggested in this paper by no means fully explore the possibilities of culturally relevant teaching. This paper describes the transformation that I went through as I reflected on my curricular and pedagogical practices and their impact on student learning. I learned to listen more carefully to my students and to be mindful of their interests and experiences. These changes required me to see both my own and my students' performance from their perspective. As a result, I not only changed what I taught but also changed how and why I was teaching it. I attempted to create a learning environment that integrated and included the many voices of my students. This approach appropriately matched the reality of the students' interests and experiences. Realizing this led me to more relevant and empowering ways of teaching mathematics.

The educational implication is that we as practicing teachers, prospective teachers, and teacher educators must reflect on our curricular and pedagogical practices. Continuous and critical reflection will challenge us to employ a variety of relevant, open-ended, challenging, and engaging learning experiences and activities for students. This allows us to meet the interests and needs of our diverse and changing student population.

Another implication is that if we want students to understand and appreciate the world in which they live, then we must offer learning experiences that strengthen and confirm who they are. We can accomplish this by challenging students, sharing some decisions with them, and allowing them to collaborate with one another. This also helps students feel confident in expressing their ideas and assessing their knowledge and understanding of the mathematics they are learning. The idea is to acknowledge that students can and do use their interests and experiences to understand mathematical concepts and ideas, to construct meaning, and to make sense of the world in which they live.

REFERENCES

Banks, James. "The Canon Debate, Knowledge Construction, and Multicultural Education." *Educational Researcher* 22 (June/July 1993): 4–14.

Beckmann, Petr. *The History of π (PI).* 2nd ed. Boulder, Colo.: Golem Press, 1971.

Brooks, Charlotte. "Teachers: Potent Forces in the Learning Lives of Black Students." In *Educating Black Children: America's Challenge*, edited by Dorothy Strickland and Eric Cooper, pp. 55–62. Washington, D.C.: Bureau of Educational Research, School of Education, Howard University, 1987.

Frankenstein, Marilyn. "Incorporating Race, Gender, and Class Issues into a Critical Mathematical Literacy Curriculum." *Journal of Negro Education* 59 (Summer 1990): 336–47.

Groza, Vivian S. *A Survey of Mathematics: Elementary Concepts and Their Historical Development.* New York: Holt, Rinehart & Winston, 1968.

Grugnetti, Lucia, and François Jaquet. "Senior Secondary School Practices." In *International Handbook of Mathematics Part I*, edited by Alan J. Bishop, Ken Clements, Christine Keitel, Jeremy Kilpatrick, and Colette Laborde, pp. 615–46. Boston: Kluwer Academic Publishers, 1996.

Jones, Phillip. "The History of Mathematics as a Teaching Tool." In *Historical Topics for the Mathematics Classroom*, 2nd ed. pp. 1–17. Reston, Va.: National Council of Teachers of Mathematics, 1989.

Kline, Morris. *Mathematics from Ancient to Modern Time.* New York: Oxford University Press, 1990.

Ladson-Billings, Gloria. *The Dreamkeepers: Successful Teachers of African American Children.* San Francisco: Jossey-Bass Publishers, 1994.

Li, Yen, and Du Shiran. *Chinese Mathematics, a Concise History.* Translated by John N. Crossley and Anthony W.-C. Lun. Oxford: Clarendon Press, 1987.

National Council of Teachers of Mathematics. *Curriculum and Evaluation Standards for School Mathematics.* Reston, Va.: National Council of Teachers of Mathematics, 1989a.

———. *Historical Topics for the Mathematics Classroom.* 2nd ed. Reston, Va.: National Council of Teachers of Mathematics, 1989b.

———. *Professional Standards for Teaching Mathematics.* Reston, Va.: National Council of Teachers of Mathematics, 1991.

National Research Council. *Moving beyond Myths: Revitalizing Undergraduate Mathematics.* Washington, D.C.: National Academy Press, 1991.

———. *Reshaping School Mathematics: A Philosophy and Framework for Curriculum.* Washington, D.C.: National Academy Press, 1990.

Nickson, Marilyn. "The Culture of the Mathematics Classroom: An Unknown Quantity?" In *Handbook of Research on Mathematics Teaching and Learning*, edited by Douglas A. Grouws, pp. 101–14. New York: Macmillan Publishing Co., 1992.

Shirley, John W. *A Sourcebook for the Study of Thomas Harriot.* New York: Arno Press, 1991.

Zaslavsky, Claudia. *Multicultural Mathematics: Interdisciplinary Cooperative-Learning Activities.* Portland, Maine: J. Weston Walch, 1987.

Teaching Mathematics to the Least Academically Prepared African American Students

9

Laura Brooks Smith

Lee V. Stiff

Melinda R. Petree

Changes in the mathematics requirements for high school graduation and entrance into college, in the technological demands of an expanding number of careers, and in the applications of mathematics in everyday living require that all students begin their mathematical preparation as early as possible and continue it for as long as possible. The study of mathematics beyond algebra 1 is, therefore, increasingly important. Yet, many African American students graduate from high school without ever taking algebra 1 or taking only the rudiments of algebra to satisfy minimal graduation requirements. In this paper we describe an approach we used to enhance African American students' ability to achieve success in the study of algebra.

There are many factors that affect the opportunities that African American students have to study algebra. Much too often, African American students are enrolled in computation-based, low-level mathematics courses in the seventh, eighth, and ninth grades and continue in non-college-preparatory or "regular" mathematics courses for the remainder of their high school careers (Heid and Jump 1993; Patterson 1989; Usiskin 1993). Despite the reform efforts in mathematics education, such "traditional" courses have proved quite resistant to changes widely touted in reform-based mathematics instruction. Computation-based high school mathematics courses offer students very little new mathematics beyond arithmetic or the simplest ideas of first-year algebra. Furthermore, teachers of such courses frequently have low expectations of their students. Consequently, students enrolled in computation-based courses gradually lose interest in mathematics and develop low self-esteem toward mathematics achievement (Schoen and Hallas 1993; Usiskin 1993; Walker and McCoy 1997).

African American students enrolled in regular prealgebra and algebra classes do not receive as much whole-class instruction as students in more-advanced classes. They complete worksheets and do individual seatwork far more often than students in college-preparatory tracks (Oakes 1985, 1995). These students simply do not have the opportunity to develop strong problem-solving and reasoning skills or make worthwhile mathematical connections. The overwhelming type of "problems" that many African American students see are replicas of computational examples provided during instruction. In fact, these "problems" are traditional "exercises" that are of little relevance or interest to most students.

Working in groups or engaging in active, manipulative-based mathematics learning in prealgebra and algebra is not a common experience for most students in school, especially African American students (Heid and Jump 1993; Stiff 1990). As a result, many African American students never experience mathematics as communication. They never reason verbally about mathematics or explain and justify their work to others. They grow accustomed to and expect

> **There are many factors that affect the opportunities that African American students have to study algebra.**

89

problems whose solutions are of the simplest form. It is not surprising that open-ended problem situations create academic discomfort in African American students who have not developed strategies for accommodating mathematical complexities.

How can we increase the opportunity African American students have to study worthwhile algebraic concepts and relationships? An investigation into the achievement of African American students suggests that problem-solving vignettes can be used to help African American students increase their mathematical power by enhancing their status as learners in the mathematics classroom (Akaishi and Saul 1991; Hale 1982; Moniuszko 1991; Stiff and Harvey 1988; Walker and McCoy 1997). We agree with others that if African American students are exposed to mathematics that is relevant to their interests and experiences and are allowed to engage more actively in their mathematics learning, they will be successful in algebra 1 and advanced mathematics courses (Kamii and Lewis 1990; NCTM 1989; Stiff 1990; Moses et al. 1989; Walker and McCoy 1997).

To illustrate, consider how the least academically prepared African American high school students in a large, urban school system were able to study more worthwhile mathematics topics, better understand those topics, and develop better attitudes toward mathematics when taught using problem-solving vignettes (PSVs). For our purposes, a problem-solving vignette describes a problem situation that is designed to engage students in real-life activities (see fig. 9.1). Printed problem-solving vignettes, like the one shown in figure 9.1, are not worksheets for students but rather a resource for teachers to help them orchestrate classroom discourse. Student activities, discussion guides, and practice sheets for specific PSVs are constructed in advance and as needed.

From the students' point of view, PSVs are not prescribed in any way beyond the general identification of a problem situation. Concepts and skills are integrated into a variety of PSVs and are revisited throughout the year as appropriate. We found that PSVs work well with African American students if the real-life activities are chosen to be of general interest to them. The effectiveness of problem-solving vignettes can be measured by the enthusiasm that students have for the problems posed and their acceptance of the open-ended instructional approach taken by the teacher. When using PSVs, students are free to direct classroom discussions and activities related to the problem situations as they see fit. Not only do they get to say which broad topics will make up the discussion, but students also determine which of those topics are important and should be pursued and which of those topics should be ignored.

For example, in one vignette in which a discussion of how the length of one's hand is related to the length of one's foot, a student asked, "Why can't we look at other body parts, like heads, arms, shoulders, and legs?" After a brief discussion, students agreed to also investigate their heights and arm lengths. Later in this thirteen-day vignette, after plotting many points by hand to investigate relationships between pairs of body measurements, such as arm span versus height, another student complained, "Why can't we use these fancy calculators to draw points?" Other students agreed, and the merits of investigating the relationships using pencil-and-paper techniques versus the graphing calculator were argued and evaluated. As a result, students used the graphing calculator, following some instruction on its use, to complete the remainder of the vignette.

All the African American students that we taught were used to computation-based mathematics courses and not accustomed to nonstructured presentations of mathematical ideas. Understandably, students were surprised and initially tentative about whether PSV instruction would really give them a say in determining the nature and direction of the mathematical discourse of the

Which Way Shall I Go?

In Raleigh, the intersection of Hillsborough and Wilmington Streets separate the northern part of the city from the southern part and the eastern part from the western part. That is, any street north of Hillsborough Street is in the northern part of the city and may have "North" as part of its name (e.g., Bloodworth or Blount). Similarly, any street south of Hillsborough Street is in the southern part of the city and may have "South" as part of its name.

Concepts to be studied: Map reading and making and determining directions; graphing, distance between two points

Materials needed: A map of Raleigh, N.C., for each group, graphing paper

Directions and activities:

A.   Can you make a similar statement about street locations and names in relation to Wilmington Street? Can you name some of the streets?

Streets that are north of Hillsborough Street and east of Wilmington Street are said to be in the northeast section of the city. Similar statements are made for other sections of the city.

B. 1. Discuss the section of the city in which your high school is located and in which your home is located. In which direction is your school from your home?

2. Do you travel in one direction to get from your home to school?

3. Draw a route from your home to school.

4. How far do you travel to school?

5. Draw a route from your school to the Civic Center, to Broughton High School, and to Saint Augustine's College.

6. Use a blank sheet of graphing paper to make the Capitol the point of origin. Locate on this grid Saint Augustine's College, Chavis City Park, and Peace College. How far is it from the Capitol to each of these locations? (We will return to this discussion soon.)

C. 1. Use a new sheet of graphing paper and let each grid represent one block of the city. (Assume all blocks are the same length.) Now assume that you leave your home and walk east for 3 blocks and then you turn and walk north for 4 more blocks. How many blocks are you from home?

2. Decide how many miles you want each grid to represent. Assume you leave Raleigh and travel to Greensboro. You then travel from there to Asheboro. How far are you from home?

3. Now, how far is it from your home to school? To Saint Augustine's College? To your best friend's home?

Fig. 9.1. Vignette: Which Way Shall I Go?

classroom or whether they even wanted such a voice. At the beginning of using PSVs students asked, "Why are we discussing this? When are we ever going to use this? What does this have to do with anything?" As the year progressed, students responded well to the freedom extended by the use of PSVs. Their comments became, "Can the range of a set of data be stated as a single number or should it be stated as, say, from 1 to 10? If I walked around a pond to approximate its circumference in feet, can I use the value of pi we discussed in class to find out how far across the pond it would be from one side to the other side? What other types of statistics are used besides the ones we hear about in sports and weather reports?" We believe that PSV instruction allowed students to take ownership of problems and that the mathematics grew in importance to students because they determined the scope and sequence of the mathematics to be learned.

In actuality, each PSV lesson was constructed with care and with expectations of several different instructional problem-solving paths that students were likely to follow. Although students did occasionally take a path that was not anticipated, the hidden structure of the PSV lessons provided a welcomed degree of teacher comfort with the open-ended instructional approach. PSVs were created to demonstrate and teach concepts and relationships by promoting mathematical investigations and explorations by students and their teacher. By carefully creating many different PSVs, we were able to recast students' entire curriculum into problem situations.

Several characteristics of the problem-solving vignettes we used make them useful in teaching algebra concepts to African American students. The first is that real-life problem settings are easily expressed using problem-solving vignettes. Since many African American students understand mathematics better when it is related to familiar events and activities, real-life problems become quite effective in the mathematics classroom (Moses et al. 1989; Silva et al. 1990).

Another aspect of problem-solving vignettes that promote mathematical growth among African American students is that PSV problem situations seldom have a single solution. Open-ended problems and projects stimulate students to think more deeply about the mathematics than problems typically found in workbooks (Kamii and Lewis 1990; Lynch et al. 1989; Silver and Smith 1990). Open-ended problems and projects provide a way to involve all students according to their interests and capabilities (Zaslavsky 1991). For the African American students in our classes, open-ended problems rooted in concrete, real-life settings worked best.

Finally, problem-solving vignettes promote active student involvement in solving problems. Most African American students prefer activity-based learning environments (Hale 1982; Stiff and Harvey 1988). Activities might include manipulating concrete objects, modeling phenomena, or gathering actual data. Students are not restricted to using predetermined methods for solving problems but are encouraged to use a variety of approaches. Eventually, our students gained in self-confidence knowing that no single approach or answer to a real-life problem situation was expected.

Students in our PSV prealgebra course included ninth-grade students who would have been placed in a typical prealgebra class, tenth-grade students who were in low-level mathematics classes in the ninth grade, and eleventh-grade and twelfth-grade students who had not yet taken prealgebra. In the typical "traditional" prealgebra course in this high school, teachers lectured and followed the sequence of lessons and examples presented in the textbook, with a heavy emphasis on numeric and algebraic computations. Worksheets, quizzes, and tests were computation-based assessments that included few, if any, open-ended problem-solving items.

By contrast, in the PSV course, each vignette was designed to present and explore at least one algebra concept. No time constraint was placed on the use of a vignette. The time spent on a vignette depended on classroom discourse and interaction. Vignettes took as few as three days to as many as twenty days to complete. The vignettes addressed topics that were meaningful to students because the topics were taken from real-life situations determined to be of interest to African American high school students. Each vignette contained several levels of questions, many of which were open-ended, many of which were based on classroom discussions. Vignettes incorporated mathematics concepts, such as percents, solving equations, or slope, that were discussed several times during the school year. Each time a concept was encountered, it was discussed from a slightly different perspective. During the academic year, all the topics that were found in the prealgebra course, including numeric and algebraic computations, were presented in the PSV classes.

Each new vignette was introduced by the teacher. Discussions followed the introduction. Although the teacher initiated the discussion, the direction of the discussion was determined by students based on their questions, responses to questions, and related comments. Over several days, as the nature of student inquiries was determined and categorized and as problem-solving paths were identified, the teacher selected prepared materials that were developed in anticipation of student responses. Deviations from the anticipated discussion

Most African American students prefer activity-based learning environments.

and instructional problem-solving paths did occur and did not always relate to mathematics. For example, when students were discussing a vignette involving maps (see fig. 9.1), many of them identified a specific community in which they lived. One student wanted to know the reason the city named the community after Ben Chavis. As a result, over the nineteen-day period in which this vignette was discussed, students received an impromptu lesson in African American history about the Wilmington Ten and Ben Chavis's participation in the civil rights movement of the 1970s, as well as instruction on map reading, map making, the distance between two points, the slope of a line, and graphing.

During the discussion of another vignette, "My Own Automobile," the anticipated lesson was to determine whether students could afford to own and maintain an automobile. The students, however, consumed an entire class period on the number of hours a week they could reasonably expect to work at a part-time job and whether it was feasible to expect a student to work forty hours a week and maintain acceptable grades while attending school. This three-day vignette, presented at the beginning of the semester, involved decimals, budgeting, using formulas, and solving simple equations. At the conclusion of this vignette, students were genuinely surprised at the difficulties associated with owning a car.

Student performance in the PSV classes was assessed in a variety of ways. Beyond the normal teacher-made assessments, the California Achievement Test in mathematics (CAT-Math), which has computation and concept dimensions, was used to measure student growth in the learning of mathematics. Classroom observations, student interviews, and audio recordings also provided anecdotal information about the PSV students and the course.

The CAT-Math was administered as a pretest at the beginning of the year and as a posttest at the end. By the end of the year, the overall mathematics scores of the PSV students along the computation dimension of the CAT-Math indicated that the African American students who were taught using PSVs developed proficiency in computation equal to that of students taught in the computation-based prealgebra courses. More important, PSV students performed better than regular prealgebra students on the concept dimension of CAT-Math (table 9.1).

Table 9.1
Adjusted Means and Standard Errors of CAT-Math Concept Dimension Scores for the PSV and Regular Prealgebra Classes

Test		Group	
		PSV ($N = 23$)	Regular ($N = 26$)
Pretest	Mean	728.65	722.21
	SE	6.44	6.09
Posttest	Mean	731.24*	710.95*
	SE	6.97	6.97
Gains	Mean	3.00	−10.25
	SE	8.40	8.40

* Significant at $p < 0.05$

Yearlong classroom observations revealed much about student behaviors in the PSV course. In the beginning of the course, students were very talkative, disorderly, and frequently off task. They engaged in small-group conversations that were unrelated to classwork. Students did not take class notes, nor did they do assigned homework. In fact, we determined that the African American students in the course were not familiar with any method for taking class notes. Students told us that they had never taken notes in any of their other mathematics classes, nor were they required to do homework. As was expected, students complained vigorously when the teacher informed them that in their PSV course they were required to take notes, keep a daily math journal, and complete homework assignments.

As the year progressed, student behavior changed noticeably. Discipline problems remained but occurred less frequently. Students more consistently took class notes and often asked whether it was appropriate to include elements of class discussions in their notes. Students wrote more and more in their math journals as weeks and months passed. From the beginning of the school year, when students literally wrote nothing in their math journals, to the end of the first semester, when journal entries began to reflect heightened student involvement (see fig. 9.2), students increasingly accepted their roles as active learners. Some students brought their journals to the teacher before class began so that the teacher could comment on their entries and make suggestions, if necessary, about material to be added. Still others would rush into the classroom before the bell sounded and write their entry so that they would be prepared when class started.

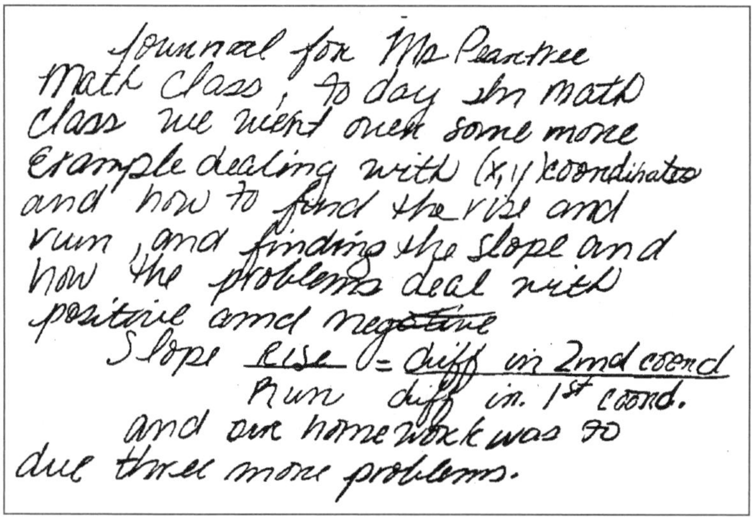
Journal for Ms Peartree
Math Class, to day in math class we went over some more example dealing with (x,y) coordinates and how to find the rise and run, and finding the slope and how the problems deal with positive and negative
Slope rise/run = diff in 2nd coord / diff in 1st coord.
and our homework was to due three more problems.

Fig. 9.2. Sample of a math journal entry

Similarly, in the second term of PSV instruction, doing homework became a habit for many students. If the teacher neglected to check homework at the beginning of class, students would often remind her to do so. As a result of improved participation in and out of class, students' questions and responses began to reflect more thought and purpose as the year continued.

Student interviews provided another perspective about the PSV course. At the beginning of the year when students were faced with a computation-based prealgebra course, the following comments were heard, "Are we doing this stuff again?" "Are you just going to give us a worksheet everyday?" and "Can't we do something else?" However, once the PSV course was fully implemented, students could be heard saying, "This is easier!" "What are we going to talk about next?" and "I think I understand now." Students expressed satisfaction in using a graphing calculator in class and asked why they had not been allowed to use calculators before. Students stated that they preferred PSV instruction to the instruction they normally received. They observed that PSV teaching methods were more interesting and more fun than other methods they had encountered, and students felt that PSV mathematics was easier to understand.

As an example of why students thought PSV mathematics was easier to grasp, consider one of the more difficult concepts to teach to prealgebra students, the concept of slope. Simply having prealgebra students memorize the slope equation does not effectively help them understand or apply the concept. However, when slope was introduced using a vignette, the meaning of slope became clear as students worked through a set of activities. In the vignette, students were asked to measure the heights and depths of a variety of sets of steps found inside and outside of the school building. As a result, students' experiences with climbing the assortment of steps found throughout the school helped them to make connections among (*a*) the meaning of slope, (*b*) the steepness of steps, and (*c*) the height and depth of a step.

Students asked such questions as "Why are there more steps going up to the second floor than steps going down to the gym level?" or "Why, inside the building, is the height and depth [respectively] of a step always the same, but outside the building, the heights and depths [respectively] are never the same?" or "Why, outside the building, is the height [of a step] always smaller [in length] than the depth?" These and other questions contributed to a lively discussion about slope, steepness, and the concepts of "rise" and "run." A few students became so interested in building regulations and specifications for steps and stairways that they decided to pursue the ideas of the vignette in a project.

Although this and other activities were very simple and straightforward to perform, the benefit of the hands-on, activity-based experiences of finding the slope of a collection of steps made the components of the slope formula come alive. Concrete experiences enabled students to understand the concept of slope in different relationships such as slope = height/depth, slope = rise over run, or slope = vertical change/horizontal change (see fig. 9.3). Once the real-life concept of slope was understood, the concept of slope was easily extended to finding the slope between two points in a plane as the PSV instruction unfolded.

The instructional approach represented by problem-solving vignettes allowed the students in our classes to address real-life problem situations at a pace consistent with their interest and understanding; promoted a hands-on, activity-based learning environment; and helped students deal with mathematical complexities more effectively. We found that once basic ideas were understood, our students quickly learned other important algebraic concepts and relationships. And, perhaps most important of all, our students' self-confidence and interest in algebra increased.

> Measurements-Rise and Run
> We measerd the width and the height of three different stairs ways. We wrote down the measurements for each set of stairs. We wrote the height and the width as a point. We used the point to graph the rise and the run. We found that the slope is equal to the rise divided by the run.

Fig. 9.3. Mathematical connection described in a math journal entry

REFERENCES

Akaishi, Amy, and Mark Saul. "Exploring, Learning, Sharing: Vignettes from the Classroom." *Arithmetic Teacher* 39 (November 1991): 12–16.

Hale, Janice. *Black Children, Their Roots, Culture, and Learning Styles.* Provo, Utah: Brigham Young University Press, 1982.

Heid, Camilla A., and Theresa L. Jump. "Females, Minorities, and the Physically Handicapped in Mathematics and Science: A Model Program." In *Reaching All Students with Mathematics*, edited by Gilbert Cuevas and Mark Driscoll, pp. 159–73. Reston, Va.: National Council of Teachers of Mathematics, 1993.

Kamii, Constance, and Barbara A. Lewis. "Constructivist Learning and Teaching." *Arithmetic Teacher* 38 (September 1990): 34–35.

Lynch, Joan K., Peter Fischer, and Sarah F. Green. "Teaching in a Computer-Intensive Algebra Curriculum." *Mathematics Teacher* 82 (December 1989): 688–94.

Moniuszko, Linda K. "Reality Math." *Arithmetic Teacher* 39 (September 1991): 10–16.

Moses, Robert P., Mieko Kamii, Susan M. Swap, and Jeffrey Howard. "The Algebra Project: Organizing in the Spirit of Ella." *Harvard Educational Review* 59 (November 1989): 423-43.

National Council of Teachers of Mathematics. *Curriculum and Evaluation Standards for School Mathematics.* Reston, Va.: National Council of Teachers of Mathematics, 1989.

Oakes, Jeannie. *Keeping Track: How Schools Structure Inequality.* New Haven, Conn.: Yale University Press, 1985.

———. "Opportunity to Learn: Can Standards-Based Reform Be Equity-Based Reform?" In *Seventy-five Years of Progress: Prospects for School Mathematics*, edited by Iris M. Carl, pp. 78–98. Reston, Va.: National Council of Teachers of Mathematics, 1995.

Patterson, Janice H. "Minorities Gain, but Gaps Remain." *Peabody Journal of Education* 66 (Winter 1989): 72–94.

Schoen, Harold L., and David Hallas. "Improving the General Mathematics Experience." In *Research Ideas for the Classroom—High School Mathematics*, edited by Patricia S. Wilson, pp. 103–18. Reston, Va.: National Council of Teachers of Mathematics, 1993.

Silva, Cynthia M., Robert P. Moses, Jacqueline Rivers, and Parker Johnson. "The Algebra Project: Making Middle School Mathematics Count." *Journal of Negro Education* 59 (Summer 1990): 375–91.

Silver, Edward A., and Margaret S. Smith. "Teaching Mathematics and Thinking." *Arithmetic Teacher* 37 (April 1990): 34–37.

Stiff, Lee V. "African-American Students and the Promise of the *Curriculum and Evaluation Standards*." In *Teaching and Learning Mathematics in the 1990s*, 1990 Yearbook of the National Council of Teachers of Mathematics, edited by Thomas J. Cooney, pp. 152–58. Reston, Va.: National Council of Teachers of Mathematics, 1990.

Stiff, Lee V., and William B. Harvey. "On the Education of Black Children in Mathematics." *Journal of Black Studies* 19 (December 1988): 190–203.

Usiskin, Zalman. "If Everybody Counts, Why Do So Few Survive?" In *Reaching All Students with Mathematics*, edited by Gilbert Cuevas and Mark Driscoll, pp. 7–22. Reston, Va.: National Council of Teachers of Mathematics, 1993.

Walker, Erica N., and Leah P. McCoy. "Students' Voices: African Americans and Mathematics." In *Multicultural and Gender Equity in the Mathematics Classroom: The Gift of Diversity*, 1997 Yearbook of the National Council of Teachers of Mathematics, edited by Janet Trentacosta, pp. 71–80. Reston, Va.: National Council of Teachers of Mathematics, 1997.

Zaslavsky, Claudia. "Multicultural Mathematics Education for the Middle Grades." *Arithmetic Teacher* 38 (February 1991): 34–39.

African American Students Conduct Mathematical Research

Miriam M. Stokes

10

When teachers combine high expectations, explicit instructions, and adequate guidance, African American students will produce and excel in mathematical research. This article describes how students in one middle school participated in mathematical research projects introduced to them and their teachers by their instructional specialist, a former high school mathematics teacher. The school was an inner-city school that served approximately 700 sixth-, seventh-, and eighth-grade students. The student population was 99 percent African American and 1 percent white and Hispanic. Although a small percentage of the students resided in nearby one-family dwellings, the majority came from two public housing projects. Ninety-one percent of the students came from single-parent homes and were eligible for the free and reduced lunch program. The mobility rate for the students was 38 percent. In spite of what appeared to be insurmountable odds, the school had a dedicated staff who shared a "vision of excellence." This quest for excellence became a reality when the school became a state School of Excellence in 1996.

The mathematics teachers in this middle school were involved in a national mathematics education project that supported and studied mathematics reform in urban communities that were economically disadvantaged and ethnically diverse. The school was one of six middle schools across the country that participated in the QUASAR Project (Silver and Stein 1996). The QUASAR Project was designed to demonstrate that it is feasible to implement instructional programs that promote the acquisition of mathematical thinking and reasoning skills by students attending middle school in these types of communities. Students who are provided with opportunities to be exposed to high-quality mathematics can potentially learn a broad range of mathematical ideas and demonstrate proficiency in mathematical reasoning and problem solving.

During the years of their involvement in the QUASAR Project, mathematics teachers and administrators at this school worked collaboratively with "resource partners" who were either mathematics educators from local universities or retired mathematics teachers from local high schools. Teachers were given frequent opportunities to interact with their resource partners and with one another to create and implement new instructional and assessment strategies that emphasized student engagement with challenging mathematical tasks, student discourse about mathematical ideas, and student involvement in collaborative mathematical activity.

One such activity designed to enhance students' problem solving, higher-order thinking, and verbal and written communication skills was a research project. While engaged in research, students were exposed to mathematical topics, skills, and concepts that would not ordinarily be taught in their regular

> **When teachers combine high expectations, explicit instructions, and adequate guidance, African American students will produce and excel in mathematical research.**

DESCRIPTION OF THE PROJECT

mathematics course. The research project, which incorporated the scientific process, was multifaceted.

Students used research methodology similar to that used in a science class. All students were asked to describe a problem in the introduction of the project. A hypothesis or purpose had to be stated, and several experiments were to be conducted, carefully observed, and recorded each time. Students also had to study and analyze data from their experiments. Finally, the students had to formulate a conclusion based on the results of the experiments.

The students are expected to conduct research over a period of time that would allow them to apply knowledge and demonstrate skills they had learned in the classroom. After the research was completed, the students could present their findings in two settings: the classroom and the local school fair. Classroom presentations provided an opportunity for students to practice their oral presentations. Class members served as judges, asked questions about the research, and made recommendations for improving the individual projects. Students who excelled in the school fair were encouraged to enter the next two levels of competition, first the city Mathematics Congress and then the state Engineering Fair.

By engaging in the mathematical research project, students gained the opportunity to demonstrate their mathematical talents and were expected to acquire or develop the following beneficial skills:

- Problem-solving techniques as a method of inquiry for open-ended problems
- Mathematical reasoning as they use the techniques of scientific research
- Verbal, written, graphical, statistical, and mathematical models to communicate their results
- Mathematical thinking and modeling as tools for solving real-world problems
- Techniques to model a situation and make predictions based on mathematical experiments

THE ROLE OF THE PARENTS AND TEACHER

The primary role of the parents or other caregivers was to serve as motivators. The parents also provided financial support and ensured that the child was working on his or her research at home. In schools where the majority of the students came from predominately low-income families, the teacher sometimes had to assume the role of the parents and donate materials and supplies that the parents could not afford. The teacher, as the main sponsor, was very instrumental in the research process. The teacher encouraged students to begin their research in a timely manner, directed them to appropriate resources, cultivated communication skills, monitored progress, and ensured that they understood the concepts being explored or presented.

RESEARCH SEMINAR

Because this was an ongoing project that required several weeks to complete, it was necessary to conduct an introductory seminar for students early in September or as early in the school year as possible. The purpose of the initial seminars for students was to discuss the steps involved in conducting the research. Teachers who had not served as sponsors before also needed training. Because the training for teachers may have already been presented during regular departmental meetings, if teachers were comfortable with their role as sponsors, the seminar was conducted for students only. The in-service program for students could be held during a single class period or, for larger groups, in an assembly program during the day or after school. Since most of the students rode the bus and could not stay after school, teachers sometimes used a portion of regular class time to present the seminar. Topics discussed included the nature of a mathematics project, topic selection, how to keep a logbook, research procedures, media resources, the research paper, the abstract, the display board, research evaluation, the educational value of research, and the presentation of the project. A video featuring a student who had won top prize at the city Mathematics Congress for four consecutive years was used as a teaching tool to demonstrate the poise, confidence, and thoroughness that students must model when presenting their research.

GETTING STARTED

The students were given a handout that detailed the procedures to follow during the research process. Specific information was given related to entering information into the logbook, writing the abstract and research paper, and preparing the display board. A schedule was presented including the deadlines for the topic, five resources, log checks, abstract, rough and final drafts of the research paper, display board, and oral presentation.

Several weeks before students had to submit the topic of their research, teachers brought in December issues of the *Mathematics Teacher*, which contain the classified index of topics for the indicated year. Other books and journals were placed on display in the room so that students could search for topics after completing their regular assignments. They were also encouraged to visit the school and public libraries to select topics. Students had to submit their topics for approval before the research began. The media specialist, who worked very closely with the classroom teacher, was given a copy of the same research assignment given to the students. The media specialist assisted the students with locating resources in the library and on the Internet. A set of related reference books was also put on reserve for students' use in the library.

The use of computers and other technology played a vital role in the research process. Computers were used to assist students in the search for references for their research papers (by way of CD-ROM, NewsBank, *Reader's Guide to Periodical Literature*). They were also helpful for word processing, statistical analysis, and generating various types of graphs. Graphing calculators also provided a means for analyzing statistical data and solving problems related to different kinds of functions.

PRESENTING THE RESEARCH PROJECT

One of the major incentives for completing the mathematics research was that students were provided the opportunity to present their research findings in the classroom among peers and in a formal setting before two or three judges. The presentation consisted of the student's giving an introduction to the project, the purpose for doing the project, the procedure used, an explanation of the data collected, and the conclusion reached. Additionally, students demonstrated how their research could benefit humanity and outlined their plans for the continuation of the project. The class presentations were given in December before students recessed for the winter holidays. The local school fair was held after the holidays, usually during the first week in January. Research projects presented during the local fair included some of the more traditional topics such as palindromes, magic squares, math and music, the Pythagorean theorem, the Fibonacci sequence, the four-color problem, even-and-odd relationships, the abacus, capture-recapture, and pi. Some of the more innovative titles included "Predicting the Winning Time in the Men's and Women's 100-Meter Race in the 1996 Olympics," "Are You Getting Your Money's Worth?" "What Is the Most Common Letter?" "The Chocolate Chip Equation," "What Is the Average Number of Licks to the Center of a Blow Pop®?" "How Many Different Ice-Cream Cones Can You Make with Ten Flavors?" "The Shadow Method," and "How Math Relates to the State Lottery."

EVALUATION

Each project was judged according to both general and specific guidelines. These guidelines included scientific thought, creative ability, thoroughness, technical skills, clarity in the oral presentation, and dramatic value. Students also used these same criteria when the projects were judged in the classroom. The judges for the fair came from higher education or the corporate world. They were encouraged to make comments, including recommendations for improvement, and to recommend students to the city fair.

CULMINATING ACTIVITY

The culminating activity was an awards ceremony where each student was rewarded for presenting a project in the local fair. All students received a certificate of participation. First-, second-, and third-place winners were awarded ribbons. Medallions were given to overall grade-level winners, and the best overall project received a trophy.

PUBLICITY

Signs and posters were displayed throughout the building to remind students of the upcoming event. Invitations were sent to parents requesting their presence and support at the local fair.

EDUCATIONAL BENEFIT

The educational benefits were enormous because each project related to some real-world situation, identified practical applications, incorporated several disciplines, and allowed the student to develop an appreciation for the scientific method. Many students seemed to blossom during this activity. Students with poor self-concepts or low self-esteem increased their self-confidence with the praise and encouragement given to them by their teachers, the resource partner, and the instructional specialist. Two eighth-grade boys who were known to the administration not for their academic prowess but for disciplinary reasons won second-place awards in two categories at the city fair. They have since reformed their thinking about getting a good education and have become role models for other students. Each of the nine teachers participated and sponsored a total of 169 students in the local school fair compared with one teacher and five projects for the preceding year. This year many of the local winners qualified and went on to participate and win in the city and state mathematics fairs.

CONCLUSION

The mathematics research project is an excellent educational opportunity for African American students to become involved in independent research and to increase their self-esteem at the same time. The project is very beneficial in that students are able to enhance their communication skills as they acquire knowledge in mathematical concepts and skills beyond that which is taught in the regular coursework. The key to the success of this project is providing directions for the students and, if needed, for the teachers. In previous years, the student participation in the local mathematics fairs was very low and teachers complained that students were not getting the parental support that they needed. This year there was an increase in the number of students who participated in the local fair as well as an increase in the number of teachers sponsoring students. We believe that the increase in participation is due to the amount of guidance and nurturing that were provided to both students and teachers through seminars and ongoing monitoring throughout the entire research process.

See the appendix for a sample project.

REFERENCE

Silver, Edward A., and Mary K. Stein. "The QUASAR Project: 'The Revolution of the Possible' in Mathematics Instructional Reform in Urban Middle Schools." *Urban Education* 30 (January 1996): 476–521.

BIBLIOGRAPHY

Edgerton, Richard T. "Analyzing Data from the Olympic Games for Trends and Inferences." *Mathematics Teacher* 89 (May 1996): 370–72.

ESPNET. Available at sportszone.com/editors/atlanta96/sports/track/index.html.

Ewbank, William. "The Summer Olympic Games: A Mathematical Opportunity." *Mathematics Teacher* 77 (May 1984): 344–48.

Foster, Alan G., Leslie J. Winters, Joan M. Gell, James N. Rath, and Berchie W. Gordon. "Scatter Plots." In *Merrill Algebra 1, Applications and Connections*, pp. 583–87. New York: Glencoe Macmillan/McGraw-Hill Publishing Co., 1995.

Haigh, William. "Graph, Guess, and Compute." *Mathematics Teacher* 80 (December 1987): 716–21.

Henningsen, Jacqueline. "An Activity for Predicting Performances in the 1984 Summer Olympics." *Mathematics Teacher* 77 (May 1984): 338–42.

Haylock, Derek W. "Sharing Teaching Ideas—a Simplified Approach to Correlation." *Mathematics Teacher* 76 (May 1983): 332–35.

Travers, Kenneth J., William F. Stout, James H. Swift, and Joan Sextro. "Fitting Rules to Data." In *Using Statistics*, pp. 179–81. Menlo Park, Calif.: Addison-Wesley Publishing Co., 1985.

Wallace, Edward C. "Exploring Regression with a Graphing Calculator." *Mathematics Teacher* 86 (December 1993): 741–43.

APPENDIX

The following is an example of a research project submitted by one student:

TITLE

Can You Predict the Winning Time in the Men's 100-Meter Race during the 1996 Summer Olympics?

INTRODUCTION

The Men's 100-Meter Race is one of the most exciting events in the track and field competitions. During these events, some of the fastest men in the world come together and compete. During the 1996 Summer Olympics in Atlanta, many great runners such as Carl Lewis and Leroy Burrell will run in the Men's 100-Meter Race. Will the record of 9.85 seconds (currently held by Leroy Burrell) be broken during the Summer Olympics or will it occur at a later competition? Is it possible to predict the winning time during the Summer Olympics in the Men's 100-Meter Race? This research will attempt to answer these questions.

PURPOSE

The purpose for completing the research project was to predict the winning time for the Men's 100-Meter Race during the 1996 Summer Olympics.

DEFINITIONS

* *Scatterplot (scattergram)* is a graph of data collected and plotted as points on a coordinate system.
* *Line of best fit* is a line that best represents the data of a scatterplot.
* *Positive correlation* implies that most of the points cluster in an upward-sloping band.
* *Negative correlation* implies that most of the points cluster in a downward-sloping band.
* *No correlation* implies that there is no connection between the points.
* *Outlier* is a value or point that stands apart from the rest of the values or points. An outlier may be omitted from the data when making predictions.

PROCEDURE

1. Collect and organize data.

Progression of the Men's 100-Meter Olympic Results

TIME	YEAR	RUNNER	COUNTRY
12.0	1896	Thomas Burke	United States
11.0	1900	Frank Jarvis	United States
11.0	1904	Archie Hahn	United States
10.8	1908	Reginald Walker	South Africa
10.8	1912	Ralph Craig	United States
10.8	1920	Charles Paddock	United States
10.6	1924	Harold Abrahams	Great Britain
10.8	1928	Percy Williams	Canada
10.3	1932	Eddie Tolan	United States
10.3	1936	Jesse Owens	United States
10.3	1948	Harrison Dillard	United States
10.4	1952	Lindy Remigino	United States
10.5	1956	Bobby Jo Morrow	United States
10.2	1960	Armin Hary	West Germany
10.0	1964	Bob Hayes	United States

9.95	1968	Jim Hines	United States
10.14	1972	Valeri Borzov	Soviet Union
10.06	1976	Hasely Crawford	T'dad & Tobago
10.25	1980	Allan Wells	Great Britain
9.99	1984	Carl Lewis	United States
9.92	1988	Carl Lewis	United States
9.96	1992	Linford Christie	Great Britain

2. Complete scatterplot.

Olympic Results for the Men's 100-Meter Race

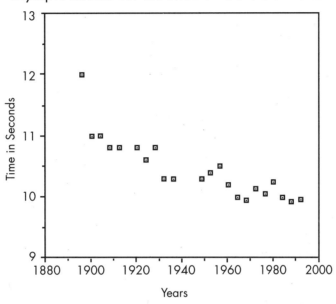

3. Use scatterplot to determine correlation.

The scatterplot shows that the data have a negative correlation and an outlier located at (1896, 12.0).

4. Find the equation of the line of best fit by using (a) mean points including the outlier, (b) mean points excluding the outlier, (c) estimation, (d) graphing calculator, and (e) computer.

Procedure for Finding the Best Line of Fit

Divide the data into two groups (1896 to 1948; 1952 to 1992). Find the average of the years (x-coordinates) and the times (y-coordinates) for each group. Next, plot the two mean points and draw a line through them. Calculate the slope for the line and determine the equation.

(a) Using the Mean Points, Including the Outlier, (1896, 12.0)

Group 1

Mean of years

$$\frac{1896+1900+1904+1908+1912+1920+1924+1928+1932+1936+1948}{11} = 1919$$

Mean of times

$$\frac{12.0+11.0+11.0+10.8+10.8+10.8+10.6+10.8+10.3+10.3+10.3}{11} = 10.79$$

The mean point: (X1, Y1) = (1919, 10.79)

Group II

Mean of years

$$\frac{1952+1956+1960+1964+1968+1972+1976+1980+1984+1988+1992}{11} = 1972$$

Mean of times

$$\frac{10.4+10.5+10.2+10.0+9.95+10.14+10.06+10.25+9.99+9.92+9.96}{11} = 10.12$$

The mean point: (X2, Y2) = (1972, 10.12)

The slope of the line of best fit using the mean points is

$$m = \frac{Y2 - Y1}{X2 - X1} = \frac{10.12 - 10.79}{1972 - 1919} = -0.013$$

Use $y = mx + b$ to find the y-intercept:

$$10.79 = -0.013(1919) + b$$
$$35.74 = b$$

Thus, the equation of the best-fitting line is $y = -0.013x + 35.74$.

Use the line of best fit to predict the winning time:

$$y = -0.013x + 35.74$$
$$y = -0.013(1996) + 35.74$$
$$y = 9.79$$

The predicted winning time using the mean points is 9.79 seconds.

(b) Using the Mean Points, Excluding the Outlier, (1896, 12.0)

Group I

Mean of years

$$\frac{1900+1904+1908+1912+1920+1924+1928+1932+1936+1948}{10} = 1921$$

Mean of times

$$\frac{11.0+11.0+10.8+10.8+10.8+10.6+10.8+10.3+10.3+10.3}{10} = 10.67$$

The mean point: (X1, Y1) = (1921, 10.67)

Group II

There is no change in the mean point. (X2, Y2) = (1972, 10.12)

The slope of the line of best fit using the mean points is

$$m = \frac{Y2 - Y1}{X2 - X1} = \frac{10.12 - 10.67}{1972 - 1921} = -0.011$$

Use $y = mx + b$ to find the y-intercept:

$$10.67 = -0.011(1921) + b$$
$$31.80 = b$$

Thus, the equation of the best fitting line is $y = -0.011x + 31.80$.

Use the line of best fit to predict the winning time:

$$y = -0.013x + 31.80$$
$$y = -0.011(1996) + 31.80$$
$$y = 9.84$$

The predicted winning time using the mean points is 9.84 seconds.

(c) Estimation

Using a straightedge, draw a line that appears to best represent the set of data. Select two points that fall on this line to determine the slope. For example, (1912, 10.8) and (1988, 9.92).

Olympic Results for the Men's 100-Meter Race

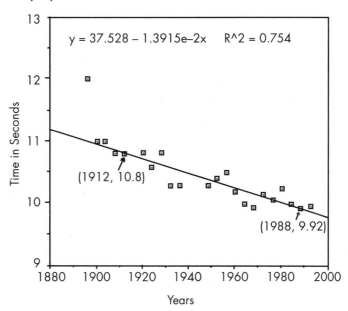

$$m = \frac{Y2 - Y1}{X2 - X1} = \frac{10.8 - 9.92}{1912 - 1988} = 0.012$$

Use the point-slope form of a line to find the *y*-intercept:

$$y = -0.012x + b$$
$$b = 10.8 + 0.012(1912) = 33.74$$

The equation for the line of best fit using estimation is

$$y = -0.012x + 33.74.$$

Substituting 1996 for *x* yields

$$y = -0.012(1996) + 33.74$$
$$y = 9.79.$$

The time using this method is 9.79 seconds.

(d) Graphing Calculator

Enter the data into the calculator, draw a scatterplot, and find the values for the equation of the line of best fit using linear regression. This procedure gives the following results: the slope of −0.014 and *y*-intercept of 37.53. Thus the equation for the line of best fit is $y = -0.014x + 37.53$. Substituting 1996 for *x* yields a time of 9.59 seconds.

(e) Computer

Entering the data into a computer using a graph maker such as Cricket Plotter, the following graph is generated.

Olympic Results for the Men's 100-Meter Race

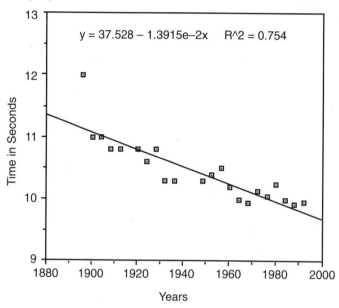

$y = 37.528 - 1.3915e-2x$ $R{\char`^}2 = 0.754$

The equation of the line of best fit generated by the computer is $y = -.014x + 37.53$. Substituting 1996 for x produces a winning time of 9.59 seconds.

5. Use the equations to make predictions and compare the results.

In conclusion, the methods using the mean points including the outlier and estimation predicted an Olympic winning time of 9.79 seconds. The procedure that used the mean points without the outlier predicted a record time of 9.84 seconds. Both the computer and the graphing calculator predicted a winning time of 9.59 seconds.

Note: Have each student discuss the reasonableness of his or her answer and the possibility of error in making a prediction based on a mathematical model.

Culturally Relevant Mathematics Teaching at the Secondary School Level

Problematic Features and a Model for Implementation

11

Lesley Wagner
Francine Cabral Roy
Elena Ecatoiu
Celia Rousseau

Acknowledging the role of culture in mathematics learning, the *Professional Standards for Teaching Mathematics* (National Council of Teachers of Mathematics [NCTM] 1991) notes the importance of including in mathematics instruction diverse cultures' contributions to the development of mathematics, the role of mathematics in society and culture, and an awareness of the influence of students' culture on their mathematics learning. These recommendations parallel several tenets of *culturally relevant teaching* (Ladson-Billings 1994) and similarly named pedagogies (e.g., *culturally congruent, culturally responsive*) advanced as avenues for engendering academic success among traditionally underserved students whose home and school cultures often conflict—a conflict that seems to suggest to students that in order to achieve in school, they must relinquish their culture and "act white."[1] This disjuncture is particularly pronounced in mathematics education, whose content has traditionally been presented as abstract and taught devoid of meaningful contexts reflective of students' lived realities. Low mathematics achievement, overrepresentation in low-track classes, unacceptable dropout rates from high school mathematics courses, and underrepresentation in mathematics and science careers, however, attest to the inadequacy of current practices for many nonwhite students. If more equitable mathematics achievement is a serious goal of educators, then mathematics instruction must begin to reflect the pedagogies that meaningfully integrate culture into the classroom.

Ladson-Billings (1994) characterizes the theoretical underpinnings of culturally relevant teaching as high academic standards, cultural competence, and the development of a critical consciousness through which students will challenge the status quo. Further underscored are the importance of the belief in the educability of all students, the development of a community of learners responsible for their own and their peers' learning, the dynamic nature of knowledge, the conviction that all students bring knowledge to the classroom that can serve as a foundation for new learning, the development of necessary skills valued by society at large, and the cultivation of relationships with students beyond classroom boundaries. Although many examples of this pedagogy exist (see, for

> **If more equitable mathematics achievement is a serious goal of educators, then mathematics instruction must begin to reflect the pedagogies that meaningfully integrate culture into the classroom.**

---

1. Schools are organized in ways that alienate African American students from their own cultural values, often attempting to resocialize African American students into mainstream (i.e., white, middle class) values, behaviors, and attitudes. As a result, many African American students "have come to equate exemplary performance in school with a loss of their African American identity; that is, doing well in school is seen as 'acting white.' Thus if they do not want to 'act white,' the only option, many believe, is to refuse to do well in school" (Ladson-Billings 1994, p. 11).

example, Ladson-Billings and Henry [1990]; Sheets [1995]; Wilkinson and Kido [1997]; Silva and Kucer [1997]), most address language arts and the social sciences, where distinct histories and diverse perspectives are more readily accessible. Conversely, mathematics in the United States has been viewed as neutral and objective. When culture does appear in mathematics classrooms, it often surfaces as an addendum to the traditional curriculum, lending the impression that this mathematics is not essential or useful in students' lives but, rather, a fun or isolated activity. When a more meaningful confluence of mathematics and culture is accomplished, the examples cited are usually confined to elementary and middle school classrooms (see, for example, Tate [1995]; Heckman and Weissglass [1994]). Demographics, however, dictate that the integration of student culture and mathematics as a nucleus of instruction is a vital necessity at *all* levels of mathematics education.

The urgency is clear. Currently, students of color represent 30 percent of the public school population (Ladson-Billings 1994), and this proportion is predicted to grow to almost 50 percent within the next twenty years (Lipman 1995). Further, students of color already make up more than 70 percent of the school enrollment in the twenty largest school districts in the nation (Ladson-Billings 1994). Conversely, demographics in the teaching force are dramatically moving away from diversity and toward homogeneity; thus, teachers will increasingly be challenged to educate students who are unlike themselves. "As the ethnic texture of the nation deepens, problems related to diversity will intensify rather than diminish" (Banks 1996, p. 76). We cannot continue to systematically ignore the failure of large groups of children and produce dysfunctional graduates in a technologically dominated future when, in the next century, these same children will compose a large proportion of the student body in this country and, ultimately, the workforce. Currently, for example, white men compose the primary pool for engineering, mathematics, and science careers (National Science Foundation 1999). However, in order to maintain a qualified pool of workers to fill these important positions, changing demographics indicate that education must prepare students of color with solid mathematics and science backgrounds. Moreover, if the claim of democracy in this country is to move beyond mere rhetoric, we must search for successful pedagogies and pertinent curricula that successfully engage *all* students and allow them to be informed participants in the democratic process. Students must recognize the power of mathematics both as a gatekeeper and as a persuasive influence in decisions that may affect them either positively or negatively. As Tate (1995, p. 483) asserts,

> Thus far, it has been the case that those few who have learned to use mathematics as a tool to guide their own decision making have stifled the voices of the large segment of the population who do not know how to counter with their own mathematically based arguments—a disproportionate number of whom are African Americans. If students learn in school to analyze and critique mathematized situations … they will be prepared for public discussions about the development and implementation of the mathematical models that are used in social decision making.

Students must recognize the power of mathematics both as a gatekeeper and as a persuasive influence in decisions that may affect them either positively or negatively.

Therefore, mathematics education for traditionally underserved students involves a twofold imperative; it must provide students with the necessary skills for entrée into upper-level mathematics courses and eventual career opportunities while simultaneously preparing them to extend the traditional conceptions of mathematics to include a critique of the ways mathematics has been used in society to advance particular agendas as well as their own use of mathematics to expose inequities, communicate their positions, and defend their rights (Tate 1994, 1995).

Many formidable obstacles block the integration of culture and the resulting call for social critique and action in the mathematics classroom. These barriers include a classroom environment premised on individualism and competition, the types and (ab)uses of assessment, the fixed hierarchy of content, tracking, and a lack of socially critical content models capable of providing students with the skills necessary to pass through the mathematics "pipeline" while concurrently engendering meaningful inquiry into society's structures. However, these barriers are not insurmountable. In this paper, we explore these obstacles and suggest alternatives that align with the tenets of culturally relevant pedagogy. Finally, we propose a socially critical model of mathematics instruction that both introduces the mathematical concepts that have traditionally been used as gatekeepers and generates an authentic call to social action.

Teacher Beliefs

Although many of the structural constraints, teacher beliefs, and classroom norms that inhibit the success of traditionally underserved students in mathematics are equally applicable in disparate disciplines and at many grade levels, other factors are unique to high school mathematics classrooms. One of the most powerful influences on student success in mathematics is the teacher's expectations. As Ladson-Billings (1994, p. 44) suggests, the "notion that all students can succeed may seem trite," but despite research supporting the importance of this belief, many minority students are labeled "at risk of failure" or "unteachable." Walker and Chappell (1997, p. 202) assert that "such labels lead one to believe that [minority] students attending urban schools cannot achieve at the same levels as other students." This belief about students' (in)ability results in a restrictive and limiting learning environment, one that contrasts sharply with the image of a classroom where all students are expected and helped to succeed. On the high school level, a teacher encounters as many as forty students a class, up to five classes a day, and embracing this belief brings daunting responsibilities for these students' success. A teacher who believes that some students are destined for failure may not be compelled to experiment with new strategies to help all students achieve, nor might she or he try to remedy problems when students encounter difficulties. This teacher can blame the student's failure on the student's lack of mathematical aptitude. In contrast, a teacher who believes that all students can succeed takes on the additional responsibility of ensuring that they do. This teacher must find ways to help struggling students; he or she invests time and effort to foster student success and takes time to discover the strengths and needs of the students. Thus, believing that all (up to 200) students can succeed carries with it a different level of responsibility than accepting that some students are predestined to failure.

The rigid structure of high school in general further impedes the implementation of culturally relevant teaching in mathematics classrooms. The 55-minute class period and the large number of students in many classes militate against opportunities for teachers to get to know their students and to discover the knowledge and skills students bring to class. The constraints of time and numbers limit the possibility that teachers can find appropriate strategies for "building bridges" to new learning. Without the chance to dig knowledge out of students (Ladson-Billings 1995a), teachers are likely to teach in a generic, traditional way that may not be advantageous for all students. Moreover, many mathematics teachers may see student knowledge as extraneous and may not believe that it is their job to pull knowledge from students and scaffold to new learning. Instead, they may conceive of teaching as telling. The student's role becomes that of a parrot, repeating back what the teacher has trained her or him to say, and the student's knowledge then is of no value. Thus, the belief that

BARRIERS TO CULTURALLY RELEVANT MATHEMATICS INSTRUCTION

knowledge flows unidirectionally from teacher to student further disconnects students from the learning process and divorces culture from mathematics learning.

CLASSROOM ENVIRONMENT

One aspect of the classroom environment that is antithetical to culturally relevant pedagogy is the individualistic and competitive nature of typical high school mathematics classes. In these classrooms, "students work mostly by themselves on individual tasks, and doing well means doing better than others" (Davidson and Kramer 1997, p. 137). This routine can cause students to feel isolated, and students who fall behind may not ask for help. Misconceptions and holes in students' understanding can easily remain unnoticed and unaddressed. This isolation can further result in students' disconnecting from the classroom process and their voices being silenced in the classroom (Walker and McCoy 1997). In contrast, culturally relevant pedagogy advocates the creation of a community of learners. This community involves more than cooperative learning with prescriptive rules to follow; it entails the establishment of an ethos of cooperation rather than one of competition. As Ms. Hilliard, a successful teacher of African American students, explains (Ladson-Billings 1994, p.72),

> From the day that they walk into my room they know they have to select a buddy. This is their learning partner for the year. A lot of times when a student is having a hard time I'll call the buddy to my desk and really give him or her an earful. "Why are you letting your buddy struggle like this? What kind of partner are you? You're supposed to be the helper." Within a couple of months I begin to see them looking out for one another. One student will hesitate before he turns in his paper and will go check to make sure the buddy is doing okay. Eventually, they begin to check very carefully and they may discover some errors that they themselves have made. Having the buddy is really just another level of learning. Those that are helping are really helping themselves.

Rather than achieving success at the cost of others, success is experienced by individuals only when success is experienced by the class as a whole. In an environment where competitive individualism is not the norm, students are respected for the knowledge they bring to the classroom, and they work together to support, teach, and take responsibility for one another.

Assessment

"And those tests! Those are the worst things ever. They don't begin to test what the kids really know" (Ladson-Billings 1994, p. 46). This lament from Ms. Winston, a "dreamkeeper," a successful teacher of African American students, addresses another curricular villain hindering the implementation of culturally relevant pedagogy in the mathematics classroom: assessment. Assessments are generally used to assign grades and to determine a student's future course enrollment as he or she competes for a limited number of spaces in higher-level classes. Knowledge on most assessments is defined narrowly, and tests are not typically used to determine a student's prior knowledge or the full extent of her or his current knowledge. Students are typically assessed individually, and success is defined according to a student's placement compared to his or her peers. This practice reinforces the notion that success and failure are individual outcomes and that it is contrary to a person's self-interest to help others.

Tracking

Unfortunately, many people still believe that mathematics is accessible only to an anointed few, and some mathematics educators and mathematicians have the expectation, even perverse pride, that not all students will succeed; in fact, they expect many to fail. A popular conception of mathematics ability as innate—"either you've got it or you don't"—continues to pervade the school system, from parents to students to teachers to counselors. Failure becomes more tolerable when it is accepted that particular students "just can't do math." Clearly, acceptance of the belief that all students can succeed in mathematics is not as trite or trivial as it may at first sound.

The belief that only an elite few students are mathematically apt often translates into a system of tracking that sorts students into mathematically capable or incapable categories. The pervasive practice of tracking, which can begin as early as elementary school (Oakes 1990; Secada 1992), severely impedes the implementation of culturally relevant teaching at the secondary school level. In high school, tracking traditionally distinguishes consumer mathematics students from algebra students. Recently, there has been a push for all students to take algebra. However, even the schools that embrace this idea often institute algebra tracks. Some schools distinguish these classes by textbook selection, resulting in different titles for these classes such as "algebra 1 method" versus "algebra 1 theory." In other schools, the text may be the same for all students, but less material is covered over a given time period in some classes. Even the *Curriculum and Evaluation Standards for School Mathematics* (NCTM 1989), which claims that all students should learn the same content topics, nevertheless promotes a differentiated curriculum, suggesting that not all students need to be exposed to the same level of mathematical rigor. Regardless of the labels, then, the reality in today's mathematics remains that tracking results in differentiation of curricular content.

Unfortunately, students in lower-track classes are disproportionately minority and students from low socioeconomic background (Oakes 1990). The emphasis in these classes is on skill building rather than on the higher-order thinking that is necessary for high-level mathematics. The hierarchy of mathematics also exists within a high-level track; that is, students must demonstrate acceptable algebra 1 skills before they can gain entry to geometry. Likewise, this strict ordering continues with the algebra 2, precalculus, calculus sequence. As a result, each juncture in mathematics education becomes a critical filter where a 50 percent decline in participation begins in ninth grade and continues to the Ph.D. level (National Science Foundation 1989, as cited in Steen 1990). These losses occur disproportionately among minority students.

When students are placed in low-level tracks or denied access to advanced courses, the system implicitly tells students, "You are not capable nor worthy of learning high level mathematics" (Ladson-Billings 1995b). In addition to self-selection, counseling, and perceived ability by teachers, oftentimes this low placement is a result of assessment tests on required skills (Oakes 1990). Secada (1990, p. 139) calls these prerequisites the "computational gate" to higher-level mathematics. When faced with low test scores or a perceived lack of ability, the mathematics teacher or counselor may introduce the tracking system as the solution. That is, they deny students access to high-level mathematics by placing them in classes that focus on skill building.

The practice of tracking directly contradicts the notion of scaffolding advocated by Ladson-Billings (1994), which is used to help students develop necessary skills. To illustrate scaffolding in practice, Ladson-Billings cites Ms. Rossi, who insists on teaching algebra to *all* her students, even one labeled "special education." She builds on the skills the students already possess and uses the more advanced students as teachers. Hence, rather than lamenting her students' lack of mastery of prerequisite skills, Ms. Rossi uses the skills the students *do* possess to build bridges to concepts they need to know to be successful with higher-level content. However, if these same students were in high school, it seems likely that they would be placed in lower-level classes. Hence, the system of tracking reifies the belief that all students, especially minority and students of low socioeconomic status, are not capable of learning advanced mathematics.

The Nature of Knowledge and Curricular Content

Rather than accepting all knowledge as fixed and undebatable, culturally relevant teaching views knowledge critically. Critical theory forms the basis for this proposition. The view advanced by Ladson-Billings (1994) advocates the use of knowledge and education to empower students to examine the social inequalities that may affect their lives. For example, Ms. Deveraux, a dreamkeeper, uses children's literature, *Mufaro's Beautiful Daughters*, to confront her students' belief that all princesses are white with blond hair. Another instance of viewing knowledge critically is evidenced in Ms. Rossi's classroom. She casts a discussion of the Gulf War in light of her students' lived realities by connecting overrepresentation of minorities in the military to the resultant effects on the African American family unit. In both of these examples, the teachers deliberately chose curriculum material that is not considered mainstream but that holds social significance in the lives and cultural backgrounds of their African American students.

Conversely, many may argue that the social significance of such issues is out of place in the value-free world of mathematics. The current secondary school curriculum upholds the traditional belief that mathematics is "a body of infallible truth far removed from the affairs and values of humanity" (Romberg 1992, p. 751). The curriculum is dominated by the algebra–precalculus–calculus sequence that is devoted to the study of the analytical symbolic formalisms of algebra. Traditionally, the subject matter is taught devoid of applications, as rote procedures. Many mathematics education reform advocates, however, are calling for the inclusion of more applications in the secondary school curriculum; yet, the mathematics taught in the algebra-to-calculus sequence is typically reserved for the world of science and engineering. For example, derivatives are usually explained in terms of instantaneous velocity. The quadratic function is typically presented as a model for the height of a ball as it drops from a given distance. Another traditional application of quadratic functions is maximizing a rectangular region by enclosing it with a known perimeter of fence. At best, these applications are socially neutral; at worst, they are elitist and irrelevant for most students. Contrast these applications with the socially critical issues present in Ms. Deveraux's and Ms. Rossi's classes discussed earlier. The socially neutral mathematics in the current secondary school curriculum clearly does not reflect all of society's quantitative demands.

Outside of school, mathematics is applied to areas other than the natural sciences, including the social sciences, business, and medicine (Steen 1990). As Tate (1994) further elucidates, mathematics beyond the classroom is used purposely to advance a particular agenda; it is never used devoid of a social or political context. Statistics is an ideal tool to analyze social issues, and therefore, should hold a more prominent role in secondary school mathematics. Although reform advocates are promoting a greater emphasis on statistics in the curriculum (NCTM 1989), schools have been slow to heed this call, at best, perhaps offering a one-semester course. Even with the recent inclusion of Advanced Placement statistics courses at the secondary school level, at most schools, calculus remains "the epitome of mathematical knowledge" (Steen 1990, p. 4).

The question arises as to why science and engineering applications dominate the school mathematics curriculum. Why are so few socially critical curricular materials available to teachers? Who shapes the curriculum? Apple (1992, p. 415) answers these questions by asserting that a conservative agenda has assumed "the most powerful leadership for school reform [and chooses] from the [reform] documents those elements that cohere with the general framework and tendencies already in motion." The socially neutral nature of the current reform materials gives credence to Apple's statement. Even the materials available that promote less traditional uses of mathematics, such as statistics, do not view the world from a critical standpoint. For example, a supplementary curriculum text published by NCTM entitled *Data Analysis and Statistics* (Burrill et al. 1992) presents activities such as taste tests and correlations between height and arm span. None of the applications, however, examine social inequalities or the realities of many minority populations.

The choice to dominate the secondary school mathematics curriculum with science applications and to ignore other more socially relevant applications is problematic. As Stanic and Kilpatrick (1992, p. 415) argue,

> Because the curriculum always represents a selected sample from an almost unlimited universe of knowledge. The main questions that guide work in the curriculum field—What should we teach? Why should we teach one thing rather than another? Who should have access to what knowledge?—are, then, fundamentally moral and ethical questions.

Hence the very knowledge culturally relevant teachers should critique is the mathematics knowledge that is valued in the mathematics pipeline. In fact, the established mathematics curriculum serves as a hindrance to culturally relevant teaching.

Classroom environment, the structure of high school in general, assessment, tracking, and curricular content are powerful barriers that teachers face in implementing culturally relevant teaching as they both reify and limit individual teacher action. Therefore, as Ladson-Billings (1994) suggests, it is necessary for teachers to be critical of the system. However, since the system is still in place and dictates what is deemed "official" and necessary knowledge, it is imperative that teachers provide their students with the necessary knowledge that enables them to pass through the pipeline.

In mathematics, the pipeline is predicated on the decontextualized world of skills, procedures, and mathematical structure. Hence, it is detrimental to student opportunity and success for teachers to implement socially relevant applications without providing the necessary skills valued in the current mathematical system. Therefore, the challenge is to incorporate these two conflicting notions. That is, culturally relevant mathematics teaching demands socially critical curriculum materials that incorporate the necessary mathematics knowledge that allows a student to progress through the mathematics pipeline. In the following section, we illustrate such an activity.

Culturally relevant mathematics teaching demands socially critical curriculum materials that incorporate the necessary mathematics knowledge that allows a student to progress through the mathematics pipeline.

A CULTURALLY RELEVANT MATHEMATICS APPLICATION

Three features guided our search for a mathematical application:

- First, believing that social critique is the most distinctive feature of culturally relevant teaching, our mathematics application is intended to make students reflect on the inequalities in society, develop socially critical thinking, and empower them to take social action.

- Second, our mathematical application is intended to teach the hard-core mathematics that the students need in order to pass through the mathematics pipeline. In other words, the application must also teach students the mainstream mathematical knowledge that appears on assessment tests and that other faculty members expect students to have mastered as they advance to subsequent mathematics classes.
- Third, this activity is intended to foster the development of a community of learners. Students will tackle these problems cooperatively; they will be encouraged to negotiate meaning with other classmates as well as be expected to assist one another in the construction of mathematical knowledge.

Socially Critical Knowledge

From the culturally relevant teaching perspective, knowledge is continuously re-created, recycled, and shared by teachers and students. Knowledge is also viewed critically (Ladson-Billings 1994). The mathematical application that we envision needs to help the students understand and participate in knowledge building and develop critical thinking about knowledge. Students will make conjectures, confront diverse views, compare different mathematical solutions, and come to realize that knowledge is not something concealed in the book (Ladson-Billings 1994); it is something that they can construct. Instead of being bombarded with prescribed algorithms, students will be challenged to think critically and to come up with conjectures and mathematical models.

In addition to students' critical view of knowledge, our mathematical example will give them insight about the inequalities that exist in our society and lead students to question traditional practices in our society and find ways in which they can act to change the society. Further, we hope students will make connections with other fields of study including history, social studies, and biology; realize that there is a connection between mathematics, their lived realities, and the world beyond the classroom; and recognize the importance of mathematics as a necessary tool for success in society. Given that mathematics is used extensively in our society, they need to realize that mathematics is a language of social power.

Necessary Mathematics

In addition to addressing important societal issues, our mathematical application deals with mathematical content that the students will need to know in order to succeed on college entrance examinations and on the path to mathematical and scientific careers. More specifically, they should be able to solve algebraic equations and systems of equations as well as to calculate derivatives and integrals. Therefore, our application seeks to help students develop the skills necessary for success in the mainstream mathematics curriculum. Thus, we tried to find an application that allows students to build on their previous knowledge. By providing them with some structural clues, we allow the students the freedom to ask questions and interpret findings on the basis of the knowledge they possess and their experiences. Beyond the societal implications, our application will also provide opportunities to learn quality mathematics for all students from diverse cultural backgrounds.

Classroom Environment

We envision our classroom setting as a cooperative one where students work in small groups. We believe that small groupings will help students overcome their intimidation and fear of mathematics, and they will feel free to ask and pose questions to their peers. The mathematics classroom atmosphere must be less rigid and cold than the traditional classroom, where students feel isolated and pressured to compete.

We encourage a community of learners rather than the competitive environment of traditional classrooms. Students will be expected to teach each other and to be responsible for each other's learning. Success is the class's success, and the failure of one member reflects on the whole group. By listening to their peers, students will also learn to respect other people's ideas and to collaborate. They will get to know each other better and learn that they can rely on classmates for help when they need it. In this environment, we hope to maximize learning for all students. We also want our students to think of practical ways to take action in order to change society, at least on a local level. We believe that this activity will actively engage all students in the learning process.

A MATHEMATICAL APPLICATION

The following mathematical application is designed for high school mathematics classrooms. It deals with data about the number of deaths and the death rates from immunodeficiency virus (HIV/AIDS) for whites and African Americans in the United States from 1987 to 1994. These data can be used in infinitely many ways in the mathematics classroom. Our suggestions are by no means exhaustive, merely suggestive of ways such data can be used in the mathematics classroom in a manner reflective of culturally relevant teaching. Because each group of students must serve as a guide to navigate the pedagogical terrain, these activities should be adapted for the unique needs and interests in individual classrooms. We further emphasize that using problems such as the following need not compromise the rigor of the mathematics taught. Moreover, we believe that the complexity of the social issues that can be raised will attract all students to participate in discussion and in the learning process. We also believe these data and the trends revealed through the mathematics will lead students to question the traditional state of affairs in our society; thus, it can form the basis of culturally relevant mathematics instruction.

Data

See the data in table 11.1.

Table 11.1
U.S. Mortality Figures for HIV Infection

	Total No. of Deaths		Rate per 100 000 people	
	White	African American	White	African American
1994	25 578	16 079	11.8	49.2
1993	23 586	13 319	11.0	41.4
1992	21 921	11 378	10.3	35.9
1991	19 850	9 437	9.4	30.3
1990	17 255	7 730	8.3	25.4
1989	15 095	6 795	7.3	22.5
1988	11 267	5 197	5.5	17.5
1987	9 328	4 040	4.6	13.8

Source: www.cdc.gov/nchstp/hiv_aids/dhap.htm. The HIV/AIDS Surveillance Report is published semiannually by the Division of HIV/AIDS Prevention, National Center for HIV, STD, and TB Prevention, Centers for Disease Control and Prevention (CDC). This report contains tabular and graphic information about U.S. AIDS and HIV case reports, including data by state, metropolitan statistical area, mode of exposure to HIV, sex, race/ethnicity, age group, vital status, and case definition category.

Questions

Notes: All questions should be discussed as a group. Each group member is responsible for learning the material. However, you need only pass in one set of answers per group. If you have questions, discuss them as a group; only then, if an answer remains unresolved, may you refer your question to other groups or to the teacher. You may also find it helpful to assign a role for each group member, such as recorder, calculator-retriever, and group facilitator.

To begin, ask students what they know about AIDS and HIV. AIDS education is common in most schools, so students should have at least tangential familiarity with these topics. Ask why information about AIDS is important in general and in their community in particular. Then distribute the data.

1. Carefully look over the data. Why do you think the data are important? What is their significance? For what purposes can you use these data? What information can you extract from this table? What kinds of arguments can you build with the data? What kind of mathematical questions would you pose? Summarize your five major points.

   Objective: After presenting our students with the data, we want them to come up with reasons why they believe the data are important. By asking them to think of ways of using these data, we want students to begin to conjecture about the data and discover ways in which they can use the data in the mathematics classroom. By confronting differing views, they will have to consider the best ways to use the data. Students may offer many perspectives on the significance of the data. We hope that they will start critically analyzing the society in which they live and other people's beliefs.

2. (*a*) On the same (*x*, *y*) rectangular system, represent the graphs of the discrete functions "rate of death" for whites and for African Americans. Represent the time variable on the *x*-axis. Explain how you determined an appropriate scale for your axes. Explain the social significance of the two graphs. List some reasons that may explain the results on the graph.

   (*b*) On the same (*x*, *y*) rectangular system, represent the graphs of the discrete functions "number of deaths" for whites and for African Americans. Represent the time variable on the *x*-axis. Explain how you determined an appropriate scale for your axes. Explain the social significance of this graph. List some reasons that may explain the results on the graph.

   (*c*) Compare the graphs from (*a*) and (*b*). What do the graphs reveal that the table does not? What are some advantages of representing the data on a graph versus the table? The table versus the graph? Were you surprised by the results of the graphs? Explain why or why not. Explain mathematically why or how the graphs in (*a*) and (*b*) are different.

   Objective: With these questions, we want to test the students' understanding about the concept of function, the difference between discrete and continuous functions, graphing skills, and the use of an appropriate scale. By representing the data for different groups of people on the same coordinate system, they will start comparing the data for the specified groups. They will realize, for example, that African Americans have greater rates of death than whites. They will probably conjecture why this is true.

3. (*a*) Using the graphing calculator (or computer program), find the best-fitting continuous model for the number of deaths in time (years) separately for whites and African Americans. What types of functions are they? Explain why and how you chose each particular model.

   (*b*) Using the graphing calculator (or computer program), find the best fitting continuous model for the rate of death in time (years) separately for whites and African Americans. What types of functions are they? Explain why and how you chose each particular model.

Objective: By asking the students to find the best-fitting continuous model for the data, we test the students' knowledge about shapes of graphs for linear, exponential, cubic, and logarithmic functions. Given the number of similar questions, they can share the task, and thus each student in the group will have a chance to use the computer or the graphing calculator. They will also learn how to collaborate and learn from other people's suggestions.

4. (*a*) Using the graph only, predict the number of deaths and death rates for both whites and African Americans for the years 1995–2000. Plot these values on your graph. Explain why you chose these predictions. What events may affect these results?

(*b*) Test your best-fitting algebraic model against your prediction. Explain how you would do this algebraically. Does your algebraic model match your predictions? If not, construct a new algebraic model that would better fit your predictions. What is this new model?

Objective: Because students will work with data beyond those that are given, students will need to explain their expectations for the future. We want our students to realize that there is a difference between choosing a particular graph to fit a data set (given for a finite number of years) and the validity of that model to predict future events, particularly in the context of changing social phenomena.

5. Using the table, find out the approximate number of whites and African Americans in the United States in 1994. Show all your work.

Objective: In order to find out the total number of African Americans and whites in the United States in 1994, the students need to use all the information in the table. The question requires the understanding of proportion and percentage concepts. We test the correct interpretation of the table and solving linear equations.

6. When is it expected that the rate of death for whites will reach 15 deaths per 100 000 whites? Explain how you can use the graph to find this solution. Explain how to use the algebraic model to find this solution.

Objective: This question tests the basic skills of solving linear or logarithmic equations.

7. Is it possible that the number of deaths for whites will ever equal the number of deaths for African Americans? Explain your reasoning. How could you use the algebraic models to obtain this answer? What are the implications of this result? What might affect these trends in the future?

Objective: We want the students to discuss the possibility of having an equal number of deaths for African Americans and whites and the social implications of this fact. According to the model that they choose, students may have different answers for this question. Because of the possible complexity of the equations (for example, they may obtain a combination of logarithmic and cubic equations), they will attempt to use technology or they may realize that they need an approximation. At the very least, we expect them to set up the algebraic equation that models the situation.

8. Using the best-fitting cubic equation for the rate of death for African Americans, find the slope of the tangent to the graph in 1990. Show all your work. If the slope of the tangent for the following years had remained unchanged, what rate of death would have been expected for 1994? Compare your result with the actual rate of death for African Americans in 1994.

Objective: This question will test the understanding of the slope of a tangent line. They will need to know the geometrical interpretation of the first derivative and the equation of the tangent to a graph. They will also realize what the social interpretation of the slope of tangent is for these particular data.

9. Using the cubic equation that best approximates the rate of death for African Americans, find the inflection point on the graph. Interpret the findings mathematically. What is the social interpretation of the inflection point on the graph?

Objective: This task requires a mastery of second derivative concepts. Students will have the opportunity to see the connection between the slope of the tangent and the inflection point on the graph. They are also asked to explain the social and historical interpretations of the existence of the inflection point on the graph.

10. Using Riemann sums, find an approximation for the number of deaths separately for whites and African Americans during 1987–1994? Give a geometrical representation for the Riemann sum. Which type of Riemann sum is best to use in this context? Use the graphing calculator to check your approximation.

Objective: These data provide a nice application of the Riemann sums. Most of the examples found in textbooks use Riemann sums only in a very abstract context. This example allows students to see both a geometrical and social interpretation of the Riemann sum. They also need to compare the advantages and disadvantages of using different types of Riemann sums.

11. Using a definite integral and the cubic model, calculate the number of deaths separately for whites and for African Americans during the same time interval. Compare your results on questions 10 and 11 for the different groups. Which one is a better approximation?

Objective: This question requires students to know the integration rules. It also provides students with an understanding of the definite integral. Students will also understand what it means to make a "better approximation."

Socially Critical Content

Of course, a curriculum that is driven solely by social inquiries will breed its own set of issues and problems. Socially relevant issues may be investigated, but the concepts that evolve from these inquiries may be mathematically vacuous; it is unclear if the skills necessary to pass through the mathematics pipeline at this level will arise naturally in classes where student experiences, interests, and culture form the basis for mathematics learning. Thus, the potential for misuse of a curriculum based on social issues may have the unintended consequence of less-demanding content that may deny students access to the normative skills needed to pass through the critical mathematics filter. Likewise, even if real-life data and contexts are used, their meaning can be obscured if they are only used to practice a skill. Frankenstein (1997, p. 13) contends,

> When no better understanding of the data is gleaned through solving the mathematics problem created from the data, using real-life data masks how other mathematical operations could be performed that would illuminate that same data. It gives a "hidden curriculum" message that using mathematics is not useful in understanding the world; rather, mathematics is just pushing around numbers, writing them in different ways depending on what the teacher wants. In addition, real-life data used out of context can wind up reinforcing stereotypes and myths about institutional structures.

The mathematical concepts embedded in the AIDS example are clearly important ones. Using these data to teach mathematical content, however, is no more advantageous than any other context, or no context for that matter, if it does not illuminate social realities and result in a call to action that is feasible for students to undertake. Thus, as the mathematical content is extracted, highlighting the relationship to students' lives should be paramount. As such, questions related to the facts revealed through the traditional mathematics instruction should permeate instruction. For example:

- What underlies these trends?
- How did these racial inequalities come about?
- Would infection rates parallel death rates?
- Are infection rates for various groups, age ranges, genders the same?
- What is the average survival time for different groups from diagnosis with AIDS?
- What is the relationship of socioeconomic status to survival time?
- Who has access to experimental treatment programs?
- What do world statistics for AIDS infection and death rates look like?
- What can students do in their community to affect these statistics?

The last question should precipitate action by students. Students may investigate the risk behaviors for AIDS infection and for other sexually transmitted diseases (STDs) and can form "AIDS Brigades" or "AIDS Troupes" to educate their peers on condom use, safer sex, needle exchange programs, and other preventive actions. AIDS is often a taboo topic among teenagers, and a peer education program would normalize discussion on this issue as well as on other STDs. Students may create posters, pamphlets, and T-shirts with information regarding the behaviors associated with AIDS infection and precautions that can be taken to minimize the possibility of infection. World AIDS Day is 1 December, so this time would be an ideal "excuse" to kick off an AIDS education campaign, perhaps with an assembly on the ways people contract AIDS, the prognosis once people are infected, preventive behaviors, and information about clean-needle programs and condom acquisition.

Furthermore, students may investigate the effect AIDS has had on their community by interviewing employees at local clinics and AIDS service centers. If they are so compelled, students may volunteer at hospices or AIDS programs in their community for shut-ins or children. They may also hold fundraisers to benefit these groups.

From their AIDS investigations, innumerable splinter explorations may also arise including access to health care, nutrition, and other health issues that may be affecting their communities, such as TB, drug and alcohol abuse, and teenage pregnancy. Using these data to teach traditional mathematics allows students, regardless of their specific interests in relation to this topic or the particular actions they take, to see that mathematics is inextricably linked to their lives, and it can lead them to be agents of change in their schools, communities, and society at large.

CONCLUSION

The HIV/AIDS example is proof that the mathematics classroom can accommodate both rigorous mathematical and socially relevant content. Not all social issues, however, are ripe for "mathematization," nor can all important mathematics be introduced through social issues. Likewise, teachers may not feel comfortable presenting and discussing particular issues with their students, nor may they have the general liberal arts background necessary to do so. Thus, the examples chosen for inclusion in the mathematics classroom will be dependent on many complex considerations. What is certain, however, is that inviting culture into the mathematics classroom clearly demands that teachers have mathematical proficiency and familiarity with a wide range of social and historical topics so that they can intertwine mathematics and culture in mathematically and socially meaningful ways.

Therefore, teachers must have training in up-to-date instructional methods based on how children learn and possess the deep subject-matter knowledge necessary to convert student interests into meaningful mathematics explorations. Teacher preparation is a principal component in the effectiveness of all teachers, but it is even more pronounced in a subject such as mathematics, which is learned primarily in school and not informally outside of school. Students in low-income, high-minority schools, however, typically have less access to qualified teachers than students in other schools (Darling-Hammond 1995). The effective implementation of culturally relevant teaching is highly dependent, then, on corresponding changes in teacher education and recruitment.

As noted earlier, curriculum is increasingly controlled by those with a conservative agenda (see Apple [1992] for a discussion of this issue) whose goal is essentially economic rebirth and who have little interest in righting the inequities confronting people of color, particularly in a domain historically viewed as acultural; thus, educators are caught in a catch-22 as Nieto (1997, p. 217) suggests:

> Schools are organizations fundamentally concerned with maintaining the status quo and not exposing contradictions that make people uncomfortable in a society that has democratic ideals but where democratic realities are not always apparent. Such contradictions include the many manifestations of inequality. Yet schools are also supposed to wipe out these inequalities. To admit that inequality exists and that it is even perpetuated by the very institutions charged with doing away with it is [a radical position].

This position is not likely to be widely endorsed by those who control curriculum construction. However, the failure of the current school system to meet the needs of a growing number of students demands that we consider alternatives. Students, particularly those who have been traditionally underserved by the school system, must recognize the relevance of mathematics in their lives and the relevance of their experiences to mathematics. Mathematics should become a tool to show students that ordinary people can change the events around them.

Achieving more equitable mathematics education is not an easy task, but if we truly believe it is a necessity, then we will invest the time and effort to present all students with a demanding curriculum, build bridges from their experiences and knowledge so that they become fluid both in their own and the accepted mathematics culture of power, and enable them to critique the status quo and constructively act on their mathematical discoveries. There are no quick fixes, but small steps may ultimately lead to a large victory.

REFERENCES

Apple, Michael W. "Do the *Standards* Go Far Enough? Power, Policy, and Practice in Mathematics Education." *Journal for Research in Mathematics Education* 23 (November 1992): 412–31.

Banks, James A. "Multicultural Education: For Freedom's Sake." In *Transforming Curriculum for a Culturally Diverse Society*, edited by Etta R. Hollins, pp. 75–82. Mahwah, N.J.: Lawrence Erlbaum Associates, 1996.

Burrill, Gail, John C. Burrill, Pamela Coffield, Gretchen Davis, Jan de Lange, Diann Resnick, and Murray Siegel. *Data Analysis and Statistics across the Curriculum. Curriculum and Evaluation Standards for School Mathematics* Addenda Series, Grades 9–12. Reston, Va.: National Council of Teachers of Mathematics, 1992.

Darling-Hammond, Linda. "Inequality and Access to Knowledge." In *Handbook of Research on Multicultural Education*, edited by James A. Banks and Cherry A. Banks, pp. 465–83. New York: Macmillan, 1995.

Davidson, Ellen, and Leslie Kramer. "Integrating with Integrity: Curriculum, Instruction, and Culture in the Mathematics Classroom." In *Multicultural and Gender Equity in the Mathematics Classroom: The Gift of Diversity*, 1997 Yearbook of the National Council of Teachers of Mathematics, edited by Janet Trentacosta, pp. 131–41. Reston, Va.: National Council of Teachers of Mathematics, 1997.

Frankenstein, Marilyn. "In Addition to the Mathematics: Including Equity Issues in the Curriculum." In *Multicultural and Gender Equity in the Mathematics Classroom: The Gift of Diversity*, 1997 Yearbook of the National Council of Teachers of Mathematics, edited by Janet Trentacosta, pp. 10–22. Reston, Va.: National Council of Teachers of Mathematics, 1997.

Heckman, Paul, and Julian Weissglass. "Contextualized Mathematics Instruction: Moving beyond Recent Proposals." *For the Learning of Mathematics* 14 (February 1994): 29–32.

Ladson-Billings, Gloria. "'But That's Just Good Teaching!' The Case for Culturally Relevant Pedagogy." *Theory into Practice*, 34 (Summer 1995a): 159–65.

––––––. *The Dreamkeepers: Successful Teachers of African American Children*. San Francisco: Jossey-Bass Publishers, 1994.

––––––. "Making Mathematics Meaningful in Multicultural Contexts." In *New Directions for Equity in Mathematics*, edited by Walter. Secada, Elizabeth Fennema, and Lisa Adajian, pp. 126–45. New York: Cambridge University Press, 1995b.

Ladson-Billings, Gloria, and Annette Henry. "Blurring the Borders: Voices of African Liberatory Pedagogy in the United States and Canada." *Journal of Education* 172, no. 2 (1990): 72–88.

Lipman, Pauline. "'Bringing Out the Best in Them': The Contribution of Culturally Relevant Teachers to Educational Reform." *Theory into Practice* 34 (Summer 1995): 202–8.

National Council of Teachers of Mathematics. *Curriculum and Evaluation Standards for School Mathematics*. Reston, Va.: National Council of Teachers of Mathematics, 1989.

––––––. *Professional Standards for Teaching Mathematics*. Reston, Va.: National Council of Teachers of Mathematics, 1991.

National Science Foundation. *Women, Minorities, and Persons with Disabilities in Science and Engineering*. Arlington, Va.: National Science Foundation, 1998.

Nieto, Sonia M. "School Reform and Student Achievement: A Multicultural Perspective." In *Multicultural Education: Issues and Perspectives*, 3rd ed., edited by James A. Banks and Cherry A. McGee Banks, pp. 387–407. Boston: Allyn & Bacon, 1997.

Oakes, Jeannie. "Opportunities, Achievement, and Choice: Women and Minority Students in Science and Mathematics." In *Review of Research in Education*, vol. 16, edited by Courtney Cazden, pp. 153–222. Washington, D.C.: American Educational Research Association, 1990.

Romberg, Thomas. "Problematic Features of the School Mathematics Curriculum." In *Handbook of Research on Curriculum: A Project of the American Educational Research Association*, edited by Philip W. Jackson, pp. 749–88. New York: Macmillan Publishing, Co., 1992.

Secada, Walter. "The Challenges of a Changing World for Mathematics Education." In *Teaching and Learning Mathematics in the 1990s*, 1990 Yearbook of the National Council of Teachers of Mathematics, edited by Thomas J. Cooney, pp. 135–43. Reston, Va.: National Council of Teachers of Mathematics, 1990.

––––––. "Race, Ethnicity, Social Class, Language, and Achievement in Mathematics." In *Handbook of Research on Mathematics Teaching and Learning*, edited by Douglas A. Grouws, pp. 623–59. New York: Macmillan Publishing Co., 1992. (Also available from the National Council of Teachers of Mathematics)

Sheets, Rosa Hernandez. "From Remedial to Gifted: Effects of Culturally Centered Pedagogy." *Theory into Practice* 34 (Summer 1995): 186–93.

Silva, Cecilia, and Stephen Kucer. "Expanding Curricular Conversations through Unification, Diversity and Access." *Language Arts* 74 (January 1997): 27–36.

Stanic, George, and Jeremy Kilpatrick. "Mathematics Curriculum Reform in the United States: A Historical Perspective." *International Journal of Education Research* 17, no. 5 (1992): 407–17.

Steen, Lynn Arthur. "Mathematics for All Americans." In *Teaching and Learning Mathematics in the 1990s*, 1990 Yearbook of the National Council of Teachers of Mathematics, edited by Thomas J. Cooney, pp. 130–34. Reston, Va.: National Council of Teachers of Mathematics, 1990.

Tate, William F. "Race, Retrenchment, and the Reform of School Mathematics." *Phi Delta Kappan* 75 (February 1994): 477–84.

———. "Returning to the Root: A Culturally Relevant Approach to Mathematics Pedagogy." *Theory into Practice* 34 (Summer 1995): 166–73.

Walker, Erica N., and Leah P. McCoy. "Students' Voices: African Americans and Mathematics." In *Multicultural and Gender Equity in the Mathematics Classroom: The Gift of Diversity*, 1997 Yearbook of the National Council of Teachers of Mathematics, edited by Janet Trentacosta, pp. 71–80. Reston, Va.: National Council of Teachers of Mathematics, 1997.

Walker, Paulette C., and Michaele F. Chappell. "Reshaping Perspectives on Teaching Mathematics in Diverse Urban Schools." In *Multicultural and Gender Equity in the Mathematics Classroom: The Gift of Diversity*, 1997 Yearbook of the National Council of Teachers of Mathematics, edited by Janet Trentacosta, pp. 201–8. Reston, Va.: National Council of Teachers of Mathematics, 1997.

Wilkinson, Phyllis, and Elissa Kido. "Literature and Cultural Awareness: Voices from the Journey." *Language Arts* 74 (April 1997): 452–66.

STEP: An Enrichment Model for African American High School Students

12

> When someone with the authority of a teacher, say, describes the world and you are not in it, there is a moment of psychic disequilibrium, as if you looked into a mirror and saw nothing.
>
> —Adrienne Rich
> *Blood, Bread, and Poetry: Selected Prose 1979–1986*

Elaine B. Hofstetter

Elaine Kolitch

Karen N. Bell

The feeling of disconnection with the ideas of mathematics and with the adults who engage in doing mathematics professionally is very real for many African American students. A sense of invisibility associated with this disconnection can exist and become a barrier to the participation of these students in mathematics and its related disciplines. As a result, students may not see themselves reflected in those who have become financially and intellectually powerful through their scientific and mathematical knowledge. Moreover, they are often not familiar with the route necessary to achieve this power. Addressing this issue, the National Council of Teachers of Mathematics in its *Curriculum and Evaluation Standards for School Mathematics* (National Council of Teachers of Mathematics [NCTM] 1989, p. 4) has stated:

> Creating a just society in which women and various ethnic groups enjoy equal opportunities and equitable treatment is no longer an issue. Mathematics has become a critical filter for employment and full participation in our society.... Equity has become an economic issue.

Since mathematical equity has economic ramifications, it becomes vital for all people to learn mathematics. In order to participate actively in society and to have a full range of career choices, individuals are best served by understanding and applying mathematical ideas to their everyday world. A disproportionate number of students within certain minority groups and among females have failed to see these connections and, therefore, continue to be a minimal presence in high school mathematics classes in the United States. These students are losing the opportunity to reach their potential and benefit from advancement to the more financially rewarding and secure positions in our technological workforce (Secada 1995; SUMMA 1995).

To address these issues, the New York state legislature passed an amendment in 1985 authorizing the use of funds to create a Science and Technology Entry Program (STEP) that assists historically underrepresented or economically disadvantaged secondary school students. New York State defines *historically underrepresented students* as those belonging to one of the following groups: African American, Hispanic/Latino, Native American Indian/Alaskan Native, or economically disadvantaged within any ethnic group (Bureau of Professional Career Opportunity Programs 1995, p. 1). The purpose of this project is to prepare these students for entry into postsecondary degree programs in scientific, technical, and health-related fields and licensed professions such as

Since mathematical equity has economic ramifications, it becomes vital for all people to learn mathematics.

architecture, nutrition, certified public accounting, dentistry, medicine, optometry, engineering, nursing, social work, and veterinary medicine.

Since 1985, we have had an ongoing STEP project at the State University of New York (SUNY) at New Paltz. Our project annually accommodates 110 students residing in the Mid-Hudson Valley and represents six school districts. A district becomes eligible for this program if it has a minimum of 20 percent minority population and agrees to provide limited financial and student support services. Since the program's inception, the ethnic composition of selected students is approximately two-thirds African American, one-third Hispanic/Latino, with a few students meeting the eligibility requirements solely on the basis of economic factors.

Students qualify for this program if they are in grades 9–12 and are currently registered in mathematics and science college preparatory courses. Project personnel inform students about the program through meetings, letters, and announcements. We give special attention to promoting women's participation by contacting individual female students and offering encouragement and support. As a result of these recruiting efforts, the program has traditionally been 60 percent female.

We require prospective STEP enrollees to fill out an extensive application form describing their academic interests and pledging to participate in all aspects of the program. Teacher recommendations serve as another factor in the selection process, and once an individual is chosen, parents are requested to take part in the program's activities.

GOALS AND OBJECTIVES

STEP is designed as an enrichment program providing an academic environment that supports and inspires high school students to remain enrolled in science and mathematics classes. It is intended to prepare students to pursue a college major in mathematics or a science-related field. We create a social environment where learning is acceptable and excellence is encouraged. Students, who may be isolated in their home schools, have the chance to find peers with similar interests and backgrounds and, at the same time, have the opportunity to network with working professionals and college personnel. The establishment of an educational community for STEP participants is an ongoing objective of our program.

The seven major goals of the program, as stated in the grant, are as follows:

- To prepare underrepresented minority and economically disadvantaged secondary school students for entry into postsecondary degree programs in scientific, technical, health-related, and licensed professions
- To assist underrepresented minority and economically disadvantaged secondary school students to enroll in professional education programs in scientific, technical, health-related, and licensed professions
- To promote the development of problem-solving skills, creative thinking, and other approaches having wide applicability in science and mathematics
- To enhance and extend students' knowledge of selected concepts, principles, and ideas spanning various areas of mathematics and science
- To motivate students to undertake full programs of study in mathematics and science and to stay with these programs
- To stimulate and heighten students' interest in science, engineering, and related health and technical fields as attractive and feasible career areas

- To motivate students to commit themselves to a full program of study of mathematics and science in high school.

PROGRAM COMPONENTS

The STEP program has several integral components all working in conjunction to enhance minority and economically disadvantaged students' learning of mathematics, science, and technology and to keep students interested in careers in these disciplines. Each year STEP offers students an opportunity to see themselves functioning in a mathematical and scientific world. This is achieved using a coordinated effort of Saturday workshops, in-school tutoring, paid internships, field trips, college advisement, and career counseling. In some years a summer precollege program is incorporated.

Saturday Academy

The Saturday Academy, the nucleus of STEP, is a daylong program with a keynote address, morning and afternoon academic workshops, and a luncheon social hour. A typical Saturday begins with all participants gathered together for a one-hour guest presentation given by a pure mathematician, scientist, doctor, individual from business and industry, college professor, or a technological expert. For the most part, these speakers are members of minority groups and have been selected to serve as role models for the students. Most often, speakers describe their profession by outlining the types of tasks performed and the educational requirements necessary to work in that field. Students typically engage in hands-on related activities or experiments as part of the presentation. Some professionals have shared personal stories about their struggles and triumphs as members of their cultural group. All sessions end with a lively question-and-answer period.

One presentation, "The Power of Knowing Mathematics," included a slide show focused on the geometric drawings of M. C. Escher along with a probability experiment. A series of Escher drawings were displayed, and their unique geometric properties were pointed out in the context of transformation geometry, optical illusions, and architecture. As part of the hands-on probability experiment, students arbitrarily tied six pieces of string, which were bound together in the center by paper, in three pairs at the top and three pairs at the bottom. Students were asked to predict the configuration of the tied strings before removing the paper. Would the result be three circles, two circles, or one circle? The guest speaker led the group through a tabulation of the results and discussed the theoretical and experimental probabilities of this exercise. Through this activity, students engaged in the practice of collecting and analyzing data in ways similar to those performed by mathematics and science professionals. Taken together, these two activities showed students how mathematics is a powerful tool for understanding elements of our world.

After the morning speaker, students are divided into classes on the basis of grade level and school district. In these classes, they receive three-and-one-half hours of instruction designed to get them actively involved in topics often not explicitly taught in their high schools. A sample of workshop topics offered in previous years include "History and Future of Measurement," "Transformation Geometry through Programming in Logo," "Discrete Mathematics," "SAT Preparation," "Using Computers to Collect and Analyze Scientific Data," "The Effects of Drugs and Alcohol on the Body," "The Use of DOS/Windows and Databases," "Using a Graphing Calculator," "Introduction to Graph Theory," "Geometric Paper Folding," "Graphing in Three Space," and "History of Number Systems."

In one workshop, the instructor gave directions in the basics of using a graphing calculator. After a review of the location of keys and the types of functions available, students were guided through several investigations of equation graphing. Beginning with the system of first-degree equations, $y = x$ and $y = -2x + 3$, students were asked to find the point of intersection using the calculator and its zoom function. Then students were given the pair of equations, $y = 0.1x^3 + 0.14x$ and $y = 3 \cos x$ and asked to find the point(s) of intersection. At first glance this pair appears to have two points of intersection; however, on closer inspection using the zoom function, it can be determined that there exists only one point of intersection. Students were asked, "Why does the original display appear to have two points of intersection when in fact there is only one?" Typical responses were, "The screen is too small" and "The dots on the calculator are bigger than a point of intersection." Students had to reason that there are limitations in using the calculator for geometric solutions of equations because of the dimensions of the pixel display in representing a theoretical point.

Continuing the investigation, students were asked to graph three equations, $y = x^2$, $y = 5x^2$, and $y = 0.25x^2$ plus three other similar parabolic equations of their choice. Students shared their observations about their equations noting that "changing the coefficient made the graph wider or narrower." Then students graphed the following equations: $y = -x^2 + 2x$, $y = x^2 - 5x$, and $y = x^2 + 3$ plus three additional equations. Students reviewed their selections and were asked, "What are your observations about the roles of each coefficient and the constant?" Common responses were, "They move the equation left and right or up and down." A similar process was employed with cubic equations. Finally students were asked to create a pair of equations that appeared to have more points of intersection than actually existed before the zoom function was used. Two such pairs created were $y = 0.3x^3$, $y = 3x + 4$ and $y = 3 \sin x$, $y = 1.33x + 7.1$.

By selecting their own equations and using the graphing calculator, students quickly perceived the relationship between equation modifications and the appearance and location of the associated graph in the coordinate plane. These activities foster the making of connections between algebraic and geometric representations, a desired outcome of both the New York State curriculum and the NCTM *Standards*. Students communicated mathematically when they discussed the results of their experimentations. Their understanding of making generalizations on the basis of empirical data suggests that they increased their mathematical reasoning and problem-solving abilities as well.

In the workshop "History of Number Systems," designed for ninth graders, participants were shown several ancient number systems so they could more fully appreciate the diversity with which numbers can be expressed. The numeration systems presented were the Egyptian hieroglyphics grouping system; the semigrouping, semipositional system of Babylonian cuneiform; and the positional number system of the Mayans. Working individually and in pairs, students practiced translating within these systems so they could observe connections among them. They performed addition and subtraction problems as a means of applying mathematical reasoning and problem solving in a unique context. To add a creative aspect to the workshop, students worked together in teams of four to design their own number systems. The results were either a grouping or positional base-ten system in which unusual and diverse symbols were created. What became evident is that students were not comfortable deviating appreciably from what they already knew. Through this exercise, students developed an understanding of the arbitrary nature of the symbols and an appreciation of the elegance of a base-ten system.

Workshops like these are characteristic of the Saturday Academy, where participants explore topics in depth through guided discovery. All workshops are conceived with three complementary frameworks in mind. First, workshops mirror and supplement the New York State mathematics curriculum where the traditional algebra, geometry, and trigonometry course sequence has been replaced by a three-tiered, spiralling mathematics curriculum. Integrated within this curriculum are topics from the areas of logic, number theory, probability, and statistics as well as the more common content strands; all these topics are revisited and investigated in increasing depth each year. Second, the workshops provide a unified context for the four major NCTM Curriculum Standards: mathematics as problem solving, mathematics as communication, mathematics as reasoning, and mathematical connections. Third, curriculum design is approached from a constructivist philosophy of learning with hands-on and exploratory activities. The activities allow for extended investigation of one topic and aim to engage students actively in the process of mathematical inquiry. Students are also instructed in how to build on their prior knowledge and experience as they reason through problem solutions and develop their critical-thinking skills.

The Saturday Academy, the heart of our program, creates a student-centered, holistic learning environment. It aims to contextualize isolated skills and to nurture the academic, personal, and social development of the students.

School District Support

In addition to the Saturday program, students receive support through their local high schools. School-based advisors, selected by the project director and participating school district administrators, act as liaisons between the grant administrators and the student participants. These advisors provide individual and group counseling and arrange for certified teachers to tutor STEP participants at their home school sites.

Large-group counseling sessions occur monthly at each school. The advisors review students' academic progress, update participants about upcoming STEP events, and provide ongoing career information. STEP advisors furnish seniors with additional guidance in completing college application forms and writing personal essays. Sometimes these advisors even accompany students to visit college campuses. Individual college and career counseling is available when requested.

Through the home schools, STEP offers small-group or private tutoring in all academic areas with special emphasis on mathematics and science. The intent of these tutoring sessions is to assist students in maintaining their commitment to, and success in, a challenging high school program.

Parental Involvement

Each year, a small group of parent volunteers serves on an advisory council and assists in promoting STEP in their local communities and with the state legislature. Throughout the years, the parent council has organized a letter-writing campaign to state leaders to voice its support of the program and to lobby for its continued existence. This has been an integral part of the successful refunding of our grant.

All parents (or other caregivers) are invited to attend the Saturday Academy so they can experience firsthand the mathematics and science enrichment activities in which their children are engaged. This encourages parents to have a stake in the program and to become more directly involved in their children's education. Furthermore, it provides them with an opportunity for offering feedback and suggestions for program improvement.

Participant Internships with Business and Industry

The capstone experience of our program is our student internship component. STEP arranges paid internships for senior students to work approximately 100 hours for local community establishments. This work experience presents students with an opportunity to connect with a mentor in their chosen field of interest. Internship placements have included work in hospital laboratories, doctors' offices, school graphic design shops, and college special services programs.

One successful internship paired a female student who wished to become a doctor with a local pediatrician in her community. She spent four hours a week after school assisting the doctor and learning about the practice of medicine directly. Another internship matched a male student who expressed an interest in the field of engineering with engineers in the laboratory of a major corporation.

The four program components (see fig. 12.1)—namely, the Saturday Academy, school district support, parental involvement, and participant internships—combine to give students diverse learning experiences that connect their academic work in school to the professional environment of the workplace. Further, the STEP program enables students to find others with similar interests and creates a support network that encourages academic excellence within a socially acceptable context. At the same time, STEP offers challenging, nontraditional academic experiences that support the integrated approach of the New York State curriculum, the four major NCTM Standards, as well as a constructivist framework.

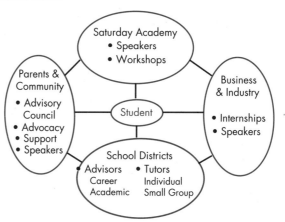

Fig. 12.1. SUNY New Paltz STEP Program components

PROGRAM EVALUATION

The two main purposes of this project are to encourage students to take a full program of mathematics and science classes in high school and to maintain and support students' initial motivation to pursue math-related careers. We evaluate these goals using qualitative and quantitative methods, with particular emphasis placed on the views of students and instructors about the efficacy of the program. More specifically, we assess the program's effectiveness through (1) student and parent surveys, (2) student and instructor interviews, (3) information about the level of student participation in regents, honors, or accelerated high school mathematics and science courses, and (4) college admissions data. As required by the state, we report grade-point averages and SAT scores for each student. These data, however, do not reflect the main activities of the program because we neither focus on preparing students for college entrance exams nor tutor students consistently in the content of their current courses. We are more committed to students' continuing registration in challenging mathematics and science courses and in stimulating and supporting the hopes of these students to enter mathematics and science careers.

STEP Educational Profiles

The program has been relatively successful in encouraging students to take a rigorous program of high school mathematics and science courses. During the period from 1991 through 1996, 496 of 544 (91 percent) students registered in regents, honors, or accelerated courses in science, and 509 of 544 (94 percent) attempted similar courses in mathematics. Overall, more than 90 percent of these students received passing grades in these courses, with approximately half receiving grades of B or better. The SAT-Math scores for seniors, aggregated over the past five years, show that about 50 percent of the students scored between 500 and 599, 25 percent above 600, and 25 percent below 500.

Collected information from STEP high school seniors about their plans after graduation shows that within the past five years, 57 seniors of 68 (84 percent) had been accepted to colleges and universities at the time they were surveyed. Some of the colleges represented were SUNY New Paltz, SUNY Albany, New York University, Penn State, Colby College, the University of Connecticut, Brown University, St. John's University, Georgia Tech, and local community colleges. The vast majority of students, when asked about their anticipated college major, expressed their intention to major in science, mathematics, premedicine, engineering, or technology; a few students reported interest in business, law, and computer science.

Saturday Academy Assessments

As part of our ongoing assessment of the Saturday Academy, we ask students and parents for written responses that rate the speaker's presentation and comment on the morning and afternoon workshop activities. These evaluations are particularly useful to instructors who use them to develop and modify future Saturday classes. Overall, these written responses have been positive, with most ratings in the good to excellent range. Open-ended comments typically focus on the enjoyment of learning about a particular topic or the value of the presentation to the consideration of a future career. A few recent comments include the following:

> I really enjoyed the presentation on telecommunication. [The speaker's] communication skills were very understandable and he made the topic interesting.

> It was a good experience learning about science observations and math equations.

> [The instructor] made me think about goals and opportunities.... He gave an important message that we all could understand and relate to—excellent, interesting, and enjoyable.

Parents who join us for the Saturday activities add insightful comments about all aspects of the program. Their observations often focus on the ways that students and instructors interact and the degree to which students are engaged in the activities. Following are examples of this idea:

> The topic for discussion in class was very good. The lecture and discussions between the instructor and the students were cordial.

> The subject seemed quite difficult, but was explained in such a way that the students had a good understanding of it at the end of the period.

> Rapport between teacher and students was great. Activities were fun and educational.

> Hands-on session, which is a great (the best) learning mode. The instructor was very knowledgeable of materials and background and handled the group with great control. [She] was very enthusiastic about the topic, which was very informative and inspiring. Students appeared to be highly motivated.

Interviews

Interviews conducted with students and instructors, especially those who have been in the program for many years, are highly valuable to us as we appraise the current structure of the program and plan for the future. As students and instructors related their experiences in STEP, some common themes emerged that captured the meaning of the program to all participants. First, the STEP program offers students the opportunity to explore new and interesting ideas in a setting that is not bound by the standardized syllabus and time allotments of the high school classroom. This allows students to see the connections among mathematical concepts and their applications to other disciplines. One instructor explained:

> What is critical is to generate interest, to maintain a high level of energy and intellectual curiosity.... We show students the value of the knowledge to us, the connections between school knowledge and how it is used.

A student remarked similarly:

> We actually learn a lot during the presentations. These instructors are very enthusiastic about what they teach.... We can see the patterns and the connections between the math formulas and how they relate to the world.

As these two individuals point out, the program not only focuses on the learning of mathematics, science, and technology but also provides opportunities for students to see how these disciplines are connected to their world.

A second recurring theme is the consistent, long-term support and encouragement offered by the staff, who project a sense of caring and respect toward the students. Comments representing this idea include the following:

> These teachers respect us. They treat you like you were mature people. If this were in a high school, you would feel you were in the same place, here, we feel more mature, more responsible. They don't belittle you or follow you around.... They never forget a face; they still remember things about my personal life from three years ago.

> These people are really dedicated. They look out for us. I figure if they are doing all this for me, I have to do something for myself.

> My counselor does everything for me. She's really my "life" counselor, helping me with the SAT, the college essay, the applications, [and] getting me free tutoring at my school.

The program's director and staff are concerned with the whole person and genuinely care about students' success in all domains. This leads to the formation of a community of responsible and mature students who possess positive attitudes toward the program and who take ownership of their decision making in both their academic and personal lives.

Some participants view the STEP program as an experience that will open doors to the future and as an avenue for academic and social advancement. Three students expressed this view:

My dad sees this program as an opportunity to advance, a way of taking an easier path. It's the whole oppression thing. He doesn't want us to go through what he went through. He wants us to push ourselves ahead. Look, you need to survive, and you need to help yourself first, before you can help others.

I want to learn more. My friends ask me, "How can you give up your Saturday to come here?" But I don't think of it as giving up my Saturday because I'm advancing myself.

They show us you can't get anywhere without college. It's a fact, we're the minority, they're the majority and they will have more power over us. But we don't have to sit and complain, we can get an education. That's the key.

The STEP students believe that education can be a means for self-advancement. They prefer to see themselves less as victims of oppression and more as responsible agents for the direction of their lives. They express hope for a successful future with an ability to recognize and seize opportunities. An IBM program manager, who has been teaching with the program since its inception, summarized his observations:

The program fortifies students' interests in math and science. It enriches their academic background. It opens a vista to the world of technology, engineering, and other careers. It allows students to see themselves as active participants in college and in careers. It provides a network of students and instructors that they can depend upon for recommendations, information, and shared experiences.

CONCLUSION

The ongoing assessment of the New Paltz STEP program allows for continuous change and improvement. Students have expressed an interest in forming links with others in similar programs across the country. The creation of a STEP home page on the Web is the beginning of efforts to introduce students to the Internet, where they can gain access to information associated with mathematics and science as well as communicate with students from other countries. Students have voiced a desire to move the program out of the classroom into the field; they want to visit laboratories, businesses, hospitals, and universities to observe professionals firsthand. The promotion of a greater partnership between schools and industry is also being pursued.

Although this program cannot alter the existing social, economic, and political inequities in society or even transform major differences in educational programs among schools, it can play a part in broadening the vision of individual students as they consider their professional opportunities. Consistent with Noddings' belief that "the preparation of students for citizenship and making of wise decisions should be the primary concern of mathematics teaching" (Williams 1995, p. 186), we can offer an avenue for helping students make informed choices about the role that mathematics and science can play in their lives. Enrichment programs such as STEP, which target minority and economically disadvantaged youth, can provide one opportunity for students to enhance their local high school experiences. The program can expand students' educational horizons, provide inspiration to others, create ambassadors who will share experiences with schoolmates, and offer role models within the college and business communities.

One parent who attended the sessions spoke about the value of the program:

The STEP program is a valuable tool/avenue for giving multicultural students the opportunity to participate in a program that has invested in the future of our children. It does "take a whole village to raise a child" and these kids need added reinforcement to instill in them an "I can succeed" attitude.

Enrichment programs such as STEP, which target minority and economically disadvantaged youth, can provide one opportunity for students to enhance their local high school experiences.

The New Paltz STEP program offers students the opportunity and support necessary for success in school and in their future professional lives. We hope they will look in the mirror and see themselves reflected as active and critical participants in an increasingly technological society.

REFERENCES

Bureau of Professional Career Opportunity Programs. _Guidelines for Submission of Science and Technology Entry Program Proposals for the Period 1996–99._ Albany, N.Y.: The University of the State of New York, State Education Department, 1995.

National Council of Teachers of Mathematics. _Curriculum and Evaluation Standards for School Mathematics._ Reston, Va.: National Council of Teachers of Mathematics, 1989.

Secada, Walter G., Elizabeth Fennema, and Lisa Byrd Adajian, eds. _New Directions for Equity in Mathematics Education._ New York: Cambridge University Press, 1995.

SUMMA Directory of Mathematics-Based Intervention Projects. _Strengthening Underrepresented Minority Mathematics Achievement._ Washington, D.C.: Mathematical Association of America, 1995.

Williams, Steven R. "A Critical Look at Practice in Mathematics and Mathematics Education." Review of _Math Worlds: Philosophical and Social Studies of Mathematics and Mathematics Education,_ edited by Sal Restivo, Jean Paul Van Bendeguin, and Roland Fischer. _Journal for Research in Mathematics Education_ 26 (March 1995): 184–88.

Part 3

Focus on Specific Methodologies

Fostering Multicultural Connections in Mathematics through Media

13

Michaele F. Chappell
Denisse R. Thompson

Past calls for making mathematics more relevant to the lives and culture of students have been echoed in recent years (Coxford 1995; Ladson-Billings 1995; National Council of Teachers of Mathematics [NCTM] 1989; Smith and Silver 1995; Tate 1995). Because mathematics classrooms consist of students from varied cultural backgrounds, it is essential that multicultural content be integrated into the curriculum at all grade levels. Specifically, the curriculum needs to incorporate the contributions to mathematics by people of color, to depict how people of color use mathematics in real-world situations, and to describe how mathematics is used in literature produced by people of color. This ensures that students have opportunities to examine the mathematical contributions of many cultures and, in particular, examine the mathematical uses and contributions within their personal culture (Shirley 1995).

Instructional materials, such as books, videotapes, audiotapes, magazines, posters, and games, are types of media with which students frequently interact. Such media help teachers create or enhance lessons by increasing students' motivation and engagement in mathematical tasks and by illustrating rich connections of mathematics to students' lives and surroundings. As a consequence, students learn mathematics in a meaningful manner.

The focus of this article is on using a variety of media to foster a multicultural connection in the mathematics classroom—in particular, media that highlight African, African American, or African Caribbean personalities or themes. We identify three categories that describe the extent to which the message evident within the given medium is integral to these cultures. First, in some media, the cultural context is essential to the message; that is, if the context were removed, the message would be fundamentally different. For example, in the book *The Village of Round and Square Houses* (Grifalconi 1986), the setting is the African village of Tos. If this context were different, the story would change and lose much of its meaning and multicultural value. We call these media examples *culturally contextual*.

Second, in some media the message presented is not dependent on the culture, although people of color portray the main characters. That is, the characters portrayed could be of any race or ethnic persuasion without changing the message within the medium. An example is *How Many Stars in the Sky?* (Hort 1991) in which a young African American boy attempts to count the stars in the sky. If the individuals were changed from an African American family to a family of another ethnic background, the message in the story remains the same and loses none of its meaning. We call these media examples *culturally amenable*; the message is not subject to the use of any particular ethnic group. Nevertheless, we advocate the use of culturally amenable media because such examples often depict broad, nonstereotypical representations of African, African American, or African Caribbean participation in society. Further, they

> **Because mathematics classrooms consist of students from varied cultural backgrounds, it is essential that multicultural content be integrated into the curriculum at all grade levels.**

illustrate worthwhile and appropriate uses of mathematics by members of these cultures.

The third category consists of media examples that are neither culturally contextual nor culturally amenable; they fall in between. Although culture is not essential to the underlying message within the medium, the use of a particular culture uniquely affects the message and students' responses to it. For instance, in the videotape *A Raisin in the Sun* (Hansberry 1961), an African American family in the 1950s agonizes over how to spend a certain sum of money. In this example, it is not essential that an African American family be faced with the decisions of how to spend this money. However, the deliberations were clearly affected by the social context of an African American family struggling to make a living in Chicago in the 1950s; perhaps that context would have been different for a family from another race or ethnic background. We call these media examples *culturally influenced.*

MEDIA AND THE MULTICULTURAL CONNECTION

Literature Media

Numerous examples of links between literature and mathematics exist (Burns 1992; Whitin and Wilde 1992, 1995; Zaslavsky 1996). Linking literature to mathematics helps to communicate the subject along several dimensions and has numerous benefits. At times, students read about situations involving mathematical concepts and see mathematics promoted in a positive manner (Sullivan and Nielsen 1996). At other times, students listen and make interpretations about those situations as they apply them to a related lesson (Curcio, Zarnowski, and Vigliarolo 1995; Karp 1994; Smith 1995a, 1995b). Sometimes students act out or dramatize mathematical scenarios found in the literature (Curcio and Zarnowski 1996). Because such links communicate mathematics in different ways, they also enable teachers to explore varied connections between topics within, and external to, mathematics. Moreover, literature media motivate students by capturing their attention and encouraging them to engage in mathematical activity that is often beyond what they normally would encounter in their typical curriculum.

Nonbook Media

In the same manner that literature media help to draw connections to mathematics, value can be found in other kinds of media. Because discussions about these types of media are not as prevalent as about literature media, teachers sometimes overlook particular examples and the opportunities for using them to teach mathematics. Considering how much students watch videos, listen to music, read magazines, and collect posters, the use of these types of media should be explored to help teachers meet particular lesson objectives. The decision to use media should be influenced by the mathematics embedded in the media and the potential of those media to enhance the study of particular mathematical concepts.

A quick-reference resource list of media suggested for use in a mathematics classroom is given in figure 13.1. Although numerous media examples are cited, we do not claim the list to be exhaustive because new applicable resources are always being generated. As shown, the figure is a matrix that cross-references mathematical content by the nature of the message presented in a particular book, video, game, or poster. Many examples pertain to varied mathematics concepts, including number ideas and operations, geometry and measurement, statistics, and patterning.

Mathematics Content	Culturally Contextual	Culturally Influenced	Culturally Amenable
Counting	• *Moja Means One* (B)* • *Count Your Way through Africa* (B) • *Ashanti to Zulu* (B) • *Emeka's Gift* (B) • *Two Ways to Count to Ten* (B) • *Board Games round the World* (B,G) • *The Games of Africa* (B,G)	• *One Smiling Grandma* (B) • *Picking Peas for a Penny* (B) • *The Hundred Penny Box* (B)	• *Afro-bets 1 2 3 Book* (B) • *Ten, Nine, Eight* (B) • *Feast for 10* (B) • *Aaron and Gayla's Counting Book* (B) • *One of Three* (B) • *Joe Can Count* (B) • *Coconut Mon* (B)
Number Operations and Ideas	• *The Story of Negro League Baseball* (B) • *Roots* (B,V) • *Roots: The Next Generation* (B,V) • *Zamani Goes to Market* (B) • *The Black Snowman* (B) • *Senefer* (B) • *Shaka: King of the Zulus* (B) • *... If You Traveled on the Underground Railroad* (B) • *Ashanti to Zulu* (B) • *The Jesse Owens Story* (V) • *Shaka Zulu* (V)	• *A Raisin in the Sun* (V) • *Cookies* (B) • *Picking Peas for a Penny* (B) • *The Chalk Doll* (B) • *Wagon Train* (B)	• *How Many Stars in the Sky?* (B) • *The Toothpaste Millionaire* (B) • *The Boy and the Ghost* (B) • *A Million Fish ... More or Less* (B)
Geometry	• *Sweet Clara and the Freedom Quilt* (B) • *The Village of Round and Square Houses* (B) • *Anansi the Spider* (B) • *Chinye* (B) • *Mufaro's Beautiful Daughters* (B) • *Shaka: King of the Zulus* (B) • *Galimoto* (B) • *Stitching Stars* (B) • *Africa Multicultural Set* (P) • *Masks of Africa* (P) • *Math of Africa* (P) • *Shaka Zulu* (V) • *The Games of Africa* (B,G)	• *Eight Hands Round: A Patchwork Alphabet* (B)	• *The Patchwork Quilt* (B) • *Octopus Hug* (B)
Measurement	• *Sweet Clara and the Freedom Quilt* (B) • *The Village of Round and Square Houses* (B) • *Why the Sun and the Moon Live in the Sky* (B) • *Senefer* (B) • *The Black Snowman* (B) • *Dear Benjamin Banneker* (B) • *Stitching Stars* (B)	• *Cookies* (B) • *Wagon Wheels* (B) • *Poppa's New Pants* (B)	
Time	• *... If You Traveled on the Underground Railroad* (B) • *Traveling to Tondo* (B)		• *Jamal's Busy Day* (B)
Statistics	• *The Negro Leagues* (B) • *The Princess Who Lost Her Hair* (B) • *Jumping the Broom* (B) • *The Jesse Owens Story* (V)	• *Tanya's Reunion* (B)	• *I Love My Family* (B)
Patterning	• *Board Games round the World* (B,G) • *Multicultural Mathematics Material* (B,G) • *Multicultural Math Classroom* (B,G) • *Multicultural Math: Hands-on Math Activities from around the World* (B,G)	• *Eight Hands Round: A Patchwork Alphabet* (B)	• *Ty's One-Man Band* (B)

*B = Book; G = Game; P = Poster; V = Video

Fig. 13.1

At the end of this article, we have included an annotated resource list. This list contains a brief description of each resource in the figure and, in most instances, brief ideas of mathematics lessons that can be implemented in the classroom; selected teacher resource books and articles are also included in this list.

Exemplars

This section presents and describes sample tasks that teachers might use in mathematics classrooms to foster multicultural connections through media. The resources have been selected on the basis of their availability and public access and are presented from different types of media including books, video-tapes, and posters. The focus is centered on media that feature African, African American, or African Caribbean personalities and themes. The authors note, however, that similar media examples may be discussed for other ethnic groups.

Literature: Two Ways to Count to Ten

Two Ways to Count to Ten (Dee 1988) is a Liberian folk tale in which the Leopard King devises a contest to determine who is worthy to marry his daughter and become king in his place. The winner will be the animal who is able to throw a spear into the sky and count to ten before the spear hits the ground. Many animals try to accomplish this feat but fail; finally, the antelope wins by counting 2, 4, 6, 8, 10. The book concludes by saying that "it is not always the biggest or the strongest, but sometimes the cleverest that wins the prize."

Rich mathematics lessons can be taught using this book. Although ostensibly a counting book, upper elementary and lower middle school students can complete somewhat sophisticated lessons based on the mathematical principles embedded in this story. Prior to reading the book, students might engage in a contest to determine who can count to a given number the fastest. Times can be recorded with a stopwatch, and the results can be tallied and possibly graphed. After reading the story, students can engage in discussions to determine different ways to count to a number. For instance, to count to 20, a student could count by 1s, 2s, 4s, 5s, 10s, or 20s; to count to 48, one could count by 1s, 2s, 3s, 4s, 6s, 8s, 12s, 16s, 24s, or 48s. However, to count to 17, one can count only by 1s or 17s. The natural extension to factors of a number as the basis for counting becomes obvious. In comparing the ways to count, students observe that some numbers can be counted in many ways whereas other numbers can be counted in only two ways. This provides another method to introduce composite and prime numbers.

After reading the story to a combined third-, fourth-, and fifth-grade class, students selected a number and wrote as many different number sentences as possible in a given time period. Below are five of thirty-four number sentences written by one fourth-grade student.

$$17 + 1 = 18$$
$$5 \times 3 + 3 = 18$$
$$18 \div 1 = 18$$
$$5 \times 6 - 12 = 18$$
$$2 \times 9 = 18$$

Such experiences offer students an opportunity to use the correct order of operations while broadening their sense of number. The complexity of the number sentences is solely dependent on the previous mathematical experiences of the students.

Literature: How Many Stars in the Sky?

How Many Stars in the Sky? (Hort 1991) is a story of a young African American boy in the city who looks out his bedroom window and wonders how many stars there are in the sky. He starts to count those visible from his window and then moves outside to continue counting. But various objects seem to block his view and hide stars. Finally his father drives him deep into the country so that many more stars are visible; at that point, he realizes it is impossible to try to count them all.

In the early elementary grades, teachers might use this book to help students think about rational counting ideas and concepts related to large numbers. The title of the book itself suggests a fundamental way in which we use number in our society, that is, to count, indicating "how many" or "how much" of some object. The count is the cardinal number of that object. Hence, this story is a way to introduce students to ideas of counting large numbers; then they could count objects around their school or home where the total would be quite large, such as a million soda can pop-tops or pieces of popcorn.

Extensions of counting ideas are possible in the upper elementary grades. The fact that the stars change their position in the sky over the course of the evening could lead to a discussion of how to count objects that are constantly moving. Such issues face biologists and wildlife managers, who often need to estimate the size of a fish population or a herd of buffalo or the number of bears living in a given region. Hence, students engage in lessons that discuss issues of tagging a sample and using the results of that tagged sample to estimate the total population. This naturally leads to concepts of ratio and proportion as well as discussions of whether or not the use of just one sample is as accurate as averaging the results of several samples. Perhaps a wildlife officer could visit the class to provide firsthand experience about the benefits and difficulties of such approaches.

At the end of the book, the young boy realizes that it really is impossible to count all the stars that exist. Consequently, this book illustrates an interesting way to introduce the notion of *infinity* and its meaning as it relates to our natural environment.

Video: A Raisin in the Sun

This classic film portrays a 1950s African American family, including the mother matriarch, her daughter, and her son with his wife and eleven-year-old boy; the family lives in a two-bedroom high-rise in a southside ghetto area of Chicago. The matriarch's husband has died, and the family is expecting an insurance check for $10 000. The plot revolves around how different members of the family want to see the money spent. The matriarch wants to use a portion of the money to buy the family a modest home and save for her daughter's medical school education; Walter Lee, her son, wants to invest the money in a liquor store.

Numerous episodes are presented from which number ideas and operations can be extracted while focusing on the processes suggested by the NCTM *Standards* (NCTM 1989, 1991). Such ideas are presented here in the form of questions teachers could ask. These ideas primarily relate to mathematical concepts appropriate at the high school level. In addition to the mathematics, social and cultural issues arise in addressing these questions; these issues provide a natural opportunity for rich connections between mathematics and other disciplines.

- In the 1950s, why was a $10 000 life insurance policy considered to be a lot of money? What were other costs during that period of time? What are typical values of life insurance policies today? What factors influence the premiums paid on these policies?

- Walter Lee mentioned that his friends who had invested in a dry-cleaning business grossed $100 000 in one year. What kinds of expenses would be incurred in this type of business? Would that have been a profitable business in the 1950s? Is a dry-cleaning business a profitable business today?

- When Walter Lee became distraught about not being able to make the investment he wanted to make, he skipped work for three days. Estimate his salary as a chauffeur and compute how much base pay he missed for those three days. Determine a typical salary for a chauffeur or taxi driver today, both base salary and tips; determine the amount of pay missed for three days' absence.

- The matriarch paid a $3500 down payment for a new house. Her daughter-in-law, Ruth, indicated that the mortgage would be no more than $125 a month. If the four adults contribute equally to the mortgage, how much would each contribute monthly and yearly? Determine the average cost of a house in your neighborhood. Compare the monthly mortgage over a 15-year loan, a 20-year loan, and a 30-year loan. Find the total cost of the house over each of these loan periods.

- The mother wanted to save $3000 for her daughter's medical school education and to place $3500 in a checking account. Determine how much interest could be earned on $3500 in a checking account, savings account, mutual fund, certificate of deposit, or other investments.

- Obtain some current tuition information from local colleges and universities. What percent of a year's tuition could be paid with $3000? What percent of a year's medical college expenses could be paid with $3000?

Poster: Masks of Africa

The poster *Masks of Africa* (Metropolitan Museum of Art) (see fig. 13.2) is a rich and engaging source around which to develop lessons dealing with a wide range of geometric concepts. The mathematical concepts to be studied and the depth at which they are studied depend on the mathematical background and maturity of the students. Here are some questions and ideas to develop a number of different lessons:

- What are the similarities and differences among the masks? Use mathematical vocabulary in your descriptions. Design your own mask and decorate it with geometric patterns.

- Which of the masks have a line of symmetry? Do any of the masks have more than one line of symmetry? Design your own mask so that it has a line of symmetry.

- Do any of the masks have rotational symmetry? Do you think a mask would have rotational symmetry? Why or why not?

- Place a grid over each of the masks. Determine the area and perimeter covered by each mask. Compare these values to the area and perimeter of the faces of the people in your class. Which of the masks cover the entire face? For those covering only a portion of the face, estimate the fraction of a face that is covered by the mask. Design your own mask and determine the area and perimeter it covers.

- Which masks contain a repeated design? Use a tessellation to design your own mask.

- Obtain information about the countries and cultures from which the masks originate as well as the ages of the masks. Develop a time line showing the introduction of such objects into a given culture. Generate a series of mathematical problems that could be asked about each country or culture.

Fig. 13.2. *Masks of Africa* poster (reprinted by permission of the Metropolitan Museum of Art)

Summary

In each of the exemplars, the focus is clearly on the mathematics. We believe the multicultural connection should be a natural result of using a wide range of resources in the classroom on a regular basis. Hence, we prefer to focus on the mathematics and let the contexts in which that mathematics is viewed foster the multicultural connection by constantly demonstrating that all groups and cultures use mathematics.

INSTRUCTIONAL ISSUES

Several instructional issues need to be considered when using media to foster multicultural connections in the mathematics classroom. It is important to avoid relegating the use of media to only certain grade levels. Often, a given media example can span many grade levels, depending on the sophistication of the mathematics studied and the manner in which the media are introduced to the students. For instance, the book *The Village of Round and Square Houses* (Grifalconi 1986) can inspire students in elementary school to design floor plans on grid paper and determine the areas and perimeters of the houses. At the high school level, students might study floor plan shapes that maximize the area for a given perimeter, possibly using spreadsheets or other technological tools. Students could even design and build three-dimensional scale models of houses. At the middle school level, students can complete activities that bridge those suggested for the elementary and high school levels.

Another instructional issue concerns the subtleness of the mathematics found in some of the media examples. In certain examples, the mathematics is explicit; for instance, in *Moja Means One* (Feelings 1971) the mathematical context clearly is counting from one to ten. However, in other examples, the mathematics is more subtle, but the medium could still be used as a springboard for doing an enriched mathematics lesson. For instance, in *Ashanti to Zulu: African Traditions* (Musgrove 1976), each letter of the alphabet is used to introduce an African word and custom. The letter *o* is used to introduce a market in which bargaining is an expected practice; the description of this letter could serve as the beginning of a lesson dealing with food purchases, costs, and estimates as different prices are negotiated and paid.

It should be noted that many of the media examples discussed here naturally lead to interdisciplinary approaches to instruction. For example, at some point in *A Raisin in the Sun*, Walter Lee says, "Money is life!" and his mother responds, "Once upon a time, Freedom was life!" At another point in the story, a representative of the homeowners' association of the area into which they were moving was willing to refund the family's $3500 down payment and pay a bonus if the family would give up their purchase in the neighborhood. In a social studies or history class, discussions could center on the social climate of the time to determine what the comments meant and why a homeowners' association did not want African American families in the neighborhood. Hence, while mathematics activities are occurring in the mathematics classroom, activities dealing with prejudice and intolerance and the political realities of the time could be conducted in the social studies classroom. In an English classroom, students of all ethnic groups could write about times when they have felt uncomfortable or unwelcome in a given situation. Approaching the media in an interdisciplinary format as suggested here promotes collaboration among teachers of different subjects; it also allows one to obtain the maximum benefit from the use of the media.

Choosing appropriate grade levels or selecting media that draw students' attention toward specific mathematics content are important instructional issues. Because many of the tasks are open-ended, it is often difficult to predict exactly what avenues students might take when discussing the plot or mathematical message found in the media. Teachers must be prepared for such alternative perspectives and be comfortable with the temporary diversions that may occur as part of the classroom discourse. Ultimately, it is the teacher's responsibility to determine what ideas to pursue while maintaining the mathematical focus and objectives of the lesson (NCTM 1991).

CONCLUSION

This article has presented ideas and resources for using media to foster multicultural connections in the mathematics classroom that feature African, African American, or African Caribbean personalities and themes. Given the growth in the ways students communicate mathematics at present, this instructional area looks very promising for creating an environment in which students see the relevancy of mathematics to their lives and culture. Moreover, it is crucial that we capitalize on every opportunity to promote every student's growth in mathematics, particularly that of students who have historically not been as successful in the discipline. Given the calls to create more successful learning environments for students of color and to make mathematics more relevant to their lives, we need to consider using mathematical messages in media to enhance learning in every way.

REFERENCES

Burns, Marilyn. *Math and Literature (K–3): Book One.* Sausalito, Calif.: Math Solutions Publications, 1992.

Coxford, Arthur F. "The Case for Connections." In *Connecting Mathematics across the Curriculum,* 1995 Yearbook of the National Council of Teachers of Mathematics, edited by Peggy A. House, pp. 3–12. Reston, Va.: National Council of Teachers of Mathematics, 1995.

Curcio, Frances A., and Myra Zarnowski. "Revisiting the Powers of 2." *Teaching Children Mathematics* 2 (January 1996): 300–304.

Curcio, Frances A., Myra Zarnowski, and Susan Vigliarolo. "Mathematics and Poetry: Problem Solving in Context." *Teaching Children Mathematics* 1 (February 1995): 370–74.

Dee, Ruby. *Two Ways to Count to Ten: A Liberian Folktale.* New York: Henry Holt & Co., 1988.

Feelings, Muriel. *Moja Means One: Swahili Counting Book.* New York: Puffin Pied Piper Books, 1971.

Grifalconi, Ann. *The Village of Round and Square Houses.* Boston: Little, Brown & Co., 1986.

Hansberry, Lorraine. *A Raisin in the Sun.* Videocassette. Columbia Pictures Corp., 1961.

Hort, Lenny. *How Many Stars in the Sky?* New York: Tambourine Books, 1991.

Karp, Karen. "Telling Tales: Creating Graphs Using Multicultural Literature." *Teaching Children Mathematics* 1 (October 1994): 87–91.

Ladson-Billings, Gloria. "Making Mathematics Meaningful in a Multicultural Context." In *New Directions for Equity in Mathematics Education,* edited by Walter G. Secada, Elizabeth Fennema, and Lisa B. Adajian, pp. 126–45. New York: Cambridge University Press, 1995.

Musgrove, Margaret. *Ashanti to Zulu.* New York: Dial Books for Young Readers, 1976.

National Council of Teachers of Mathematics. *Curriculum and Evaluation Standards for School Mathematics.* Reston, Va.: National Council of Teachers of Mathematics, 1989.

————. *Professional Standards for Teaching Mathematics*. Reston, Va.: National Council of Teachers of Mathematics, 1991.

Shirley, Lawrence. "Using Ethnomathematics to Find Multicultural Mathematical Connections." In *Connecting Mathematics across the Curriculum*, 1995 Yearbook of the National Council of Teachers of Mathematics, edited by Peggy A. House, pp. 34–43. Reston, Va.: National Council of Teachers of Mathematics, 1995.

Smith, Jacquelin. "A Different Angle for Integrating Mathematics." *Teaching Children Mathematics* 1 (January 1995a): 288–93.

————. "Threading Mathematics into Social Studies." *Teaching Children Mathematics* 1 (March 1995b): 438–44.

Smith, Margaret S., and Edward A. Silver. "Meeting the Challenges of Diversity and Relevance." *Mathematics Teaching in the Middle School* 1 (September-October 1995): 442–48.

Sullivan, Emilie P., and William Nielsen. "Fictional Literature in Mathematics." *Mathematics Teaching in the Middle School* 1 (January-February 1996): 646–47.

Tate, William F. "Mathematics Communication: Creating Opportunities to Learn." *Teaching Children Mathematics* 1 (February 1995): 344–49, 369.

Whitin, David J., and Sandra Wilde. *It's the Story That Counts: More Children's Books for Mathematical Learning, K–6*. Portsmouth, N.H.: Heinemann, 1995.

————. *Read Any Good Math Lately? Children's Books for Mathematical Learning, K–6*. Portsmouth, N.H.: Heinemann, 1992.

Zaslavsky, Claudia. *The Multicultural Math Classroom: Bringing in the World*. Portsmouth, N.H.: Heinemann, 1996.

ANNOTATED RESOURCE LIST

Books

Culturally Contextual

Aardema, Verna. *Traveling to Tondo: A Tale of the Nkundo of Zaire*. New York: Dragonfly Books, 1991.

A civet cat is traveling to another village to get married. Along the way, he meets several friends who wish to travel with him, but each must wait for certain events to happen before they are able to continue on the journey. Mathematical lessons can involve time, including the proper sequencing of events, the amount of time needed to complete certain tasks, or the time of day at which certain school events occur.

Brashler, William. *The Story of Negro League Baseball*. New York: Tichnor & Fields, 1994.

This book details the history of the men and the teams that made up Negro League baseball. This book serves as a nice complement to the Margolies book referenced later.

Dayrell, Elphinstone. *Why the Sun and the Moon Live in the Sky: An African Folktale*. Boston: Houghton Mifflin Co., 1968.

In this folktale, the sun and the water are friends. The water is invited to visit the sun, but as the water comes in with his friends, the sun must keep moving higher and higher in the house. Eventually, the sun and the moon must reside in the sky. Lessons might deal with measurement ideas in terms of the height of the water at a given point in time or rates of change involving graphs of the water height at given points of time. Students might repeat these investigations by using a fixed measure to fill containers of different sizes; the rate of change in the height of the liquid can be connected to the volume of the container.

Dee, Ruby. *Two Ways to Count to Ten: A Liberian Folktale*. New York: Henry Holt & Co., 1988.

This story revolves around a contest in which the winner is the animal who can count to ten in a given time period. The winner is the animal who chooses to count by twos. Prior to reading this story, students could have a contest to see who can count to ten the fastest. After reading the story, discussions can occur about different ways to count to ten, thus introducing ideas of factors and their multiples. Students can take a given number and write as many different number sentences for that number as possible in a given time period.

Feelings, Muriel. *Moja Means One: Swahili Counting Book.* New York: Puffin Pied Piper Books, 1971.

This book counts from 1 to 10, introducing Swahili words and customs.

———. *Zamani Goes to Market.* Trenton, N.J.: Africa World Press, 1990.

The story describes a young boy's first trip to the market. Mathematics lessons relating distance, time, and rate are possible. In addition, students might investigate the prices at which one should sell goods in order to earn a particular profit.

Grifalconi, Ann. *The Village of Round and Square Houses.* Boston: Little, Brown & Co., 1986.

In the African village of Tos, the women live in round houses and the men live in square ones. The story tells the legend of how this came to be. A mathematics lesson might revolve around perimeters and areas of houses in the given shapes.

Haskins, Jim. *Count Your Way through Africa.* Minneapolis: Carolrhoda Books, 1992.

Counting from 1 to 10, the book introduces Swahili words for the numbers and aspects of the culture of those speaking the language. The book notes that more than 800 languages are spoken throughout Africa, with Swahili as the official language of Kenya and Tanzania.

(The title of this book treats Africa as though it is a country rather than a continent composed of many countries and cultures. Nevertheless, we have included the book because the content connected with the counting words is quite rich and the author describes the use of Swahili throughout Africa.)

Hopkinson, Deborah. *Sweet Clara and the Freedom Quilt.* New York: Dragonfly Books, 1993.

A young slave girl uses a quilt to construct a map describing the path to freedom along the Underground Railroad. Students can design maps describing locations of various places in the room or around school. Distances, orientation, and so on would all come into play.

Levine, Ellen. ... *If You Traveled on the Underground Railroad.* New York: Scholastic, 1988.

This book contains a number of two-to-three-page chapters dealing with various aspects of slavery and with escape along the Underground Railroad. Lessons are possible relating to the use of maps, the time needed to travel a given distance, costs for a trip today, and so on.

Lumpkin, Beatrice. *Senefer: A Young Genius in Old Egypt.* Trenton, N.J.: Africa World Press, 1991.

This book tells the story of Senefer, a carpenter's son who grew up to be a famous mathematician and engineer in the time of the pharaohs. Lessons are possible dealing with number sense, alternative computational algorithms, area and volume of the Pyramids, including ratios and comparisons of the different Pyramids.

Lyons, Mary E. *Stitching Stars: The Story Quilts of Harriet Powers.* New York: Charles Scribner's Sons, 1993.

This book highlights the artistic quilts made by Harriet Powers that currently hang in the Smithsonian Institution and the Museum of Fine Arts, Boston. The techniques used to depict the stories in the quilts suggest a strong African and spiritual influence. The author uses the context of slave quilting on Georgia plantations to portray Powers's story. Mathematics lessons of the following are possible: geometry and spatial sense in designing quilt squares; measurement including ratio and proportions to design appliqués; the use of patterns in storytelling; and problem solving in assessing costs, and so on.

Margolies, Jacob. *The Negro Leagues: The Story of Black Baseball.* New York: Franklin Watts, 1970.

This book describes the history of the black baseball leagues and contains a wealth of statistics about the teams in the leagues.

McDermott, Gerald. *Anansi the Spider: A Tale from the Ashanti.* New York: Henry Holt & Co., 1972.

Five sons use their individual talents to hunt and find their father when he becomes lost. In addition to ideas related to directions and mapmaking, the geometry in the book designs provides many opportunities for lesson development.

Mendez, Phil. *The Black Snowman.* New York: Scholastic, 1989.

A young boy dislikes being black. With his brother's help, he builds a snowman from dirty snow. But when a kente cloth is placed on the snowman, the snowman comes to life. Adventures set in as the snowman helps the young boy develop courage and an appreciation for his heritage. Lessons might relate to similarity and volume issues in designing a snowman and the amount of money made from recycling cans, bottles, and other such items. Students might consider the amount of landfill space that can be saved by recycling and might investigate recycling plans in their community.

Mollel, Tololwa M. *The Princess Who Lost Her Hair: An Akamba Legend.* Troll Associates, 1993.

This African tale describes a princess with long beautiful hair. Through selfishness, she loses her hair and faces shame. With the help of a poor young man, she learns kindness and generosity of spirit; when her hair returns, she has learned to share with others. Students might measure the length of hair for all students in a class; various statistics can be calculated and graphs displayed. Students might also record their hair length for a given period of time and determine different rates of growth. Students might also plant different seeds and measure the differences in the growth rates of the plants.

Musgrove, Margaret. *Ashanti to Zulu.* New York: Dial Books for Young Readers, 1976.

Each letter of the alphabet is used to introduce an African word and custom. Many of the descriptions can be used as starting points for mathematics lessons. For instance, the letter *o* is used to introduce a market in which bargaining is practiced. This might serve as the beginning of a lesson dealing with food purchases, costs, and estimating as different prices are negotiated.

Onyefulu, Ifeoma. *Emeka's Gift: An African Counting Story.* New York: Cobblehill Books, 1995.

The setting for this book is southern Nigeria. On his trip to see his grandmother, Emeka sees lots of things he would like to buy as presents, but he has no money. Lessons involving counting, shopping, saving money, and so on, are all natural extensions from this book.

Onyefulu, Obi. *Chinye: A West African Folk Tale.* New York: Viking, 1994.

In this folktale, a mean daughter and a good daughter are both given a set of directions. The one who follows the directions properly receives great wealth. The book could be used as a springboard to deal with the importance of providing clear and accurate descriptions of mathematics as well as clear directions on how to design a given geometric figure. Students might describe a hidden figure to a partner who attempts to build the figure; comparing the two figures built provides a concrete opportunity to discuss the importance of clear communication.

Pinkney, Andrea Davis. *Dear Benjamin Banneker.* San Diego: Gulliver Books, 1994.

This book describes the life and some of the accomplishments of Benjamin Banneker, one of America's first black mathematicians and scientists. The story describes the development of his almanac and his correspondence with Thomas Jefferson. Interdisciplinary lessons connecting mathematics and astronomy are natural extensions of the book, as are lessons illustrating the use of mathematics in survey work.

Stanley, Diane. *Shaka: King of the Zulus.* New York: Morrow Junior Books, 1988.

This book is a biography of the life and exploits of the great Zulu warrior Shaka. In addition to the geometry lessons possible through the African art, other number sense and operations activities are possible while exploring Shaka's strategies with his army.

Steptoe, John. *Mufaro's Beautiful Daughters: An African Tale.* New York: Lothrop, Lee & Shepard Books, 1987.

The life experiences of two sisters come into play as each goes to the city to present herself as a candidate to become the wife of the king. Geometric designs abound throughout the book and can serve as a basis for lessons. Problem solving can also be addressed through the book.

Williams, Karen Lynn. *Galimoto.* New York: Mulberry Paperback Books, 1990.

A young African boy collects pieces of wire in order to make a galimoto, a toy vehicle made of wire. Lessons might involve students' building toys or structures from objects of their choosing or determining the time needed to save money for a desired toy.

Wright, Courtni C. *Jumping the Broom.* New York: Holiday House, 1994.

A young African American girl discusses slave life on a plantation as the slaves prepare for a wedding where the couple will jump the broom. Students might collect data about special foods eaten at celebrations or holidays and determine an appropriate manner in which to display the data. Students might also plan a class party, being careful to estimate the amount of food needed and the costs.

Culturally Influenced

Brenner, Barbara. *Wagon Wheels*. New York: Harper Trophy, 1978.

After the Civil War, an African American family moved from Kentucky to Kansas because of the promise of free land. This story describes a number of their adventures, including a trip of 150 miles by three children in search of their father. Students might investigate their normal walking speed and determine the time needed to walk from home to school or to some other location.

Flourney, Valerie. *Tanya's Reunion*. New York: Dial Books for Young Readers, 1995.

A young African American girl visits the farm where her grandmother grew up. Students might design a survey to determine how many states or countries the individuals in the school have visited and then display the results in an appropriate manner.

Jaspersohn, William. *Cookies*. New York: Macmillan Publishing Co., 1993.

This book traces the story of the development of Famous Amos Cookies and describes the cookie-making process. Students can investigate the costs of starting and running such a business, the amount of raw foodstuffs used and purchased every day in making the cookies, the amount of payroll for a factory, and a host of other items. Students might even begin their own small company at school.

Linden, Ann Marie. *One Smiling Grandma: A Caribbean Counting Book*. New York: Dial Books, 1992.

Students count from 1 to 10 using themes set on one of the Caribbean islands.

Mathis, Sharon Bell. *The Hundred Penny Box*. New York: Puffin Books, 1975.

An African American woman, one hundred years old, has a book with one hundred pennies, one for each year of her life. The pennies remind her of stories in her life. The book can be used for counting.

Medearis, Angela Shelf. *Picking Peas for a Penny*. New York: Scholastic, 1990.

Set in the 1930s, an African American family picks peas for a penny a pound. Later, the children go to the general store to select their purchases. This book can be used to compare costs in the past to costs now and projected costs in the future, to discuss how much time is needed to earn a given amount of money, and to decide how to spend one's earnings or allowance.

———. *Poppa's New Pants*. New York: Holiday House, 1995.

A father buys a pair of pants that are much too long and requests someone in the family to hem them. Everybody seems to be too busy, but three different individuals cut and hem the pants in the middle of the night. Because so much is cut off, the pants now fit the son instead of the father. Mathematics lessons connecting measurement ideas are a natural extension to the story.

Paul, Ann Whitford. *Eight Hands Round: A Patchwork Alphabet*. New York: Harper-Collins Publisher, 1991.

Each letter of the alphabet is used to identify a quilt pattern. Two of the patterns, Tobacco Leaves and Underground Railroad, deal with African American culture during the slavery period. Problem solving, geometry, and patterning can be developed around the designs represented in these quilt patterns.

Pomerantz, Charlotte. *The Chalk Doll*. New York: Harper Trophy, 1989.

A mother shares with her daughter aspects of her life while growing up in Jamaica. Many of the individual stories can be used to develop mathematics lessons dealing with the amount of material and costs to make a rag doll, measurement in cooking, and how birthday money is spent.

Walter, Mildred Pitts. *Ty's One-Man Band*. New York: Scholastic, 1980.

A young boy finds a man named Ty who claims to be a one-man band. Ty uses a variety of different objects to make music and interesting sound patterns. Students might collect numerous objects and classify them on the basis of the types of sounds they make.

Wright, Courtni C. *Wagon Train: A Family Goes West in 1865*. New York: Holiday House, 1995.

After the Civil War, an African American family travels west to seek freedom and free land. Many adventures occur while traveling with the wagon train. Interdisciplinary connections abound as students investigate the length of time to cross the country by wagon train, the proportion of people who made the trip successfully, the amount of food or money needed for such a trip, and the weather characteristics in the different states.

Culturally Amenable

Bang, Molly. *Ten, Nine, Eight*. New York: Mulberry Books, 1983.

This is a reverse counting book picturing African American characters.

Falwell, Cathryn. *Feast for 10.* New York: Clarion Books, 1993.

In this counting book, the numbers from 1 to 10 are counted twice—once in the store and once in the kitchen at home.

Flourney, Valerie. *The Patchwork Quilt.* New York: Dial Books for Young Readers, 1985.

As a grandmother stitches a quilt, she shares all the memories related to the individual scraps of material composing the quilt. A mathematics lesson can be designed around quilts, including the geometry and patterns inherent in many quilts.

Greenfield, Eloise. *Aaron and Gayla's Counting Book.* New York: Black Butterfly Children's Books, 1993.

This book provides examples of counting from 1 to 20.

Hort, Lenny. *How Many Stars in the Sky?* New York: Tambourine Books, 1991.

A young boy wants to count the stars in the sky, but the lights of the city are distracting. After a trip to the country, he realizes that it is impossible to count all the stars. This book can be used as an introduction to large numbers and to the concept of infinity.

Hudson, Cheryl Willis. *Afro-Bets 1 2 3 Book.* Orange, N.J.: Just Us Books, 1987.

African American children are pictured with various objects in this book, counting from 1 to 10.

Hudson, Wade. *I Love My Family.* New York: Scholastic, 1993.

Genealogy is discussed as family members arrive from many places to attend a reunion. Students can collect data about their families and the families of students throughout the school (number of brothers, sisters, cousins, aunts, grandparents, etc.) and then determine ways to display that data.

————. *Jamal's Busy Day.* Orange, N.J.: Just Us Books, 1991.

Jamal describes his parents' jobs and the aspects of his own job—attending school. A mathematics lesson can relate to students' sequencing the events of their day, determining the fraction of their day spent on certain activities, and creating circle graphs to describe how their day is spent. Students can make comparisons of the graphs from different students and develop a variety of mathematical problems related to the graphs.

Johnson, Angela. *One of Three.* New York: Orchard Books, 1991.

An African American girl has two sisters. She describes the many ways in which she is one of three. Students might write similar books for different numbers.

McKissack, Patricia C. *A Million Fish ... More or Less.* New York: Alfred A. Knopf, 1992.

A young boy goes to the bayou and catches a million fish. However, on the way back home, he runs into a number of obstacles and loses all but three fish. His story is one more tale to add to the many other strange tales of the bayou. Students might estimate the length of time needed to catch a million fish, the volume and storage space for this many fish, and might check the numbers in the story to determine whether or not the boy's arithmetic is correct.

Merrill, Jean. *The Toothpaste Millionaire.* Boston: Houghton Mifflin Co., 1972.

A young African American boy becomes upset about the cost of toothpaste and sets out to remedy the situation by making his own at a cheaper price. Lessons involving business costs, including costs of materials, can be built around this story.

Milstein, Linda. *Coconut Mon.* New York: Tambourine Books, 1995.

This counting book counts from 1 to 10, all in the context of coconuts on a Caribbean island.

Ormerod, Jan. *Joe Can Count.* New York: Mulberry Paperback Books, 1986.

An African American boy counts from 1 to 10.

Pringle, Laurence. *Octopus Hug.* Honesdale, Pa.: Caroline House, 1993.

A father develops an octopus game in which he hugs and wrestles with his kids in a variety of ways. Geometry ideas, specifically transformations and size, are all embedded within the book and can be used to develop mathematics lessons at the elementary school level.

San Souci, Robert D. *The Boy and the Ghost.* New York: Simon & Schuster Books for Young Readers, 1989.

A young African American boy from a poor family sets off for the city to earn some money to help his family. He meets a stranger who tells him that he can be wealthy if he can spend the night in a haunted house. He manages to spend the night, and the ghost in the house leads him to a treasure, half of which he may keep and half of which is to be given to charity. Mathematics lessons can relate to how a given amount of money would be divided, the measurements of the hole in which the money was buried, and the boy's strategy for remaining in the house with the ghost.

Video

Gast, Harold. *The Jesse Owens Story*. Paramount Pictures, 1984.

> This video chronicles the life of this star athlete from his high school years through the 1936 Olympics through his accomplishments later in life. Mathematics lessons might focus on Olympic records, the length of time records have held, and the rate of change of the record. Interdisciplinary connections are available through exploring the social and political contexts with which Owens had to contend.

Haley, Alex. *Roots*. Miniseries. American Broadcasting Corporation, 1977.

> This miniseries traces the history of an African American family from the time when the first member was brought to the United States as a slave until shortly after the Civil War. Mathematics lessons might connect to money brought in from the blacksmith trade of one of the family members, the money earned by Chicken George in the cockfights, and the economics of cotton growing.

————. *Roots: The Next Generation*. Miniseries. American Broadcasting Corporation, 1979.

> This miniseries continues the history of Haley's family to the present time. Mathematics lessons might focus on business issues as Will Palmer becomes the owner of the local lumber company.

Hansberry, Lorraine. *A Raisin in the Sun*. Videocassette. Columbia Pictures Corp., 1961.

> An African American family receives a $10 000 insurance check and must decide how to spend it.

Shaku Zulu. Starmaker Entertainment, 1989.

> This miniseries highlights the life and exploits of the Zulu warrior-king Shaka.

Posters

Africa Multicultural Set (available from Dale Seymour Publications)

> Art, textiles, sculpture, architecture, and other aspects of African life are illustrated and described on the posters.

Masks of Africa. New York: Metropolitan Museum of Art. (Available from Dale Seymour Publications)

> This poster contains pictures of a number of African masks hanging in the Metropolitan Museum of Art.

Math of Africa. (Available from Dale Seymour Publications or Key Curriculum Press)

> This large poster illustrates mathematical contributions from Africa.

Games

Bell, Robbie, and Michael Cornelius. *Board Games Round the World: A Resource Book for Mathematical Investigations*. Cambridge, England: Cambridge University Press, 1988.

> This book devotes an entire chapter to a variety of mancala games. In addition to describing the rules for playing the games, the book includes a number of questions to be used for mathematical investigations.

Krause, Marina C. *Multicultural Mathematics Materials*. Reston, Va.: National Council of Teachers of Mathematics, 1983.

> One of the activities in this book is the game of wari, a two-row variation of a game played by the Asante people in Ghana.

Prior, Jennifer. *The Games of Africa*. New York: Harper Festival, 1994.

> This book describes a number of African games, including mancala, yote, sey, achi, and a Guinean string puzzle.

Zaslavsky, Claudia. *The Multicultural Math Classroom: Bringing in the World*. Portsmouth, N.H.: Heinemann, 1996.

> This book contains an entire chapter on games from many cultures, including African games.

————. *Multicultural Math: Hands-on Math Activities from around the World*. New York: Scholastic Professional Books, 1994.

> Included in the multicultural activities are several African games, specifically oware, shisima, and igba-ita.

Teacher Resource Books and Articles

Multiculturalism in Mathematics, Science, and Technology: Readings and Activities. Menlo Park, Calif.: Addison-Wesley, 1993.

> Several chapters of activities in this book connect to the mathematics and science contributions of African Americans, such as Benjamin Banneker, George Washington Carver, Charles Richard Drew, and Ernest Just, as well as to ancient Egypt.

Reimer, Luetta, and Wilbert Reimer. *Mathematicians Are People, Too.* Vol. 2. Palo Alto, Calif.: Dale Seymour Publications, 1995.

> One chapter in the book contains a story of the life of Benjamin Banneker, a famous African American mathematician.

Reimer, Wilbert, and Luetta Reimer. *Historical Connections in Mathematics.* Vol 2, *Resources for Using History of Mathematics in the Classroom.* Fresno, Calif.: AIMS Education Foundation, 1993.

> One chapter in this book deals with Benjamin Banneker and includes a brief story highlighting his important mathematical contributions together with several pages of activities appropriate for middle school students.

Shirley, Lawrence H. "Activities from African Calendar and Time Customs." *Mathematics Teaching in the Middle School* 1 (January-February 1996): 616–20.

> A number of activities with the calendar and time are described.

A Slave Ship Speaks: The Wreck of the "Henrietta Marie." Mel Fisher Maritime Heritage Society, 1995.

> This book details the history of the *Henrietta Marie*, a slave ship that sank off Florida, as well as the history of slave practices. Mathematical details in the book can be used as springboards for rich lessons in measurement and problem solving.

Smith, Jacquelin. "A Different Angle for Integrating Mathematics." *Teaching Children Mathematics* 1 (January 1995): 288–93.

> This article describes a lesson with the book *Jumping the Broom.*

———. "Threading Mathematics into Social Studies." *Teaching Children Mathematics* 1 (March 1995): 438–44.

> Mathematics lessons dealing with several books having an African American theme are described in this article.

Smith, Sanderson. *Agnesi to Zeno: Over 100 Vignettes from the History of Math.* Berkeley, Calif.: Key Curriculum Press, 1996.

> A number of the chapters in this book contain historical notes and activities related to African and African American themes.

Zaslavsky, Claudia. *Africa Counts: Number and Pattern in African Culture.* New York: Lawrence Hill Books, 1973.

> This book looks at the history and development of mathematical ideas and applications by the people of Africa.

———. "Multicultural Mathematics Education for the Middle Grades." *Arithmetic Teacher* 38 (February 1991): 8–13.

> A number of connections to African life are described in this article.

———. "People Who Live in Round Houses." *Arithmetic Teacher* 37 (September 1989): 18–21.

> This article would be a useful supplement when conducting lessons related to *The Village of Round and Square Houses.*

———. "Symmetry Along with Other Mathematical Concepts and Applications in African Life." In *Applications in School Mathematics*, 1979 Yearbook of the National Council of Teachers of Mathematics, edited by Sidney Sharron and Robert E. Reys, pp. 82–97. Reston, Va.: National Council of Teachers of Mathematics, 1979.

> Geometrical applications, particularly with symmetry, are described in this article.

Using Flags to Teach Mathematics Concepts and Skills

14

Joan Cohen Jones

The National Council of Teachers of Mathematics (NCTM) 1995 Yearbook, *Connecting Mathematics across the Curriculum*, stresses the importance of connecting mathematics to other topics in the curriculum and to cultural referents. By linking mathematics to other disciplines, students and teachers develop an appreciation for its many real-world applications. Curricular materials that provide multicultural connections to mathematics stimulate the learning of traditional curricular topics and encourage students' success by making mathematics relevant to the world in which they live.

It can be difficult for teachers to think of mathematical applications to other disciplines that interest elementary school students and also make relevant cultural connections. We tend to think erroneously of mathematics as culturally neutral and gender-free, and the applications that come to mind often refer back to our own European-influenced experiences with mathematics (Shirley 1995). With this in mind, I have developed a series of curricular units for preservice and in-service elementary school teachers that model integrated curriculum within a multicultural context. Preservice and in-service teachers have been quite enthusiastic about the interdisciplinary lessons, often remarking that linking mathematics with topics like geography, literature, and history serves to enhance their own understanding of mathematics. Class discussions focus on developing ideas for integrated curricula that do not shortchange mathematics topics. The preservice teachers in my classes have taught successful lessons modeled from these units to elementary school students, grades 2–5, during their field experiences. In-service teachers have used the activities in their classrooms with positive results.

A secondary goal in presenting interdisciplinary, multicultural curricular activities to preservice and in-service teachers is to facilitate their ability to evaluate how their own lives have been influenced by culture and ethnicity. The interdisciplinary units effectively encourage discussions on definitions, interpretations, and goals of multicultural education, as well as the myths and misperceptions that surround the topic.

I will discuss, in detail, a unit that has been quite successful with preservice and in-service teachers and their students, "Flags of Sub-Saharan Africa."

Curricular materials that provide multicultural connections to mathematics stimulate the learning of traditional curricular topics and encourage students' success by making mathematics relevant to the world in which they live.

UNIT OVERVIEW

This unit focuses on the history, flags, and geography of the forty-four countries that make up sub-Saharan Africa. Flags are used as physical models to introduce mathematics concepts and skills at the elementary school level (grades 2–5). The related lessons detailed below can be presented as an interdisciplinary unit or explored as individual lessons.

Mathematics Concepts and Skills

Classification by attributes, set intersection, data collection and analysis, fractions, decimals, percentages, area

Interdisciplinary Connections

Social studies, geography

Social Studies and Geography Concepts and Skills

Identification of countries on a world map, historical information about sub-Saharan Africa, identification and classification of flags

Materials

1. A classroom-sized world map or map of Africa.

2. A reference book on flags, such as *Pocket Guide to Flags* (Crampton 1992), which provides pictorial examples of flags and brief historical information about individual countries

3. Large reproductions of several flags of sub-Saharan Africa, using poster board or 12″ × 18″ construction paper

   I chose the flags of Benin, Chad, Ethiopia, Gabon, Ghana, Guinea, Ivory Coast, Madagascar, Mali, Mauritius, Nigeria, Sierra Leone, and Uganda because, with the exception of Ghana and Uganda, the flags consist of stripes of different colors (see fig. 14.1). The flags of Ghana and Uganda have stripes with embedded designs. Flag reproductions can be taped across the front chalkboard or around the classroom.

4. An index card for each country that contains a brief history of the country, including its former and present name, date of independence, and a description and some information about the country's flag

   An index card for Ghana might read, " The Gold Coast joined with British Togo and achieved independence in 1957, calling the newly unified country Ghana. Ghana's flag consists of three equal-sized stripes of red, gold, and green, with a black star embedded in the gold stripe. These colors were chosen because they are similar to the colors used in the Ethiopian flag. The black star was first introduced by Marcus Garvey, an African American who led a 'back to Africa' movement in the 1920s and 1930s." (*Note:* The depth of information on the index card should be adapted to the grade level.)

5. Sets of index-card-sized reproductions of flags of sub-Saharan Africa (for lesson 2 only), one set for each group of students

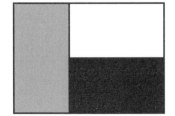 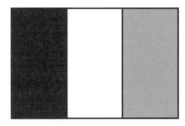 

Red

Green

Gold

Fig. 14.1. *From left to right:* flags of Benin, Guinea, and Ethiopia

Cultural Connections

Cultural relevance can be established through a discussion of the meaning and significance of the Pan-African colors of red, gold, and green, which appear in most of the flags of sub-Saharan Africa, as well as kente cloth from Ghana. These colors have, in recent years, become a symbol of African American pride and unity and are familiar to many African American students. Teachers and students, however, may not be aware of the origin or historical significance of these colors. Red represents blood shed in captivity; gold represents the mineral wealth of Africa; green stands for Africa's lush vegetation. These three colors were first used together in the flag of Ethiopia, one of the two countries of sub-Saharan Africa that was never colonized by Europeans (the other is Liberia).

Creating Context

As an introduction to the lessons described below, my students and I read children's books in class. *The Black Snowman* is an excellent book about a magical piece of kente cloth that helps an African American child take pride in his ancestry. A piece of kente cloth, given to me by one of my students after her trip to Africa, enhances the storytelling. Next, we read Maya Angelou's *Kofi and His Magic*, about a young boy who lives in Bonwire, Ghana, and is training to be a weaver. Students find it interesting to compare and contrast the story of the African American child with the story of the African child. This leads into a discussion of the history of kente, the colors in kente cloth, and their connection to the colors used in the flags of sub-Saharan Africa. This type of activity creates a context for the lessons. African American students have been very interested in the flags, especially when flags are introduced by first discussing the significance of their colors.

LESSON ONE

Distribute individual index cards with country and flag descriptions to student pairs. Each student pair reads the index-card description to the class and attempts to identify the flag from its description on the card. If the pair succeeds in identifying the flag, they attempt to identify the country on a map. If they do not succeed, volunteers from the class will try. This is not a trivial exercise, since several flags of sub-Saharan Africa are quite similar. For example, both Ethiopia and Guinea have flags with stripes of green, gold, and red.

As each flag and country are identified, ask students to describe the flags fully in their own words. Ask questions such as "How many stripes? What direction are the stripes? What colors are used in the flag? Are any colors repeated? What shape is the entire flag? What shapes are found in the flag? Does this flag look similar to others we have seen?"

LESSON TWO

Students in the lower grades (second and third) can explore properties of relationships with the following activities. Students work in small groups. Provide each group with a set of index-card-sized reproductions of the flags. Ask each group to sort the flags into two categories and describe their categories and reasoning to the class. Focus discussion on attributes used for sorting. Next, ask each group to sort the flags into three or more categories and describe their categories and reasoning. Sorting into two groups often provides uniform results. The two countries with designs embedded in stripes usually form one group, the rest of the countries form the other group. However, sorting into more than two categories yields interesting results. For example, students typically sort with respect to the attributes of number of stripes, type of design, or colors of stripes. One such selection is (1) stripes only (three or fewer), (2) stripes only (more than three), and (3) stripes and design. Ask students to explain their reasoning and identify the attributes used for sorting.

For a final activity, also appropriate for upper grades, select two intersecting attributes, such as (1) stripes only and (2) red, green, and gold stripes. Keep the attributes secret. Draw two large intersecting circles on the chalkboard, one circle for each attribute. Tape one set of index-card-sized flag reproductions on the chalkboard. Ask your students to select flags from those taped on the chalkboard and place them in the appropriate circle or intersection of circles. After all the flags have been correctly placed, ask students to describe the attributes. Informally discuss the concept of the intersection of sets. Conclude with a discussion of the similarities between flags and comparisons to the flag of the United States. The index-card-sized reproductions of the flags can be made into a bulletin-board display.

LESSON THREE

Collect data on the different flags. Ask students to count the number of red, gold, green, white, or blue stripes in the various flags. Display data in a bar graph color-keyed to the stripes in the flags or a line plot. Analyze both the numerical and graphical representations of the data. Find the mode. Extend the lesson by displaying historical data graphically. For example, display dates of independence for the countries of sub-Saharan Africa in a bar graph or stem-and-leaf plot.

LESSON FOUR

Flags can be used to model fractions as regions partitioned into equal-sized subregions. I generally introduce flags in my mathematics education classes as a final fraction model. Before beginning the lesson with preservice teachers, I ask my students to summarize the different models they have learned for fractions. After we discuss Cuisenaire rods, pattern blocks, tangrams, and fraction strips, I say: "We are going to use flags to provide a new model for fractions. Look at the flags of Benin, Guinea, and Ethiopia. For each of these flags, are all stripes equal-sized? What is the total number of stripes? How many stripes do you see of each color? What part of the whole does each equal-sized stripe represent?" For example, the flag of Guinea has three equal-sized stripes, one of which is red. The red stripe is a subregion that is one-third of the whole flag. Students easily grasp that the red stripe can represent the fraction one-third.

Next, my students are asked to compare the flags of Guinea and Ethiopia. Each flag has equal-sized stripes and one red stripe covering one-third of the flag, but the red stripes in the two flags do not appear to be the same size. Indeed, the areas of the two red stripes (and the two flags) are different. I ask my students whether each red stripe represents one-third. This question is confusing for some students. They learned fractions in elementary school by drawing pies of the same size and partitioning the pies into smaller pieces. It is often difficult for them to understand that two fractions representing one-third may refer to wholes of different sizes. To clarify, I ask the following question: "Kenya and her mother each ordered a pizza and ate one-third of it. Kenya claims that she ate more pizza than her mother. Could Kenya be correct?" Most students agree that Kenya could have ordered a bigger pizza than her mother. The discussion about Kenya's pizza usually helps students appreciate that one-third can represent different amounts, depending on the whole. Finally, I ask students to represent one-third in at least five different ways. They usually draw circles, squares, grids, or strips and shade one-third.

This lesson can be extended by reproducing the flags on 10×10 grid paper. Ask students to estimate the fractional size of each stripe and check their estimates by counting grids. Using the grid paper, introduce decimals and percents. Care should be taken when flags are rectangles and not squares. Grid paper can still be used, but students should carefully decide how many grids determine the whole flag. Another extension involving grid paper is area. Here, a meaningful comparison can be made between the red stripe on the flags of Guinea and Ethiopia.

LESSON FIVE

To bring closure to the unit, ask students to make their own flags, individually, with partners, or in small groups. Offer as much direction as needed. Suggested activities include asking students to design flags that use four different colors at most or asking students to design flags with two or four equal sections, with each equal section colored differently. Dot paper nicely facilitates this activity. Ask students to write descriptions of their flags and to explain why they chose their colors or design. Next, ask your students to justify how their flags meet the assigned criteria. Finally, sort the student-made flags. Do any patterns seem to reappear in different flags? Compare student-made flags to the flags of sub-Saharan Africa. Ask students to select their favorite student-made flag as a class banner.

For upper grades, an interesting extension is a student-run model United Nations, where "delegates" from sub-Saharan Africa meet to discuss some predetermined topic. Another extension is a time line chronicling independence for the countries of sub-Saharan Africa.

FINAL REMARKS

The lessons described above serve a dual purpose. They can be presented to preservice and in-service teacher education classes to increase their awareness of multicultural issues and supply successful models of hands-on integrated curricula. They can also be taught to students in grades 2–5. The mathematics content, based on traditional topics from the elementary school curriculum, is linked with other content areas to create multicultural, integrated curricular materials that make mathematics relevant to ethnically and culturally diverse students.

Although the mathematics should not be shortchanged for the sake of the other content areas, the interdisciplinary nature of the unit lends itself to rich extensions that will enhance the learners' experience. For example, the songs, music, art, textiles, and recreational children's games of sub-Saharan Africa can be explored concurrently with the lessons described above. Children's literature from Africa or about African and African American history and culture can also be included for enrichment. An annotated bibliography has been included for interested readers.

ANNOTATED BIBLIOGRAPHY

Aardema, Verna. *Bimwili and the Zimwi.* New York: Dial Books for Young Readers, 1985.

This story tells of three sisters in a Swahili village, especially the youngest, Bimwili, and her adventures.

———. *Bringing the Rain to Kapiti Plain.* New York: Dial Press, 1981.

A delightful folktale from Kenya, discovered more than seventy years ago and retold with a refrain that gives the story the rhythm of a familiar nursery rhyme.

Addison, John. *Ancient Africa.* New York: John Day Co., 1970.

This is a nonfiction book, suitable for upper elementary school grades, with interesting information about ancient kingdoms, including the Ashanti kingdom of Ghana.

Angelou, Maya. *Kofi and His Magic.* New York: Clarkson N. Potter, 1996.

This is the story of Kofi, who lives in Bonwire, the Ashanti weaving center, and is training to be a weaver. The book has wonderful pictures and is fun to read.

Feelings, Muriel. *Moja Means One: Swahili Counting Book.* New York: Dial Press, 1971.

This Caldecott Award–winning counting book uses unique aspects of East African culture to teach counting from 1 to 10 in Swahili.

Ford, Juwanda G. *A Kente Dress for Kenya.* New York: Scholastic, 1996.

This is the story of Kenya, who wears a dress of kente cloth to her school for "show and tell" and tells her class her favorite Anansi story.

Humphrey, Sally. *A Family in Liberia.* Minneapolis: Lerner Publications, 1987.

This book provides a richly detailed nonfiction account of a real family living and working in Liberia.

Jacobsen, Karen. *Ghana.* Chicago: Children's Press, 1992.

This is a nonfiction book for young children that describes Ghana and its people.

Kroll, Virginia. *Wood-hoopoe Willie.* Watertown, Mass.: Charlesbridge, 1992.

This American Book Award winner tells the story of a loving family celebrating Kwanzaa while appreciating their African musical heritage.

Mendez, Phil. *The Black Snowman.* New York: Scholastic, 1989.

This engrossing Christmas story is about a young boy who finds pride in his African heritage with the help of a magical piece of kente cloth.

Musgrove, Margaret. *Ashanti to Zulu: African Traditions.* New York: Dial Press, 1976.

This is a beautifully illustrated picture book. For each letter of the alphabet, interesting information about an African ethnic group or country is given.

REFERENCES

Crampton, William. *Pocket Guide to Flags.* New York: Crescent Books, 1992.

National Council of Teachers of Mathematics. *Connecting Mathematics across the Curriculum,* 1995 Yearbook of the National Council of Teachers of Mathematics, edited by Peggy A. House. Reston, Va.: National Council of Teachers of Mathematics, 1995.

Shirley, Lawrence. "Using Ethnomathematics to Find Multicultural Connections." In *Connecting Mathematics across the Curriculum,* 1995 Yearbook of the National Council of Teachers of Mathematics, edited by Peggy A. House, pp. 35–43. Reston, Va.: National Council of Teachers of Mathematics, 1995.

African Networks and African American Students

Claudia Zaslavsky

15

This article introduces the topic of *networks*, an aspect of graph theory that rarely fails to engage people of all ages and ethnic and racial backgrounds, from the elementary school grades to adults. Since many of the examples illustrated in this article are based on African culture, this topic may have a special fascination for African Americans as they reclaim their African heritage.

The concepts involved in graph theory are just beginning to find a place in the precollege curriculum in the United States, although Great Britain and other countries have long included them. We are surrounded by examples of problems that have been solved by applying graph theory: plotting pipelines for oil and water transmission; laying out systems of streets, roads, and telecommunications; designing printed circuits; planning the most efficient methods for delivering the mail and picking up the garbage.

This article will describe traditional networks of several African peoples, rich sources of mathematical ideas. As the concepts of graph theory are developed, suggestions will be offered for related classroom activities based on these concepts. Several additional topics will receive attention: number patterns and symmetry, among others, illustrating the interrelatedness of various aspects of mathematics. Finally, I will outline and provide references for some applications to our culture, at several levels of difficulty.

Grade level is not specified in the activities. Student success seems not to be correlated with grade level or mathematical achievement. In fact, a twelfth-year student in my high school decided to instruct an eighth-grade class in network theory, using African examples, as her senior-year project and was chagrined to discover that some eighth graders could handle the material more easily than she could!

NETWORKS OF THE CHOKWE OF ANGOLA

The Chokwe (Tshowke, Tchokwe) people, who live mainly in northeast Angola and neighboring regions, have long had a tradition of drawing networks in the sand, called *sona* (singular: *lusona*), to illustrate stories. These may be creation legends, morality tales, riddles, or actual human dilemmas. One purpose for these networks was to teach the children the history, moral principles, and cultural traditions of their people. First the storyteller, always a man, would mark a set of equidistant dots in the sand with his index and ring fingers. As he related his tale, he illustrated it by drawing a continuous line around the dots, being careful not to touch them or to hesitate as he executed the network.

The simple illustration in figure 15.1 poses a riddle: This [object] can accompany dancers and send messages [a two-headed drum].

Figure 15.2 depicts the marks left on the ground by a chicken when it is chased (Gerdes 1988, 1999; Kohl 1995). A version of this design graces the cover

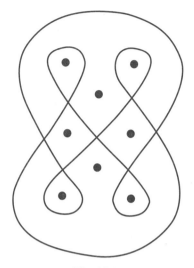

Fig. 15.1

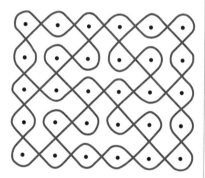

Fig. 15.2

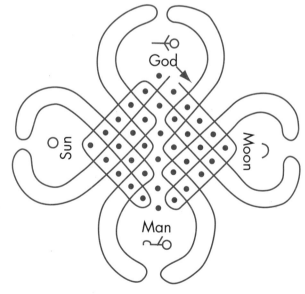

Fig. 15.3

of Chavey (1992), a study of graph theory and its applications for secondary school students.

Figure 15.3 illustrates a Chokwe creation myth involving the path to the god Kalunga and tells why the sun and the moon continue to appear every day, whereas humans eventually die. The storyteller relates this tale as he draws the path.

Once upon a time the Sun went to pay his respect to the god Kalunga. He walked and walked until he found the path that led to Kalunga. When he arrived, Kalunga gave him a rooster and said, "See me in the morning before you leave." In the morning the rooster crowed and woke the Sun. Then the Sun went back to Kalunga, who said, "I heard the rooster crow, the one I gave you for supper. You may keep him, but you must return every morning." That is why the Sun goes around the earth and appears every morning.

The Moon also went to visit Kalunga. He, too, received a rooster, and it woke him the next morning. When he returned with the rooster under his arm, Kalunga said, "I see that you did not eat the rooster I gave you yesterday for your supper. That is good. You must come back to see me every twenty-eight days." That is why we see the full moon every twenty-eight days.

Then Man went to see Kalunga and was given a rooster. But Man was very hungry after his long trip. He ate part of the chicken for supper. The next morning the Sun was already high in the sky when Man awoke. He quickly ate the rest of the rooster and hurried to see Kalunga, who then said to him with a smile, "Where is the rooster I gave you yesterday? I did not hear him crow this morning."

Man was afraid. "I was very hungry and I ate him," he said.

Then Kalunga said, "That is all right, but listen. You know that the Sun and the Moon have been to see me. Each of them received a rooster, just as you did, but they did not kill theirs. That is why they will never die. But you killed yours, and so you must die as he did. And, at your death, you will come back to see me."

And so it is. Haven't the Sun and the Moon always appeared, just as in the days of our great grandparents? But men and women do not live forever (Zaslavsky 1981).

Activities for Students

1. *Tracing.* Distribute copies of one or more of the Chokwe networks. Tell the story associated with each figure. Then ask students to trace the design without lifting the pencil or going over a line *segment* more than once, although they may *cross* a line. Figures 15.1 and 15.2 may be started any place, whereas the arrow in figure 15.3 indicates the starting point. The line being drawn is continuous, and it is generally best to draw each line as far as possible in one direction before changing directions.

2. *Copying.* Once students have learned to *trace* the figure, ask them to *copy* the figure on another sheet of paper. First they draw the pattern of dots as a guide. Note that the dots in figure 15.2 form a 5×6 rectangle, whereas the array in figure 15.3 is a 6×6 square (Zaslavsky 1993, Activity #54).

3. *Symmetry.* Students may examine the figures for symmetry. Figure 15.1 has both vertical and horizontal symmetry. To prove this, have the students fold the design along one line (axis) of symmetry and hold the figure up to the

light to see that one half fits exactly over the other half. Then follow the same procedure with the other line of symmetry. Students should also notice rotational symmetry; when the figure is given a half turn (180°), it looks the same as in the original position. In fact, any figure that has two perpendicular lines of symmetry also has 180° rotational symmetry. [Is the converse true? If a design has 180° rotational symmetry, does it necessarily have two perpendicular axes of symmetry?] Challenge students to find other examples of these types of symmetry.

Figure 15.2 has vertical symmetry only. Ask students what that fact leads them to believe about the chicken's path. Figure 15.3 also has vertical symmetry, once the starting and finishing points are connected.

Kohl (1995, pp. 58–83) breaks down the procedure for drawing a variety of *sona* into simple steps. He presents other types of networks for analysis.

Gerdes (1988) has studied the Chokwe *sona* extensively and has developed many activities based on the mathematical concepts inherent in these designs —number patterns, arithmetic progressions, several types of symmetry, graph theory, similarity, and the geometrical determination of the greatest common divisor of two counting numbers. Since the appearance of that article, he has published several books on the Chokwe *sona* (see Gerdes [1999], pp. 156–205).

Tip for teachers: It is a good idea to try all the network activities before assigning them to students. They may be more challenging than they look! Students enjoy the challenge and the sense of achievement that comes with solving a difficult problem.

NETWORKS AND GRAPH THEORY

My fifth-grade teacher fired my interest when she presented the network in figure 15.4a and challenged the class to draw the figure in one sweep of the pencil, without retracing. I spent many hours (instead of doing assigned homework) trying to convince myself that points *A* and *B* were the only possible starting and finishing points. Figure 15.4b can be drawn in one sweep starting anywhere, but figure 15.4c cannot be drawn in one sweep, no matter where you start. Figure 15.4d cannot be drawn in one sweep because it consists of two unconnected line segments.

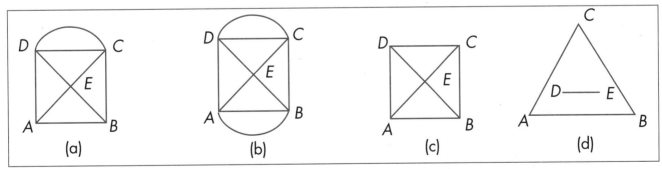

Fig. 15.4

A network consists of a set of points (*vertices*) and the line segments (*arcs* or *edges*) connecting them. In figure 15.4, the points *A*, *B*, *C*, *D*, *E* are the vertices of each of the four networks. The line segments connecting pairs of points are the edges. The study of such networks is called *graph theory* (not to be confused with algebraic graphs or graphs of statistical data). Figures 15.4a, 15.4b, and 15.4c are all *connected graphs*; each vertex is joined to another vertex by one or more edges. Figure 15.4d is an *unconnected graph*.

CHILDREN'S NETWORKS IN ZAIRE

The Bakuba (Kuba) people live along the Kasai River in Zaire. Early in the twentieth century Emil Torday, a European ethnologist, described their customs, particularly those of the Bushoong, a subgroup known for their beautiful artwork. One day he observed a circle of young Bushoong children drawing in the sand. "I was invited to sit down, and one of them, Minge Benegela, divested himself of his loincloth and offered it to me as a seat. This bettered Sir Walter Raleigh's action, as my young gallant was devoid of all other clothing. The children were drawing, and I was at once asked to perform certain impossible tasks; great was their joy when the white man failed to accomplish them," as he wrote in his book (quoted in Zaslavsky [1973], p. 105).

The impossible task was to draw two networks without lifting the finger or retracing a segment. Figure 15.5 shows one of the networks. These children were imitating the weaving patterns of their elders, the patterns in the fishing nets drying on the banks of the river and in the embroidered raffia cloth that has become a hallmark of the Bakuba people. The task was difficult but not impossible. The Bushoong children had done it! From the everyday tasks of the village, these children themselves had devised a game so sophisticated as to baffle the learned European anthropologist. What better way to learn mathematics?

Figure 15.6 shows simpler versions of figure 15.5, a growth pattern for this type of design. The first network consists of one small square. The second network has two small squares in its longest row, the third has three small squares in the longest row, and so forth.

Figure 15.7 shows another figure that the Bushoong children drew. In this network, several rows and columns consist of ten small squares each, whereas the other rows and columns are shorter.

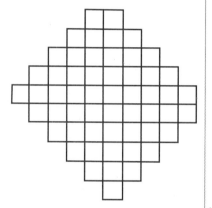

Fig. 15.5. Bakuba network

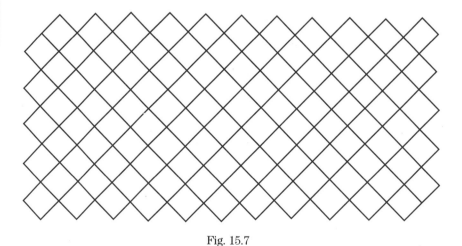

Fig. 15.7

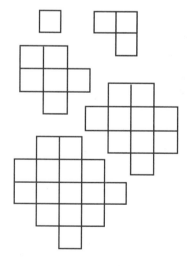

Fig. 15.6

Activities for Students

(Students should work in groups and compare their solutions.)

1. *Trace and copy.* The challenge, again, is to trace these designs in one sweep of the finger or pencil without going over a line segment more than once. Start with the smaller networks (fig. 15.6). Are there specific starting and finishing points or can one start anywhere? Then ask students to copy the figures on grid paper.

2. *Draw the missing networks.* The largest network in figure 15.6 has five small squares in the longest row and the longest column. The Bushoong children drew a similar figure having ten small squares in the longest row or column (fig. 15.5). Challenge the students to draw the missing figures on graph paper, similar networks having six, seven, eight, and nine small squares in the longest row or column. Mark each starting point and finishing point. Can they be interchanged? How are they different from other points in the network?

3. *Growth pattern.* Refer to the growth pattern of the networks in figure 15.6. Have students count the small squares in each figure and relate the total to the number of squares in the longest row. They might arrange their data in a table. Can they find a growth pattern for the number of squares? They should discover that the sums of the squares in each figure, taken in order, are the triangular numbers 1, 3, 6, 10.... The result may not be so surprising when we realize that the triangular numbers are the sums of the consecutive counting numbers: 1, 1 + 2, 1 + 2 + 3, ..., exactly the number of squares in the rows of each network (Zaslavsky 1993, Activity #55). Advanced students might find a formula for the sum of the squares, given that the longest row has n squares. [$S_n = (1/2)n\,(n + 1)$, the sum of the first n integers.]

4. *Symmetry.* Ask the students to analyze the networks in figures 15.5 and 15.6 for symmetry. They will find that each figure has just one axis of symmetry. The starting point of the network lies on one side of the axis, and the finishing point lies on the other side. The axis of symmetry bisects the distance between them.

5. *Enlarge and enhance.* Suggest to students that they draw figure 15.5 so large that it fills almost an entire sheet of graph paper. How many squares are in the longest row? They might color the small squares in an attractive pattern. A more difficult alternative is to draw the design on colored construction paper or oak tag and glue contrasting yarn over the pencil lines. Of course, only one continuous length of yarn is required for each network.

6. *Analysis.* Challenge students to carry out an analysis of figure 15.7, similar to that in questions 1 to 4 above.

   a) Have them devise a growth pattern for the network in figure 15.7. To generalize, for a network having n squares in the longest rows, the formula is $S_n = n(n + 1)$. Can students see why the formula holds?

   b) Analyze the networks for symmetry. Students will find that those designs having an even number of small squares in each of the longest rows have 180° rotational symmetry, whereas those with an odd number have one axis of symmetry halfway between the starting and finishing points.

TRACEABLE NETWORKS

You may have discovered that all the African networks presented thus far can be drawn without lifting the pencil or going over a line segment more than once. You may, however, go *through* a vertex more than once. Such networks are called *traceable* (or *traversable* or *unicursal*). You may also have discovered that some networks, such as the Bakuba examples in figures 15.5, 15.6, and 15.7, have only two possible starting and finishing points. If you start at one point, you finish at the other. You can start the Chokwe drum and the chicken's path (figs. 15.1 and 15.2) at any point, and you will finish at the same point.

How can you determine, without actually tracing the pattern, whether a network is traceable? Examine figure 15.5, the design that the Bushoong children drew in the sand. There are exactly two vertices at which three edges meet. One of these is the starting point, the other the finishing point. Look at the other vertices; either two or four edges meet at each one. The Chokwe myth illustration (fig. 15.3) starts at a point in the "God" quadrant and ends at another point in the same quadrant. Only one edge meets each of these vertices.

A vertex at which an even number of edges meet (two, four, six, etc.) is called an *even* vertex. A vertex at which an odd number of edges meet (one, three, five, etc.) is called an *odd* vertex.

To sum up, a network is traceable if and only if it is connected and it meets one of the following conditions:

- All the vertices are even; the starting point, which is also the finishing point, can be anywhere.
- Exactly two vertices are odd and all the others are even; one odd vertex is the starting point and the other is the finishing point.

See Zaslavsky (1993) for blackline masters of activities incorporating many of the suggestions above. For further discussion, see Zaslavsky (1973, 1991, and 1996).

Ascher (1991, pp. 31–65) considers African and other networks from both the mathematical and anthropological points of view. She describes the mathematics of the designs, as well as the cultural traits of the peoples who make them, in extensive and meticulous detail.

Activities for Students

1. *Identifying traceable networks.* Challenge students to discover the conditions under which networks are traceable by presenting several different patterns, some traceable and others not. In figure 15.8 are some of the African networks I have used with students, based on designs in Williams (1971). All are traceable except the Bida wall relief, which has eight odd vertices and therefore requires four distinct lines.

Benin bronze plaques, Nigeria

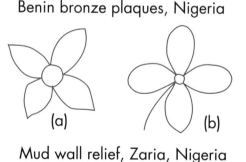

(a)   (b)

Mud wall relief, Bida, Nigeria

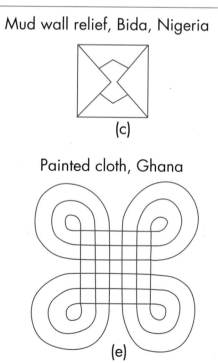

(c)

Mud wall relief, Zaria, Nigeria

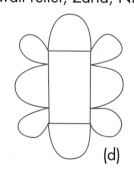

(d)

Painted cloth, Ghana

(e)

Fig. 15.8

2. *A piece of string.* Let students experiment with a length of string to create various traceable networks (Zaslavsky 1981). By manipulating the string, students discover that one end of the string is the starting point and the other is the finishing point, unless the two ends are joined (fig. 15.9).

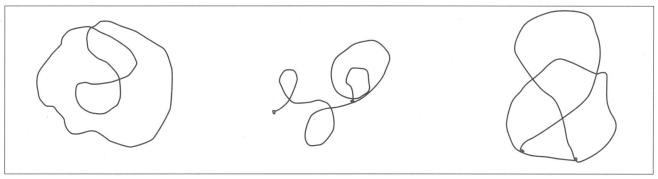

Fig. 15.9. A piece of string

3. *Network designs.* Suggest that students draw network designs on paper and ask their classmates to determine whether they are traceable. They may want to include several connected networks that cannot be traced with one continuous line. How many separate lines does each nontraceable example require? [To determine the number of separate lines, count the odd vertices and divide that number by 2.]

4. *Networks with odd vertices?* Ask students to decide whether it is possible to draw a connected network with exactly one odd vertex or with an odd number of odd vertices. [Impossible. Think of the network as a walk or a drive by car. What goes out must come back. You might come back to the starting point, making that vertex even, or to some other point, creating two odd vertices, the starting and the finishing points.]

APPLICATIONS IN OUR CULTURE

Graph theory is becoming increasingly important in present-day life. The points may represent cities on a map, and the line segments would be the roads connecting them. A *network* may describe the route of a letter carrier delivering mail or a truck picking up garbage, where the arcs represent the city streets and the vertices are their intersections. Television, telephone, and radio networks are other examples, and increasing numbers of people are getting to know the meaning of being "on the Net." Networking implies communicating.

The Swiss mathematician Leonhard Euler is considered the father of graph theory, with his solution in 1736 of the famous problem of the Seven Bridges of Königsberg (NCTM 1984, Chavey 1992). A park in the town of Königsberg (in the German state of Prussia) lay on two sides of a river, with two islands between. Seven bridges connected these regions. The townspeople loved to stroll through this park on their holidays. The question was raised about whether one can cross each of the seven bridges exactly once and return to the starting point. By analyzing a diagram in which each region is represented by a point and each bridge is an edge joining two vertices (fig. 15.10), one finds that not only is it impossible to return to the starting point but also at least one bridge must either be omitted or else be crossed twice to complete the stroll. The graph is an example of a mathematical model used to solve a real-world problem.

Glidden (1996) suggests further investigations based on the Königsberg bridge problem. "What if instead of visiting every vertex, we want to traverse

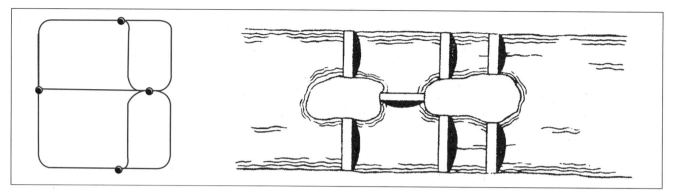

Fig. 15.10. The seven bridges of Königsberg

every edge? Does anything interesting happen when we add or remove edges? Vertices? What happens if we connect a vertex to itself? Can a situation be found in the real world in which an edge would connect a vertex with itself?" Glidden gives as an example the pedestrian pathways in a zoo.

Jacobs (1982, pp. 6–17) analyzes the path of a billiard ball on tables of various dimensions. It turns out that in some cases, the ball describes paths amazingly similar to those in figures 15.5, 15.6, and 15.7, the Bushoong children's drawings. The analysis involves prime and composite numbers as well as graph theory.

Folio (1987) describes a seventh-grade activity to chart the course of a cold epidemic through a classroom. She introduces the subject with this statement: "[Graph theory] can also be used to trace the spread of information, rumors, and disease in search of an original source" (p. 204). Each student becomes a vertex of the graph. Arrows on the edges indicate whether the cold was passed to the student or by the student to another person. Graphs in which the edges have direction are called *directed graphs*.

Perham and Perham (1995) offer an example of directed graphs as applied to decision making in history. The sixteenth-century Portuguese explorer Ferdinand Magellan, in his search for financial backing for his explorations, was rejected by the Portuguese king and sought aid from King Charles I of Spain, bitter rival of Portugal. The many factors that influenced King Charles, both directly and indirectly, are portrayed by a directed graph. As the authors state, the graph is "a storehouse of interconnected information that can be altered to accommodate new information, insights, and evaluations" (p. 109). A similar analysis can be applied to other events, both historical and contemporary, such as the civil rights movement and the campaign for the abolition of slavery.

Chavey (1992) is a rich source of problems on networks for secondary school students. Here is his introduction to a section of his book entitled "Examples of Applications" (p. 9):

> The problem that started Euler thinking about graph theory involved people trying to walk over a collection of bridges, and many real-world problems involve the same type of travel but for more serious purposes. For example, mail carriers need to travel down sidewalks, visiting every house. Garbage collectors, street cleaners, and snowplows must travel down every road in a city. Police cars might wish to patrol the city by driving down every road. Parking meter attendants need to travel down selected sidewalks to collect money (or to distribute tickets). Inspectors of many types might wish to inspect every road in a city, or every flight for an airline, or every route of the bus system, or every connection in a computer network. All of these problems can be expressed in terms of graphs and can be solved by finding an appropriate "drawing" of the graph.

Chavey deals with many of these situations, as well as others, introducing such concepts as—

- *Eulerian circuit:* a traceable graph that starts and ends at the same point;
- *Eulerian path:* a traceable graph that starts and ends at different points;
- *deadheading:* repeating edges that have already been traveled;
- *directed graphs:* graphs in which the edges have arrows indicating the direction to be followed, as with the cold epidemic.

Shyers (1987) gave her article an intriguing title: "You Can't Get There from Here—an Algorithmic Approach to Eulerian and Hamiltonian Circuits." A Hamiltonian circuit is a path that goes through each vertex exactly once and returns to the starting point. A traveling salesperson might want to determine the most efficient Hamiltonian circuit for his business.

Readers can refer to the many books and chapters on graph theory now available.

Activities for Students

1. *Plan an automobile trip.* Distribute a road map (or a section of a map) to each group. Suggest that they plan a trip that will take them to several specific cities. What route would involve the least amount of driving? The route should be traceable, since they don't want to retrace their path, and they certainly cannot convert a car into a plane!

2. *Look around you.* Invite students to discover examples of networks in their environment—in designs, maps, systems of streets and roads, the route of the mail carrier or the garbage truck. They might discuss the meaning of "TV network" or analyze a "coverleaf" highway intersection. Students might undertake investigations to analyze the efficiency of garbage collection or mail delivery in their neighborhood compared with other areas.

3. *Generalize.* Ask students to consider the questions raised by Glidden (1996), quoted above. Can they make generalizations and justify them?

HOW STUDENTS BENEFIT MATHEMATICALLY

I have used African network materials with elementary and secondary school students, with teachers of various grades, and with parents—for example, at the New York Urban League's Math and Science Fair. These materials never fail to interest and challenge the participants for many reasons, among them the following:

- The topic is different from the dull, dreary drill that so often constitutes mathematics teaching for African American students. Many of the activities do not require the use of previously acquired skills or computational ability.

- Students have the opportunity for real problem solving using hands-on activities. They look for patterns and arrive at generalizations based on their own explorations and analyses. They acquire the mathematical power that will prepare them for high school and college mathematics, particularly for the discrete mathematics courses now becoming part of the curriculum, which generally include graph theory among the topics.

- Students work in cooperative learning groups, compare their solutions, and discover that there are many ways to arrive at correct answers.

- The activities are open-ended, permitting each student to take them as far as she or he is capable. They allow accommodation to individual differences in style and pace of learning.

- These activities relate both to the African heritage of the students and to their own environments. Children learn to appreciate the common mathematical elements in diverse cultures and take pride in the contributions of African people, even of children. As one sixth grader commented in his evaluation: "As you probably don't know I feel very strongly and am in deep thrust [*sic*] with my black people, and the math has made me feel better."

- Mathematics is integrated with other subject areas—science, social studies, language arts, fine arts—making all these areas more meaningful.

- These activities foster a positive attitude toward mathematics; students are both fascinated and challenged. Some insist that "it's so much fun, it can't possibly be math!" An African American ninth grader commented: "I like the way they learn math in Africa better than the way we learn it here," in the mistaken belief that I was illustrating school mathematics as taught in Africa. Unfortunately, most African mathematics curricula demonstrate a neglect of their own cultural heritage in favor of European and American models (Zaslavsky 1991).

REFERENCES

Ascher, Marcia. *Ethnomathematics: A Multicultural View of Mathematical Ideas.* New York: Chapman & Hall/CRC, 1991.

Chavey, Darrah. *Drawing Pictures with One Line: Exploring Graph Theory.* Lexington, Mass.: COMAP, 1992.

Folio, Catherine. "Charting a Classroom Cold Epidemic." *Mathematics Teacher* 80 (March 1987): 204–6.

Gerdes, Paulus. *Geometry from Africa.* Washington, D.C.: Mathematical Association of America, 1999.

———. "On Possible Uses of Traditional Angolan Sand Drawings in the Mathematics Classroom." *Educational Studies in Mathematics* 19, no. 1 (1988): 3–22.

Glidden, Peter L. "Teaching Applications: Will the Pendulum of Reform Swing Too Far?" *Mathematics Teacher* 89 (September 1996): 450–51.

Jacobs, Harold R. *Mathematics: A Human Endeavor.* New York: W. H. Freeman & Co., 1982.

Kohl, Herbert. *Insides, Outsides, Loops, and Lines.* New York: W. H. Freeman & Co., 1995.

National Council of Teachers of Mathematics. "Networks." *Student Math Notes*, September 1984.

Perham, Arnold E., and Bernadette H. Perham. "Discrete Mathematics and Historical Analysis: A Study of Magellan." *Mathematics Teacher* 88 (February 1995): 106–12.

Shyers, Joan H. "You Can't Get There from Here—an Algorithmic Approach to Eulerian and Hamiltonian Circuits." *Mathematics Teacher* 80 (February 1987.): 95–98, 148.

Williams, Geoffrey. *African Designs from Traditional Sources.* New York: Dover, 1971.

Zaslavsky, Claudia. *Africa Counts: Number and Pattern in African Culture.* Chicago: Lawrence Hill Books, 1973. (Revised 1999)

———. *The Multicultural Math Classroom: Bringing in the World.* Portsmouth, N.H.: Heinemann, 1996.

———. "Multicultural Mathematics Education for the Middle Grades." *Arithmetic tTeacher* 38 (February 1991): 8–13.

———. *Multicultural Mathematics: Interdisciplinary Cooperative-Learning Activities.* Portland, Maine: J. Weston Walch, 1993.

———. "Networks—New York Subways, a Piece of String, and African Traditions." *Arithmetic Teacher* 29 (October 1981): 36–43.

Part 4

Focus on Future
Mathematicians and
Mathematics Educators

Struggling toward Diversity in Graduate Education

A Reflective Exercise

16

Howard C. Johnson
Peter T. Englot

Today, American higher education reels as the ground shifts under its feet. Following an era of stability, in which many of its underlying assumptions went unquestioned, higher education now finds itself astride the turbulent boundary of colliding societal forces. The debate about affirmative action is just one of those forces, but one that has some unique characteristics. Whereas issues such as tenure, institutional governance, and fiscal accountability have proved to be as contentious within higher education as their analogues are in society at large, in the debate over ethnicity-sensitive admissions, the higher education community seems to speak with one voice. (This is not to say, of course, that there is complete unanimity within higher education on the goals of such programs and policies. However, those who speak for American higher education on a superinstitutional scale appear to be in almost complete unanimity.) The education community has spoken out resoundingly against the Hopwood decision, rendered in the fifth circuit of the federal court of appeals, and against Proposition 209's passage in California. This voice comprises myriad individual strains, certainly, but also the collective strains of higher education associations. Meanwhile, outside the ivy-covered walls, the Hopwood decision has been greeted warmly in many quarters, and Proposition 209 was a popular initiative, being the result of a statewide referendum. Although the ramifications of these phenomena, legal and otherwise, are still being worked out, they have effectively proscribed the use of ethnicity in college admissions decisions within their jurisdictions. It seems fair, then, to characterize the debate over affirmative action as one in which higher education speaks in direct opposition to a powerful, though by no means unanimous, strain of popular sentiment.

How is higher education to respond to this conflict? Certainly, we could give in to the urge to simply express incredulity that anyone could wish to exclude consideration of ethnicity in college admissions. We can find many examples of such an approach to conflict in contemporary political rhetoric: toeing the party line, nationalism, and saber rattling constitute examples of the same brand of rhetoric, varying only in degree and scope. However, although this approach to conflict may build internal unity, it is not likely to result in productive dialogue among those who hold opposing points of view. It seems to us that if we are genuinely interested in resolving the current conflict over affirmative action, we must speak to, rather than at, our opponents in this debate. As obvious as the right answer may appear to us within higher education, we must take the time to explain ourselves thoroughly to those who think differently from the way we do. In fact, a similar strategy has been advocated by the American Council on Education in a new report on college costs (Ikenberry 1998). Also similar is the sentiment expressed in a recent report from the Institute on American Values, a group of largely conservative scholars that includes others such as Cornel West. Their report, *A Call to Civil Society*, advocates rebuilding that "sphere of our communal life in which we answer together the most important questions: what is our purpose, what is the right way to act, and what is the common good" (Institute for American Values 1998). We believe that to be incredulous is to withdraw from civil discourse.

However, it is indeed difficult to prepare for civil discourse on this subject. There is a strong temptation to allow our visceral reactions to carry our message. Further, it is not easy to find the terms with which to begin such a discourse. The rhetoric of divisiveness is so prevalent in our society today that it is not as though we may simply refer to a catalog of well-practiced forms of expression to guide us in approaching ideological opponents. Consequently, we feel compelled to try to discover a process by which we might prepare for opening a civil dialogue on the subject of affirmative action in higher education. This essay is an attempt to do just that.

> **The rhetoric of divisiveness is so prevalent in our society today that it is not as though we may simply refer to a catalog of well-practiced forms of expression to guide us in approaching ideological opponents.**

It seems to us that a good first step would be to offer some externally verifiable observations of the context of our concerns. Demographic data about participation in higher education seem to us to fit that criterion. It also seems that we should offer some of our own interpretations of the data, which are evidence of our position on causes. Also important for us to get on the table are the assumptions that underlie our interpretations. Although exposing all such assumptions merely through self-examination is difficult, if not impossible, we will make an earnest attempt. We will then describe some of the ways that we have acted on our beliefs about this subject. Finally, we will summarize and discuss next steps that might be taken.

FACTS OF UNDER-REPRESENTATION

There are a number of readily accessible sources of data on the status of minorities in higher education. One that is particularly useful, and from which we will draw most of our data here, is *Minorities in Higher Education* (Carter and Wilson 1997). Although the wealth of data makes extensive analysis possible on the situation of each major minority group, as well as all combined, we will restrict our comments to African Americans for the purpose of this discussion. (In fact, the American Council on Education [ACE] has adopted a like strategy for its publication series, providing in-depth analysis of one particular minority group each year.)

It is useful to know at the start that of the total population of the United States (265 185 000) in 1996, African Americans represented 12.7 percent, or 33 618 000 (Carter and Wilson 1997, p. 103). With this as a backdrop, we may examine some facts about the participation of African Americans in secondary and postsecondary education.

- Of 25- to 29-year-olds in 1975, 84.4 percent of whites and 71.0 percent of African Americans had completed high school. In 1995, those percentages were 87.4 and 86.5, respectively (Carter and Wilson 1997, p. 74).

This appears to give us cause for celebration, since African Americans had nearly achieved parity with whites by 1995 in terms of high school completion. However, the data on college completion rates for African Americans indicate that celebration today would be premature.

- Of 25- to 29-year-olds in 1975, 22.8 percent of whites and 10.7 percent of African Americans had completed four years or more of college. In 1995, those percentages were 26.0 and 15.3 respectively (Carter and Wilson 1997).

If we try to get a clearer picture of what has been happening in postsecondary education, we find the following:

- From fall 1984 to fall 1995, undergraduate enrollment of whites grew by 3.8 percent, whereas the enrollment of African Americans grew by 34.0 percent. Graduate enrollment of whites grew by 18.0 percent over the same period, whereas graduate enrollment of African Americans grew by 77.0 percent (Carter and Wilson 1997, p. 78).

These data reflect very impressive growth in raw numbers. As a society, we must strive to understand what we have done so well as to have produced such outcomes. It seems to us no coincidence that these gains have occurred during the period in which affirmative action programs in undergraduate education flourished. Unfortunately, other data show us quite clearly that much work remains to be done.

- In 1995, African American enrollment in postsecondary education was as follows: 1 334 000, or 10.9 percent, of the total of 12 232 000 undergraduates; and 119 000, or 6.9 percent, of the total 1 732 000 graduate students (Carter and Wilson 1997).

The picture emerging from the data above is one in which African Americans appear to be approaching parity in educational attainment with whites primarily at the secondary school and undergraduate levels while continuing to be dramatically underrepresented at the graduate level. (Remember that African Americans represented approximately 12.7 percent of the total population in 1995.) The following economic data show us why this should be of great concern to us:

- In 1994, the average annual salary for 1993 bachelor's degree recipients who were employed full time one year after graduation was $24 195. Their average annual salaries, by field of study, were as follows: health professions—$31 302; engineering—$30 948; business and management—$27 069; mathematics, computer, and physical sciences—$25 414; biological sciences—$22 763; social sciences—$22 082; public affairs and social services—$22 042; humanities—$21 307; history—$21 047; psychology—$19 463; education—$19 280; and other fields—$21 619 (National Center for Education Statistics 1997).

- In 1995, the mean annual earnings for persons age 18 and over, by level of education, were as follows: professional degree—$82 749; doctoral degree—$67 685; master's degree—$46 332; bachelor's degree—$37 224; associate's degree—$26 363; some college—$20 728; high school—$20 248; not a high school graduate—$13 697 (U.S. Census Bureau 1996).

- In 1994, of the 28 025 master's degrees granted in the United States in health professions, 1 496, or 5.3 percent, were awarded to African Americans; of the 29 754 in engineering, 682, or 2.3 percent, were awarded to African Americans; of the 93 437 in business, 5 213, or 5.6 percent, were awarded to African Americans (Carter and Wilson 1997, p. 91).

- In 1995, of the 7 913 doctoral degrees granted in the United States in life sciences, 155, or 2.0 percent, were awarded to African Americans; of the 6 007 doctoral degrees granted in engineering, 54, or 0.9 percent, were awarded to African Americans; of the 2 654 doctoral degrees granted in professional fields, 112, or 4.2 percent, were awarded to African Americans (Carter and Wilson 1997, p. 95).

The picture that we get from the preceding data is much less optimistic than that regarding educational attainment at the secondary school and undergraduate levels. What these data show is that African Americans are still dramatically underrepresented in graduate education and that this underrepresentation has grave economic consequences. Clearly, we must conclude that African

Americans do not enjoy a level of economic prosperity that is equal to the majority of the U.S. population. Further, we conclude that it appears that African Americans' economic *opportunity*—as measured by present enrollment in graduate education—will not improve greatly in the very near term.

CONSTRICTION IN THE PIPELINE TO ECONOMIC OPPORTUNITY

The reasons for the underrepresentation of minority students in graduate education are deeply rooted in the fabric of American education and society. Although our professional focus is on the graduate level, we would be remiss to ignore the depth of the problem. We could marshal statistics similar to those we already have presented showing that not enough minority youth progress from elementary and junior high school to high school and not enough graduate from high school. It is our experience that many of those who do graduate have received no encouragement, inadequate counseling, and inadequate preparation to continue on to college. One means of homing in on solutions to the pipeline problem is to look at one of the gates by which access to undergraduate and graduate study is controlled: standardized exams.

While still in high school, students are confronted with the Scholastic Aptitude Test (SAT). The Scholastic Aptitude Test (renamed the Scholastic Assessment Test) has dominated undergraduate admission testing in the United States. The SAT is and has been the most prominently used examination of its kind. The primary use of the SAT is to evaluate individual students' skills in the areas of vocabulary, reading speed and comprehension, and effectiveness with mathematical concepts and principles. It is thought to make a significant contribution to the evaluation of students' capacities to perform collegiate-level work.

Nevertheless, there is a compendium of research pertaining to the question of whether, in fact, the SAT is an effective measuring device of the skills for which it was originally designed. In addition, the College Board has been increasingly under pressure to modify the SAT to respond to the long-standing concern about gender and race bias. There is no argument that the examination has been gender- and race-biased in its nature, and the College Board has conceded that point. For example, in 1986 the Educational Testing Service, which creates and administers the SAT, introduced a "Differential Item Functioning" (DIF) procedure to identify questions that are biased. This procedure has led to modifications to the examination in recent years aimed at diminishing the effects of inherent bias. The changes have been minor, but they do constitute an attempt to respond to some of the critics. However, the predictive value of the SAT has become more and more suspect over the years; its use by most college admissions offices has declined with respect to the prominence and influence of the test in admission decision making.

Although the College Board readily acknowledges that the SAT, taken by itself, is not an especially useful tool in predicting college performance of applicants, there does appear to be value in taking the exam into account in combination with an applicant's record of high school achievement as a means of attempting to predict success. However, it is clear that the SAT has very limited value in the assessment of students from traditionally underrepresented groups. The SAT mathematics section score is unreliable, even in combination with the high school record, in predicting college performance of women. This is evident in the myriad examples of women and students from underrepresented groups who have been judged to be borderline admission cases but who have gone on to high academic achievement. (Conversely, the reliability of admission heuristics relying heavily on SAT scores also is thrown into doubt by the myriad examples of students whose scores foretold high achievement but who went on to drop out.) Thus, gatekeeping mechanisms such as the SAT have contributed to constricting the movement of women and students from underrepresented groups into undergraduate study; to what degree, precisely, we will never know.

At the level of undergraduate study, new constrictions in the educational pipeline are introduced that reduce the flow of these populations into graduate study. There is a vast literature on the experience of these groups during undergraduate study; delving into it is beyond the scope of the present essay. Let us focus for the moment, then, on the movement we see out of the undergraduate section of the pipeline, as reflected in the demographics of Graduate Record Examination (GRE) test takers. As we saw in the preceding section, far too few African American undergraduates make it to graduate school, and this is especially true for African American males. In 1996, more than two-thirds of African American GRE test takers were female. Further, the ethnic distribution of older examinees differs from the distribution of younger examinees; the greatest differences are seen in the African American and the Asian American composition. Half of all minority GRE test takers over age 30 are African American compared with 37 percent of minority test takers under age 30. One-fourth of the younger minority cohort are Asian American compared with only 10 percent of the older cohort.

We might be inclined to take the fact that African Americans are approaching representative levels of enrollment in high school and in undergraduate study as a sign that all is well. However, the acknowledged problems with the SAT and the demographics of GRE test takers prompt us to be concerned that attention must be paid at early levels of education to enable and encourage more African Americans to pursue advanced education. Efforts at the graduate level can only be effective if coordinated with others that are focused on earlier sections of the educational pipeline.

EXAMINING ASSUMPTIONS

All the preceding contextual observations have contributed to our conviction that affirmative action efforts focused on increasing the representation of African Americans in graduate education, as well as other underrepresented groups, merit our vigorous support. We recognize, however, that our sentiment did not simply materialize from the data. Our view of the data is from a particular perspective. We know that if we are to make ourselves more understandable to opponents of affirmative action, we must be prepared to not simply leave it at that. We must try to expose our underlying assumptions about global social issues, higher education, and graduate education specifically. Our first pass at this attempt produces the following assumptions.

Assumptions

- The world today increasingly depends on people with advanced scientific and technological knowledge to address a growing range of existing social and economic concerns. Such people are needed to develop new technologies and industries that will reduce environmental pollution, combat disease and hunger, and develop new sources of energy.

- Graduate education is designed to perpetuate the creation of new scholarship by creating new scholars—individuals with the capacity to learn independently, to redefine continually our understanding of the world, to identify and attack new problems, and to teach what they have learned to others who are from many walks of life.

- The experience of sensing, comprehending, and embracing difference is indispensable for the development of functional adults in American society.

This is so today and becomes more so every day as the dynamics of population growth metamorphose American society into one that is decreasingly homogeneous on a number of indexes.

- Inalienable human rights such as those made explicit in the Declaration of Independence—life, liberty, and the pursuit of happiness—are the foundation of social justice. To make these rights manifest in American society today and into the foreseeable future entails ensuring that all people have an equal opportunity to prosper economically.

- The representation of minority groups in higher education reflects the degree to which members of those groups have equality of economic opportunity with the majority.

- It is in the realm of possibility that someday legislation that outlaws discrimination will catalyze the evolution of a society in which all truly have equality of opportunity. We are not there yet. Consequently, affirmative action is required to compensate for the continuing effects of systemic discrimination. To defer action to a future point in time is to gamble with the lives of the present generation of minorities and those of their children.

- We conclude from the above that affirmative action in higher education—particularly at the graduate level—remains a critical tool for promoting equality of opportunity, one that we must continue to vigorously support.

This is the first time that we have articulated all these assumptions. We admit that we wonder—along with the reader, no doubt—how that can be? The best response that we can muster is that we have not had to articulate them before because in our community—our campus and, more generally, higher education—we have had implicit support from those around us in developing the programs founded on these assumptions. Many would remark, no doubt, how curious it is that this could happen in an academic environment, in which it is our very business to peel back the layers of surface phenomena to discover what lies beneath. And yet, we believe that we are far from alone in this experience.

This is, again, a first pass at uncovering our assumptions, but we immediately observe some interesting things about them that warrant comment. One is that they constitute moral positions that seem to hint at even deeper morals. For example, they would seem to militate against social Darwinism, which holds that only those who are "strongest" at the moment should survive. We might even be inclined to add an assumption to the list having to do with a sentiment that we must help our fellow human beings who face deprivation and injustice. Interestingly, our assumptions also imply the existence of other possible points of view and conclusions that one might draw about how to act on those points of view. Since none of our assumptions is grounded in externally verifiable fact, their logic admits of opposition.

We must not let go of this last point too easily. By articulating our own assumptions, we have created a window through which we might view the positions of those who oppose assumptions like ours and the actions that follow from them. This is not a trivial accomplishment. For although we may not agree with those who hold other points of view, we now have an idea of where to look for crucial points of departure. Reflection on our assumptions, then, seems to be an important step in preparing ourselves for civil debate.

THE SYRACUSE CONTEXT

We have translated our observations of the social context and our sentiments (represented by the assumptions we have now articulated) into professional action in particular ways. It is action restricted to the domain of a graduate school, but it reveals an awareness of the role that graduate school plays in society generally. We believe that we are members of a professional community that can have considerable impact in working to ensure equality of economic opportunity.

As the designated advocate for graduate education across Syracuse University, the Graduate School provides both leadership and support to individual departments and faculty members in recruitment and retention. We have interpreted that broad mission as including a charge to promote the recruitment, retention, and graduation of highly qualified students from ethnic groups that historically have been underrepresented in graduate education. Below we describe the most visible of our efforts to carry out this charge on our campus.

The Corporate Access Partnership Program

The Corporate Access Partnership Program (CAPP) is a joint effort by the Syracuse University Graduate School and corporate sponsors from around the nation to provide a comprehensive support system for students from underrepresented groups who wish to obtain a graduate (usually master's) degree. Since being founded in 1989, CAPP has successfully launched more than forty students on their professional careers.

CAPP is a fellowship program that selects fellows to be sponsored by corporations on the basis of those corporations' human resources or philanthropic priorities. Corporations also have the option of sending current employees to graduate school full time through CAPP. Typically, students receive a full-tuition scholarship and stipend of at least $9000 for the academic year. In the summer, each fellow interns under the guidance of a mentor with his or her corporate sponsor. Throughout their graduate programs, fellows have access to a variety of support services organized by the Graduate School. These include special travel and research grants, tutoring, social events, and other services developed to meet the needs of fellows.

CAPP fellows have been sponsored in the following programs: aerospace engineering; business administration; computer engineering; electrical engineering; environmental engineering; information resources management; instructional design, development, and evaluation; law; materials science; media administration; newspaper journalism; and telecommunications and network management. Corporate partners in CAPP have included ALCOA, Apple Computers, Associated Spring, Consolidated Natural Gas, Digital Equipment Corporation, General Electric, IBM, Kodak, Lincoln Life, Lockheed/Martin, Motorola, the Newhouse Foundation/Syracuse Newspapers, Niagara Mohawk Power Corporation, Procter and Gamble, Scientific Atlanta, and Texas Instruments.

The Upstate New York AHANA Graduate Forum

This annual event for African, Hispanic, Asian, and Native Americans (AHANA) is coordinated by a consortium of institutions in upstate New York led by the Syracuse University Graduate School; the other institutions involved are the State University of New York (SUNY) at Binghamton, Ithaca College, the Rochester Institute of Technology, and SUNY at Albany. The forum is hosted annually by one of the coordinating institutions and centers on a graduate fair that draws students from across New York State and graduate-school recruiters from around the country. More than a mere fair, however, it also gives undergraduates from underrepresented groups the opportunity to participate in workshops on strategies for success in graduate school, from the application process through graduation. A popular feature is the faculty-led seminars on the nature of graduate study in various disciplines. Initiated in 1988, the forums now have been replicated by consortia of schools in New York City and California.

African American Fellowships

African American Fellowships are university-funded awards for African American graduate students (U.S. citizens or permanent residents) whose graduate study requires the integration of African American and Pan African studies and who will make an intellectual contribution to the life of the Syracuse University Department of African American Studies.

These fellowships are intended primarily to provide a means of helping graduate programs recruit outstanding African American applicants when they do not have the means to do so themselves. (The Department of African American Studies currently does not have a graduate program.) The African American Fellowship Committee considers the nomination of truly outstanding individuals for multiyear awards (first-year fellowship; second-year teaching assistantship in the Department of African American Studies; third-year fellowship), but the majority of the awards are for a single year only. Each fellow's home academic department is expected to support him or her in subsequent years. No person can hold an African American Fellowship for more than two years.

All students who hold these awards must be in residence on the Syracuse University campus during the fellowship year and be actively engaged in coursework toward the completion of their degree requirements. No awards will be given to students who are registered for research or dissertation credit only. All who hold the awards must take at least one graduate course with the Department of African American Studies per semester.

Project 1000

The Syracuse University Graduate School annually provides tuition scholarships to help support some of the graduate students who enroll after having applied through Project 1000, a national initiative to increase graduate enrollment of Latinos and Latinas. The funds used for these scholarships come out of a small, discretionary tuition budget that must be used to address needs across the entire range of graduate programs offered at Syracuse (about 60 doctoral and 190 master's programs).

It bears pointing out that these efforts, although specific to Syracuse University, are replicable (if not already existing in some form) on other campuses. For example, the coordinating institutions for the AHANA Forum include two public universities, each of which has hosted the forum. Those institutions also participate in a state-funded fellowship program that is very similar to our African American Fellowship Program. It is our understanding that such programs may be found in several other states and at a number of other individual institutions. Finally, the reader should note that Project 1000 is a national program in which many private and public institutions participate. Thus, it appears to us that there is nothing to stop any institution that offers graduate programs from developing a multifaceted response to a concern about underrepresentation.

CONCLUSION

We find the reflective exercise in which we have engaged here to have been helpful in several ways. First, it has served to remind us of the foundations of our beliefs about why it is appropriate for us to invest so much energy in developing programs to promote diversity in graduate education. Second, it has helped sensitize us to possible sources of contention over the issue of affirmative action. Our work in higher education does not require such sensitivity daily because of the consensus in favor of affirmative action within the higher education community. Obviously, we could do much more to explore the sources of contention, but we believe that we now have at least begun to prepare ourselves for civil debate on the subject. Finally, we have found an opportunity to remind ourselves that the struggle to achieve diversity in our professional domain, graduate education, begins much earlier in the educational pipeline.

On the latter point, we feel compelled to offer encouragement to readers who have committed their professional lives to those earlier parts of the pipeline. It is well known that the impact of primary and secondary education is felt throughout later education, indeed for a lifetime. Clearly, increased graduate enrollment of African Americans and members of other underrepresented groups can be stimulated by efforts focused on the early levels of education. The data that we have marshaled in this essay show that economic opportunity is greatest in academic areas in which African Americans are very poorly represented—health professions, engineering, and business and management. It also happens that these academic areas are mathematics-and-science intensive. We know from our own professional experience that persistence in graduate education is high among those who view their education instrumentally, as a means to a career end, whether that be a professional or academic career. It seems, then, that today our greatest need in this regard at the primary and secondary school levels is for interventions that will stimulate lifelong interest in applications of mathematics and science. Consequently, we encourage efforts that will help youngsters to envision themselves in rewarding careers that entail excellence in mathematics and science.

We hope that this exercise will prove useful to others—particularly those outside of higher education—in opening paths to constructive engagement in the conflict over affirmative action in higher education. For our part, today we find the case for our work specifically, and affirmative action generally, even more compelling than we had before, and we look forward to opportunities to engage opponents of affirmative action in constructive dialogue on the subject.

Clearly, increased graduate enrollment of African Americans and members of other underrepresented groups can be stimulated by efforts focused on the early levels of education.

REFERENCES

Carter, Deborah J., and Reginald Wilson, *Minorities in Higher Education.* Washington, D.C.: American Council on Education, 1997.

Ikenberry, Stanley O. *Too Little Knowledge Is a Dangerous Thing: What the Public Thinks and Knows about Paying for College.* Washington, D.C.: American Council on Education, May 1998.

Institute for American Values. *A Call to Civil Society.* New York: Institute for American Values, 1998.

National Center for Education Statistics. "Employment Status of 1992–93 Bachelor's Degree Recipients One Year after Graduation, by Field of Study and Occupational Area: 1994." In *Baccalaureate and Beyond Longitudinal Study, First Follow-up Survey*, August 1997. Available at www.nces.ed.gov.

U.S. Census Bureau. "Mean Annual Earnings for Persons Aged 18 and Over, by Level of Education, 1996." *Current Population Reports* P20-489 (available at www.census.gov). Washington, D.C.: Government Printing Office, Document 803-005-00091-5, 1996.

Changing the Faces of Mathematics Ph.D.'s

What We Are Learning at the University of Maryland

17

Duane A. Cooper

As of late 1998, the University of Maryland's mathematics department boasts twenty-one black graduate students, most of whom are pursuing the Ph.D. This number stands in stark contrast to the national totals of five to nine who earn the degree in a typical year. In this chapter, we examine the actions that gave rise to this large concentration of graduate students and the efforts that fostered the development of a sense of community. We hear the graduate students' voices of experience and analyze their comments as they pertain to elements of success previously studied for black graduate students. We learn: one individual can make a tremendous difference, though departmental commitment is recommended; a black presence on a department's faculty, staff, and student community can attract students to matriculate; academic and social peer support are vital for many students to survive the hard work of a mathematics Ph.D. program, especially the transitional first year; mentorship before and during graduate school is important to influence and academically prepare students to pursue the Ph.D. and to facilitate progress toward the degree; and some maintenance of support mechanisms is needed. For those who might consider similar efforts, significant points to ponder are provided.

M y heart swelled one afternoon while walking down the fourth floor corridor of the Mathematics Building. There, at the octagonal table by the stairwell, were seated a half-dozen black[1] graduate students, talking mathematics and working together on homework. Or maybe they were preparing for an examination; it doesn't matter. It was a sight I would witness repeatedly that semester.

This communal study was nothing like my graduate experience, and mine was more racially supportive than many. As a young graduate student at Berkeley, I was fortunate to have the counsel of more advanced black graduate students, to whom I could turn for sound advice on mathematical and more general matters. As an old graduate student, I was able to return the favor to those who followed. However, I rarely had camaraderie with black peers enrolled in courses or preparing for major examinations concurrently with me.

Nationally, such clusters of black graduate students are few and far between. The numbers of black graduate students pursuing Ph.D.'s in mathematics are small, and the numbers of those attaining the degree are particularly tiny. In my crowning year, 1993, about one-half of 1 percent of all this country's mathematics Ph.D.'s were earned by African Americans; specifically, 5 of 1146 (National

---

1. In this chapter, *black* will be used primarily instead of *African American* because the findings and implications are not restricted to American students. Persons identified as African American in this work are either known to be from the United States or designated as such in a cited study. Furthermore, although it is the author's conviction that racial groups, Black and White, should be capitalized, they are lowercased in this publication to conform to NCTM's style.

179

Those numbers were typical of the decade 1986–95, in which just 58 of the 9520 Ph.D.'s in mathematics were awarded to African Americans.

Science Foundation 1995). That year was not an aberration, since those numbers were typical of the decade 1986–95, in which just 58 of the 9520 Ph.D.'s in mathematics were awarded to African Americans. The percent improves to about 1.5 percent if we add the 14 black Ph.D. recipients that decade who were U.S. permanent residents and the 69 more who studied here on temporary visas.

During the 1998–99 academic year, twenty-one black students were working in the graduate programs of the Department of Mathematics at the University of Maryland; most of them are pursuing the Ph.D. Furthermore, Maryland has produced two recent African American mathematics Ph.D.'s, one in 1996 and another in 1998. The current group of twenty-one is widely believed to be the largest concentration of black mathematics graduate students at one institution, rivaled only by the population at Howard University, a traditionally black institution. Even allowing for attrition, if this population has reasonable success, it is evident how they alone could boost the meager 1986–95 statistics cited above when similar data appear for the decade 1996–2005.

But attrition is a major consideration. In Maryland's mathematics department, attrition rates are not documented, but informal numbers suggest that two-thirds to three-fourths of all Ph.D.-intending students do not complete the degree, since the department, with nearly 250 graduate students, tends to admit about 60 students a year but graduates closer to 15, maybe 20, a year. In a national examination of mathematics graduate education (Case and Blackwelder 1992), 63 black mathematics graduate students were documented as having entered programs in the 1990–91 academic year; 8 received Ph.D.'s that year. In a follow-up study, Case and Blackwelder (1993) found that 17 of 43 (40 percent) of those entering students had left their programs with no degree at all by June 1992.

"Between 100 and 200" seems to describe the number of black graduate students currently pursuing Ph.D.'s in mathematics in the United States. Among the data gathered in a 1995 survey (Mathematical Association of America 1997) by the Mathematical Association of America (MAA) and the National Association of Mathematicians (NAM) of mathematical sciences departments and their minority graduate students, 190 African American students were reported in 134 mathematics and applied mathematics departments with doctoral programs. The students, though, were not categorized by degree sought as pursuing master's degrees or doctorates, so considerably fewer than the 190 were probably Ph.D. students. However, the 134 departments are only 69 percent of the 194 such departments in this country, so other African American students were likely not counted.

Whatever the precise numbers, the three-digit number of black students pursuing Ph.D.'s in mathematics does not compare well with the typically single-digit numbers of black mathematics Ph.D.'s granted each year. And the three-digit number of students does not represent a sudden surge in enrollments according to the MAA-NAM (1997) survey, which alluded to a previous study (Case and Blackwelder 1992) when asking and answering: "Did the total number of minority doctoral students increase dramatically between 1991 and 1995? Most evidence indicates this did not happen" (p. 11).

Although some of the large group at Maryland have dropped from the program or are considering doing so, many of the students have advanced to the research stage or are passing major checkpoints en route to the Ph.D. Though the final accounting will come after some more years have passed, the remaining sections of this chapter serve to give some insight into elements of successes achieved thus far.

WHAT IS WRITTEN ABOUT GRADUATE STUDENT SUCCESS? ... IN MATHEMATICS?

Not much has been written specifically about success for mathematics graduate students, although journals are peppered with articles about African American graduate students and about graduate students, in general. This literature speaks of assorted factors, including peer support, hard work, scholarly collaboration, mentoring, and prior educational preparation as important elements of graduate success.

One of the perceived strengths of the large concentration of black mathematics graduate students at Maryland is the potential for significant peer support in a setting that often lends itself more to isolation. The benefits derived from peer groups are supported as a significant factor in Asera, Velasquez, and Cortez (1994), a report that gathered stories and advice from various mathematicians and mathematics graduate students from groups underrepresented in the profession. This work's conclusion was that peer support and hard work are essential ingredients for surviving a mathematics Ph.D. program.

Related to the matter of peer support is that of scholarly collaboration. Anderson (1996) and Conrad and Phillips (1995) suggested that collaboration holds promise for countering intellectual and social isolation among graduate students, though these works present no compelling evidence that collaboration is *necessary*. An internal Department of Mathematics report (Kudla et al. 1997) at Maryland also spoke well of collaboration in its recommendations: "Several graduate students told the Review Committee that collective work in preparation for the written exams greatly increased the chances of success, and that students who were isolated frequently had difficulty on the exams" (p. 7).

Additionally, mentoring has been cited as a significant predictor of black graduate students' success. Smith and Davidson (1992) examined specific ways in which faculty mentoring and peer networking affect black graduate students' professional development. Hall and Allen (1982) considered in their study another angle—that students' perceptions of opportunities for being mentored were the most salient predictors of achievement.

The MAA-NAM survey (1997) of minority graduate students in the mathematical sciences categorized the students' responses about the people who have helped guide them and the ways in which they have done so. Many people and ways were cited as influential, but heading the list of "persons instrumental in pursuit of your goals" were professors from the undergraduate institution, followed by professors from the graduate institution. Giving encouragement and bolstering confidence emerged as the most frequently mentioned ways in which individuals were helpful to students.

Along with mentoring, Wilson (1988) cited prior educational preparation as a significant predictor of the success of black graduate students. Besides preparing students academically, the undergraduate educational institutions also play a role in whether or not black students continue for graduate study. In particular, compared to figures for undergraduate institutions overall, traditionally black institutions produce disproportionate numbers of students who persist toward doctorates in sciences and engineering (Solorzano 1995), even though most African American students attend predominantly white institutions. As for the performance of the students from traditionally black institutions, the work of Anderson and Hrabowski (1977), though dated, addressed many of the same perceptions that exist today when comparing educations received and resources available at minority and majority institutions, yet their study concluded that black graduate students from predominantly black colleges had success equal to that of the black students who hailed from predominantly white institutions.

> **Peer support and hard work are essential ingredients for surviving a mathematics Ph.D. program.**

HOW DID A COMMUNITY OF BLACK MATHEMATICS GRADUATE STUDENTS DEVELOP?

The University of Maryland's Department of Mathematics

Located just a few miles northeast of the nation's capital, the Department of Mathematics at the University of Maryland is one of the largest in the nation and enjoys an excellent reputation for scholarship and productivity. In its 1995 comprehensive review of doctoral programs, the National Research Council (1995) ranked the department eighteenth out of 139 nationwide, seventh among public universities, and first among public universities in the eastern United States. Figures from 1997 placed the department's population at 245 graduate students and 83 graduate faculty.

The department offers three Ph.D. programs, in mathematics (MATH), in applied mathematics (MAPL, pronounced "maple"), and in statistics (STAT). The MATH program is regarded as an outstanding graduate program, very highly respected nationally and internationally, according to the campus's Graduate Program Review Committee (1997). The committee also lauded MAPL as a high-quality graduate program with significant national standing among leading U.S. public research universities. Most of the requirements for the three degree programs are the same. The graduate students are divided between degree programs in about a 7:5:2 ratio, with 124 students in the MATH program, 86 in MAPL, and 35 in STAT. Recent data show that the time spent in pursuit of Ph.D.'s in the department is increasing: "The average student ... now takes slightly over 6 years to finish a Ph.D." (Kudla et al. 1997, p. 10).

One Professor's Efforts

One of the department's eighty-three graduate faculty is Raymond L. Johnson, for many years the department's only black professor. Johnson, who was instrumental in bringing forth Maryland's large black mathematics community, identified principal areas in the development of that community: departmental commitment, social support, informal networks for the transmission of information, and a diverse environment.

It was during Johnson's five-year tenure (1991–96) as department chair that the large cluster of black graduate students arrived. Asked, "How'd you do it?" he was quick to clarify that he alone did not bring those students to matriculate.

> I would strongly urge that I didn't do it; the Department did it. ... I did not participate in reviewing the folders [of applicants]. The Department made the decisions on whom to admit. This was important for me, because I could then go back to them and ask for help. If I had made the admissions decision, I would have felt under more pressure to take the lead in helping the students cope with academic issues.

Though he denies credit for bringing in the students, several cite Johnson as a reason they elected to come to Maryland for the Ph.D., having met him in recruitment settings like Undergraduate MATHFest, an annual conference sponsored by the National Association of Mathematicians designed to inform black mathematics majors about, and inspire them to consider, graduate and career opportunities in mathematics.

Johnson saw the need to work proactively to nurture a sense of community among a group of black graduate students early in his years as chair:

> A critical mass does not necessarily mean that you have a community. It takes work to turn a group into a community. There are many forces calling on them to

take individual responsibility that work against their naturally forming a community.

Indeed, when a problem arose, he was struck by the realization that three black students who had entered the program together barely knew one another. As chair, he was able to provide departmental support to sponsor initial social gatherings to assemble the students. Today, such gatherings are sustained by the black graduate student community for occasions like celebrations of achievements of program milestones or for no particular reason other than just to get together.

The mere presence of a substantial number of black students will not ensure success in their degree programs. To be successful, they need to use effectively informal departmental networks. Beyond their own community development, Johnson believes the black graduate students should make efforts to participate in, and benefit from, the department's graduate student grapevine of information. He offers this example of a ramification when black graduate students do not have access to reliable information:

> A poorly taught course affects all students in it but can be especially devastating for black students. The reason is that white students can fall back on their informal networks in such a case, whereas the black students do not have access to those networks and are left with fewer resources with which to cope.

During his term as department chair, Johnson met with the black students regularly for a couple of years. He describes his efforts to develop the black student community as a specialized information network.

> [I met] with the black graduate students about once a month to provide reliable information and to validate the information/misinformation they [had] received. I do not believe you have to be black to do this; [more important,] it is critical that you be able to look at the students and say/believe that they belong in your school.... I used my meetings with the black students as an opportunity to assist in their professional development by introducing them to other black Ph.D.'s, from a variety of professions, to expose them to the idea that there are many things that can be done with a math degree.

> I think that I was able to help make a difference in how they saw the first two years, so that not everyone was unfriendly and uncaring.... I was able to help them contact the right person, call the right office when they needed help.

Johnson also suggests that a diversity of faculty and staff creates a more satisfying environment for the black graduate students.

> I think the fact that we had a diverse staff helped the students decide to come here and helped make them feel comfortable about staying. I think that the fact that they had Duane and Dawn to talk to, being more near their ages, and having just gone through what they are going through, helped them.

In fact, the young black faculty have provided mathematical assistance, hosted informal gatherings, and coordinated job opportunities, though the primary roles, as needed or wanted, have been to offer advice and advocacy. ("Duane and Dawn" above are Duane A. Cooper, author of this chapter and assistant professor in the Department of Mathematics with a joint appointment in the Department of Curriculum and Instruction, and Dawn A. Lott-Crumpler, assistant professor at the New Jersey Institute of Technology in the Department of Mathematical Sciences. Both were postdoctoral research fellows at Maryland, Cooper from 1993 to 1995 and Lott-Crumpler from 1994 to 1997.)

The established community of black graduate students serves to attract new students to the program and to guide them along. And now there are twenty-one. As Johnson concludes:

> The fact that we got to a critical mass is because new students recognized the value of coming where others could help inform them about practices and people.

WHAT DO THE GRADUATE STUDENTS' VOICES OF EXPERIENCE SAY?

A Profile of the Group

By late 1998, twenty-one black graduate students with different national and educational backgrounds were studying in the mathematics department's graduate programs. This number includes a couple of students who are not enrolled during the current term but who remain in active pursuit of their degrees. More than half are in the MAPL program in applied mathematics; the others are split fairly evenly between the mathematics and the statistics programs. All but one of the twenty-one students have had a goal of a mathematics Ph.D., although a few have shifted their sights to obtaining the M.A. instead. Some of these talk of possibly continuing for the Ph.D. at another time and place.

Sixteen of the twenty-one students are U.S. citizens. Of those, a majority hail from Maryland and other states along the East Coast, though the group contains a few each from southern and midwestern states. Other black graduate students have their origins in Ghana, Haiti, Kenya, Mauritania, and Tanzania.

Thirteen students developed their collegiate mathematical foundations at black institutions, including three each from Spelman College and Clark Atlanta University, both members of the Atlanta University Center in Georgia. The others came from predominantly white institutions, though one of these earned a master's degree at Clark Atlanta before coming to Maryland. About half of the students entered the program here already having a master's degree, and the other half came with only the bachelor's. Most of the students are young, in their twenties, since a large majority of them came to Maryland either directly from their previous degree programs or having taken just one year away from school to work.

Of the twenty-one students in this black community, eleven are fairly far along in their Ph.D. programs. Six have advanced to candidacy. Another three have passed three written qualifying exams. These exams, tests of graduate material, serve as this department's major "hurdle"—"a necessary sieve" (Kudla et al. 1997, p. 8)—to be cleared by prospective doctoral candidates. Two others have passed two of the requisite three examinations, with only one to go. None of the characteristics of this group's profile seem significant in examining which students succeed in their programs, since the backgrounds of these eleven reflect those of the group at large.

Reasons They Are Here

Fourteen black graduate students responded to a questionnaire designed to elicit thoughts and information about this Ph.D. program, what brought them here, and where they might go from here. Of these fourteen, nine were from the group of more advanced students. A particular goal of the instrument was to gain insight into just what is significant about the unique concentration of black graduate students in this mathematics department.

Five items arose as common reasons that these students elected to come to Maryland for the Ph.D. One was the black presence and its supportive environment in the department. Another reason, cited by four of the fourteen, was the recruitment and presence of Raymond Johnson. Other repeatedly cited reasons were the academic reputation of Maryland's Department of Mathematics, the flexibility of the program with options available to pursue mathematical interests, and the location. Those for whom location was important either liked College Park's proximity to immediate family, were already living in this area, or thought they would like to live in the Washington, D.C., metropolitan area.

The reasons the students elected to pursue a Ph.D. in mathematics, wherever that might be, were remarkably diverse; no three students gave the same reply. Among those reasons mentioned were these: to gain understanding of mathematics and to gain respect; always having loved mathematics; interest in mathematics research; serving a need for more nonwhite professors; desire not to enter the workforce yet; desire to teach college; perhaps because "that was expected of me"; and having wanted a Ph.D. since they were young. The latter reason, cited by two students, yielded this intriguing recollection:

> My goal was a Ph.D. from third grade (honest!). This was because I always enjoyed math even when I was in elementary school.... My father would tell me each year how less than a handful of blacks were getting Ph.D.'s in math each year and I wanted to be one of those few.

Peer Support and Academic Collaboration

An earlier section alluded to the belief that peer support is important to success in a mathematics graduate program. The Maryland group gives credence to this notion. A large majority of them tell of ways that they view peer support as special and important. This support comes largely, though not exclusively, from their fellow black students and largely consists of academic collaboration and social support. Some of this support is in the form of counsel and encouragement, much like they get from senior mentors. One student who finds peer support "extremely helpful" declares that one reason she chose Maryland was the "family" feeling she received from the black students. She adds, "Having a support system really keeps you sane and motivated."

Another student remarks. "It is essential to talk to others who share your cultural perspective. Also ... it helps to know that others are as lost as you are."

The potential for academic collaboration among black students is probably the most unique feature of the large number studying here. At other institutions that have several blacks, the students are often scattered among different entry classes so that they are not taking key courses and preparing for major examinations at the same time. There is an uneasy two-way street of black students who are reluctant to approach white students or Asian students about academic collaboration and of whites or Asians who are resistant to being approached. No matter how many times we sing "We Are the World," many black students find the most comfort and can relax, not fearing condescension or disrespect, in the company of other black students.

Many students are taking advantage of the opportunity to enroll in classes together when they share common requirements or common interests. Although being "the only one" in a class is the national norm, some of the numbers here are staggering. When asked in what portion of their coursework were there two or more black students in their classes, the following replies were received, mostly from advanced students: "100 percent"; "100 percent"; "95 percent"; "9/10"; "all except one class"; "all but two." One student remarks:

> There have only been two classes where I was the only black student. I admit that I took all of my other classes because another African American student was taking it. Since many of the African American students here are in the same area, we

Many black students find the most comfort and can relax, not fearing condescension or disrespect, in the company of other black students.

185

usually schedule our classes where we can take them together. When I was in the classes by myself, I worked in a pair with someone of another race.

A few other students report having been the lone black in more than half of their courses. These students tend to have different mathematical interests or to have entered the graduate program at a time when there were few other black students.

All the students have participated in study groups. Some study groups are all black and others are multiracial. Even in the latter instance, an interesting phenomenon sometimes occurs, as one student recounts:

> When I met with a group, it was usually multiracial. However, if the group had another black member, the two of us would meet at other times outside of the large group.

Most of the black students, even those who express a preference for studying alone, participate in groups, regardless of whether or not other black students are taking the class. However, a few black students report that they use study groups for their coursework *except* when they are "the only one," in which case, they work individually. .

When preparing for the important written qualifying examinations, a few say they did so alone, though most report having studied with others at least some of the time. The consideration of individual versus group study evoked some interesting comments.

> I prefer to study on my own. It takes me a lot longer to learn the material but I do learn it much better. [When working with others,] I have primarily studied with black students. I have been fortunate enough to have at least one black student in all of my classes. However, I have joined study groups with other students.

Another discusses her transition from individual to group work based on her level of comfort.

> During my first two years, when I was the only black [in my courses], I studied alone; later, I began studying with others. I had met more people and felt more comfortable approaching them about classwork.

Another describes how she strikes a balance that affords her the benefits of both individual *and* group study.

> It takes a combination of both to be most effective for me. I must first study on my own to know exactly what it is that I am not strong on. The group helps me to strengthen my weak areas.... My study groups have mainly consisted of other African American students even though [a mentor] advised against it.

Mentorship

Support from peers can be important and so can support from more-senior individuals—mentors. Mentorship appears to be helpful to our graduate students not only in facilitating their progress through the Ph.D. program but also in helping them decide to pursue a Ph.D. in the first place.

Asked about any particular persons or courses or experiences that influenced the decision to pursue a doctorate in mathematics, more than half of the graduate students credit professors from their undergraduate days as the influence or as an influence on their matriculation at the graduate level. Particularly striking is that six of the eight graduate students who came from traditionally black undergraduate institutions give such credit to former professors. However, only two of the six who went to college at predominantly white institutions claim influence by persons there, and one of those two credits only a black administrator on his campus. The significant role played by undergraduate faculty is consistent with an aforementioned finding of the MAA-NAM survey (1997).

Beyond guidance of our black students to pursue the advanced degree, mentorship is important during graduate study. Some undergraduate professors continue to be mentors for their former students who are now at Maryland. Other graduate students report that the department's black faculty and post-doctoral fellows, some nonblack faculty members, other campus personnel, and mathematicians from outside this university have been helpful to their development. The primary ways in which mentors have assisted students are by giving advice and encouragement.

These two components—advice and encouragement—of mentorship were manifested in a wide range of ways. Mentors have given advice to students on things like selecting courses, choosing thesis advisors, handling programmatic difficulties, dealing with external pressures, and preparing for examinations. Students have received encouragement to "hang in there," to attend conferences, and to apply for funding or internship opportunities. Mentors have also encouraged students by bolstering flagging confidence and by sharing common experiences.

Other ways mentors have helped include alerting students to employment opportunities, resolving procedural matters, providing advocacy, developing friendships, and helping with the mathematics. Some students credit whites with mentoring them, though not all have benefited from guidance across racial lines, like the student who comments:

> Professors have tuned me in to opportunities I didn't know about. The Office of Minority Affairs has done the same. Upper-level grad students have been very helpful in assisting with coursework. Note: In *all* cases, these people were black.

Some students do not feel that they have benefited greatly from mentoring during their time here, but many have found it extremely valuable:

> I don't think I could've survived without having mentors because they are there to let me know that they had to go through some of the same things and sometimes worse. It makes one feel good to know that there are people out there that believe in you, that have your best interests at heart, and who will go to bat for you.

Another student adds:

> I doubt I would have had such a positive experience anywhere else.

Help with subject matter most commonly comes from senior graduate students, who often assume two roles as both peer supporter and mentor. They regularly help newer students by explaining concepts and sharing old notes, homework assignments, and examinations for study guides. One student states:

> Friends … are not only important for keeping up your spirits but even more critical is the fact that there are times when you will not be able to get everything done on your own. Having someone to ask "just show me how to do this" is very helpful as long as it doesn't become a habit.

Current mathematics department leadership has continued to support attendance by our black graduate students at regional and national conferences where peer support and mentorship opportunities are available. At Undergraduate MATHFest, our students serve in a mentoring capacity to the black mathematics majors from various institutions. On other occasions, like the annual Conference for African American Researchers in the Mathematical Sciences, our students are mentored by the mathematicians in attendance.

No Primrose Path

The graduate students are nearly unanimous in agreement, some emphatically, with the notion that the mathematics Ph.D. program is hard work and requires hard work in order to succeed. About half say that it is harder than they expected, whereas the others feel they had a good sense of the effort required when they entered the program.

Responses to "Do you think you were well-prepared for our graduate program when you entered?" were quite interesting. Though a considerable majority answered yes, there were very few *firm* yesses. Many responded with phrases like "yes and no," "somewhat," and "yes, but...."

One of the advanced students who is firmly satisfied with his own preparedness for Ph.D. study here worries that some of the newer students have been arriving without some of the theoretical foundation on which they should be building.

> Students need to be better prepared for the more difficult/theoretical classes. I'm sure students are told they should take the most challenging classes they can find as undergraduates, but it still doesn't seem to be happening. It may be too much after the fact to address this once a student is already here.

An example of one such student might be the one who says:

> I was more geared towards application at [my undergraduate institution]. Here, even the MAPL courses are heavy in theory.

Some of those who report that they felt prepared with adequate mathematical backgrounds say that their unpreparedness was for the level of hard work demanded by the program, the pace and workload of the courses.

> I think I was prepared intellectually; however, I was not prepared to put in the long hours and to make the many sacrifices necessary to succeed in graduate school. In fact, it's truly taken every one of [my years here] to (1) know what areas I want to study, (2) gain a better understanding on how to study this material, and (3) learn to make the sacrifices (e.g., late hours, working on weekends).

Students do not seem displeased with the program's heavy demands, though. The two matters about which there is considerable unrest are the qualifying examinations and the climate. The qualifiers, also known as the *comprehensive examinations*, are currently a source of debate among students and faculty alike. Questions have been raised about the reasonableness of the examinations offered in certain fields and whether or not they are being crafted with the expressed purpose "to indicate that the student has the basic knowledge and mathematical ability to begin advanced study" (Kudla et al. 1997, p. 8) in mind. Some students of all races have been meeting unsettling circumstances trying to pass the exams. One student at the Ph.D. dissertation stage reflects:

> I think the comprehensive exams are unnecessarily difficult. The comprehensive exams challenged my desire to love math.

Although some are fairly pleased with life in the department ("They are doing a pretty good job here at Maryland"), quite a few negative feelings were aired about the atmosphere of the department. That environment includes students with "competitive attitudes," professors who can be "unfriendly" and "condescending," program directors who seem "out of touch," and a general climate that is "cold" in which it is "easy to get lost." Informal discussion suggests that this environmental matter is a general issue affecting the graduate student population at large. One can imagine, though, how isolated black students could be

"I think I was prepared intellectually; however, I was not prepared to put in the long hours and to make the many sacrifices necessary to succeed in graduate school."

"chewed up and spit out" in the absence of the existing supportive community of black mathematics graduate students.

Attrition

In 1998, one black student received the Ph.D. from the University of Maryland's Department of Mathematics; three others earned the M.A. and left the department. As previously mentioned, some of the other black students have shifted their sights from earning a Ph.D. to attaining an M.A. instead. Here is the sentiment of one such student:

> I'm no longer sure if I want to stay here for as long as [earning a Ph.D.] takes, or even why I'd want to.

This student, though, hopes to get the M.A. and a job, with a possible return to another institution's Ph.D. program in operations research down the road.

Even though this student will apparently be lost to other opportunities, it is not such a sad tale because, in a fairly short time in the program, the lack of desire to pursue the Ph.D. was realized, a sense of future direction has been established, and an advanced degree will likely be earned. Some students' exits from the program have been much more painful. Not all students will see the doctoral process to completion, especially in this department where Ph.D. program attrition seems to be in the neighborhood of 70 percent or so. Indeed, by comparison, the cluster of black mathematics graduate students might be doing pretty well.

Let us examine what has become of the fourteen Ph.D.-intending black graduate students who entered the Department of Mathematics in 1993 and 1994. There is cause for optimism that seven of the fourteen might successfully achieve the doctorate. Six of those seven have passed all three qualifying examinations and are, thus, well on their way; three of these have advanced to candidacy. The seventh student has passed two of three qualifying examinations, so although not having cleared the main barrier to success in the program, the student is quite close, and the degree certainly seems attainable. Of these seven students, three came to Maryland with a master's degree, and all four others have earned the M.A. while here.

The remaining seven did not proceed as well through the Ph.D. program. Four of them received the M.A., and one other continues part-time work toward that degree. Five of the seven are gainfully employed. The other two now study in Ph.D. programs at other universities, one in statistics, the other in engineering.

It seems, then, that those black students entering in 1993 and 1994 will produce about six or seven Ph.D.'s, a pretty good rate when compared to departmental trends. This is by no means conclusive. Not only must we wait a few more years to determine how many actually finish, but it will also be appropriate to see if other entering classes of black students fare as well. Indeed, numerous black students from more recent entering classes have encountered difficulties, dropping out or progressing very slowly in the program. These difficulties coincided with a decline in the faculty support and community-building activities from which the 1993 and 1994 classes benefited. The lesson appears to be that the maintenance of formal support mechanisms, especially in the students' first years, is important to the sustained progress of the black graduate student community. One advanced student reflects on the importance of a solid beginning:

> I strongly believe that the first year is crucial. If a student makes it through the first year with a positive "yes, I can" attitude, then there's a good chance [the student] will make it through the program.

Despite some difficulties, the numbers are encouraging enough to suggest that something good is happening here. If all the aforementioned seven black students, six of whom are African American, succeed and attain a mathematics Ph.D., we at Maryland will have matched the typical annual *national* numbers for African American mathematicians from just two entering classes of students.

WHAT FACES MIGHT BE CHANGED?

The literature speaks to the disproportionate numbers of African Americans pursuing Ph.D.'s who attended college at a traditionally black institution (Solorzano 1995). The influence of undergraduate faculty at these colleges and universities was highlighted earlier when discussing the effects of mentors on our graduate students. The mathematics departments of these institutions have a crying need for more black faculty with doctorates to similarly inspire current and future generations of undergraduates.

Many argue because of job market conditions of the 1990s that we do not need as many mathematics Ph.D.'s. Well, let it resound loudly and clearly: *We need more black ones.* Black mathematicians are needed to deliver quality instruction and provide invaluable guidance to students at traditionally black institutions. There is also a need for greater black representation all across the spectrum of opportunities for persons holding doctorates in mathematics.

Of the fourteen graduate students who responded to a questionnaire for this chapter, half speak of either definitely or possibly teaching mathematics at a black institution, some on graduation and others "down the line." This includes six of the nine respondents who are more advanced in the program. The students express a broad range of career interests. Some plan on business or consulting work. Other students look forward to doing mathematics in a corporate or government setting. Other expressed goals include working at research universities and teaching at liberal arts colleges.

WHAT CAN OTHERS DO?

I conclude with some recommendations of others and with my advice for faculty, administrators, students, and others interested in increasing the participation of blacks in graduate mathematics study. At the end of his correspondence for this chapter, Raymond Johnson suggested the following actions that other concerned mathematics departments could take:

> They should invite students to campus, show off their diverse staff (if they have one) and their diverse faculty. I think schools should strive to be involved with education of minority students only if they can get to a critical mass. Schools having one isolated student are doomed to fail often.... A department that attracts a critical mass has to then work with the students to help them develop a community.

The MAA-NAM (1997) survey concluded with a set of nine recommendations of their own, based on existing programs across the country, for graduate mathematics departments to enlarge the pool of minority graduate students. The extensive list will not be recreated here, but elements of their recommendations are reflected in some of the efforts that occur or have occurred at Maryland. Those include mentorship for new students, the recruitment of prospective graduate students by current students, information on community opportunities beyond the department's walls, the sponsorship of student-faculty gatherings, and the recruitment of minorities and women for tenure-track faculty positions.

The influence of undergraduate professors on students' pursuit of, and progress toward, the mathematics Ph.D. was expounded in this chapter. Professors of undergraduates at *all* institutions should be aware of the significance of their guidance on the development and the future endeavors of their college students. Aware that we do need more black mathematics Ph.D.'s, they should identify the potential, polished or raw, in black students they encounter. The professor can then encourage the student to consider the possibility of earning a Ph.D. in mathematics, share a variety of reasons the student might do so, express his or her confidence in the student's potential to attain the doctorate, and suggest courses and actions that might facilitate the student's pursuit of this goal, if desired.

Arguments for faculty diversity at predominantly white institutions should be enhanced by the Maryland graduate students' reports about mentors and influential individuals, if those institutions are committed to serving students well. Although whites and others have played significant roles in mentoring a number of our students, much of the important guidance our black students received in their undergraduate and their graduate days came from other blacks. In spite of those who would say of race that "it shouldn't matter," substantial evidence suggests that it *does* matter.

Undergraduate students who are considering graduate school in mathematics should study hard and enroll in courses to give them the strongest possible mathematical foundation. For instance, extra efforts should be made to excel in core upper-level courses in analysis and algebra.

Departments and individuals who are trying to make a difference should maintain an awareness that the students, though of common heritage, are *individuals* with different needs, different wants, and most important, different ways to achieve success. Faculty should strive to create a framework through which the students find support and determine how best to maneuver the program on the basis of personal study preferences and social inclinations. This framework to foster development of a community can allow for individual distinctions but still pay special attention to common difficulties like isolation and inadequate advising and promote the benefits of academic collaboration and mentorship.

> Professors of undergraduates ... should identify the potential, polished or raw, in black students they encounter.

REFERENCES

Anderson, Ernest, and Freeman Hrabowski. "Graduate School Success of Black Students from White Colleges and Black Colleges." *Journal of Higher Education* 48 (1977): 294–303.

Anderson, Melissa. "Collaboration, the Doctoral Experience, and the Department Environment." *Review of Higher Education* 19 (1996): 305–26.

Asera, Rose, Elinor Velasquez, and Ricardo Cortez. "Diversity in Mathematics." Unpublished manuscript, Dana Center for Mathematics and Science Education, University of California, Berkeley, 1994.

Case, Bettye Anne, and M. Annette Blackwelder. "Doctoral Department Retention, Expectations, and Teaching Preparation." *Notices of the American Mathematical Society* 40 (1993): 803–11.

———. "The Graduate Student Cohort, Doctoral Department Expectations, and Teaching Preparation." *Notices of the American Mathematical Society* 39 (1992): 412–18.

Conrad, Linda, and Estelle Phillips. "From Isolation to Collaboration: A Positive Change for Postgraduate Women?" *Higher Education* 30 (1995): 313–22.

Graduate Program Review Committee. *Building Cornerstone Programs of Excellence: Report of the Graduate Program Review Committee.* College Park, Md.: University of Maryland, 1997.

Hall, Marcia, and Walter Allen. "Race Consciousness and Achievement: Two Issues in the Study of Black Graduate/Professional Students." *Integrated Education* 20 (1982): 56–61.

Kudla, Stephen, John Benedetto, William Goldman, R. Bruce Kellogg, David Kueker, Jonathan Rosenberg, and Paul Smith. *Graduate Program Review Committee Final Report, 1997*. College Park, Md.: University of Maryland, Department of Mathematics, 1997.

Mathematical Association of America (MAA) and National Association of Mathematicians (NAM). *Survey of Minority Graduate Students in U.S. Mathematical Sciences Departments*. Washington, D.C.: Mathematical Association of America, 1997.

National Research Council. *Research-Doctorate Programs in the United States, Continuity and Change*. Washington, D.C.: National Academy Press, 1995.

National Science Foundation. *Selected Data on Science and Engineering Doctorate Awards: 1995*. NSF 96-303. Arlington, Va.: National Science Foundation, 1995.

Smith, Emilie, and William Davidson. "Mentoring and the Development of African-American Graduate Students." *Journal of College Student Development* 33 (1992): 531–39.

Solorzano, Daniel. "The Doctorate Production and Baccalaureate Origins of African Americans in the Sciences and Engineering." *Journal of Negro Education* 64 (1995): 15-32.

Wilson, Reginald. "Developing Leadership: Blacks in Graduate and Professional Schools." *Journal of Black Studies* 19 (1988): 163–73.

Developing Future Mathematicians

18

Janis M. Oldham

Though educators in the United States would like to produce more home-grown mathematicians, the reality is that starting from the freshman year in high school, approximately half the students enrolled in mathematics courses each year choose not to enroll the very next year, dropping out of the mathematics pipeline that could eventually lead to a Ph.D. (National Research Council [NRC] 1989, p. 7). For minority students, including African Americans, the dropout rate is even higher. An often proffered explanation of why this is true cites traditional teaching methods that expect the student to listen and imitate and do not take into account the way students learn mathematics. Research has shown that students learn mathematics through personal, intellectual engagement that allows them to create an understanding (NRC 1989, p. 6). The purpose of this paper is to discuss the effort of faculty at North Carolina Agricultural and Technical State University (NCA&TSU) to improve instruction in upper-level mathematics courses in order to give our mathematics majors an improved opportunity to learn and understand mathematics, better preparing them for graduate school in the mathematical sciences, keeping them in the pipeline.

Improvement must come in teacher-student interaction and in student-student interaction. Instruction must be relational (Skemp 1978), teaching mathematical principles and engaging the students in mathematical thinking. In addition, all students must become inducted into the "mathematics culture," so that student-to-student interaction reinforces their learning. Students who are a part of the mathematics culture (1) engage in long hours of contemplative individual work; (2) spend much time carefully reading mathematics texts or articles; (3) develop patience with the difficulty and effort in making progress in attaining new results or understanding new concepts; (4) have ability to interact with other mathematicians and verbally discuss mathematics; (5) understand the difficulty in knowing when something is proved correctly; (6) are able to learn in a lecture format; and most of all, (7) possess commitment and perseverance (Baldwin 1995). In studying the minority (including African American) students who participated in the University of California at Berkeley's Summer Mathematics Institute, it was noted that about a third of the students lacked a mathematical "learning community" experience as part of their college experience. These students did not see themselves as part of a mathematics community, locally, nationally, or globally. Yet research indicates that students working together in intentionally structured academic and social communities learn material more enthusiastically (Asera 1995). This culture is what some faculty at NCA&TSU are seeking to develop among their mathematics majors.

Although this effort was primarily led by the Professional Mathematics Curriculum Committee (PMCC), of which I am a member, full support of the entire mathematics department is necessary to make systemic change (e.g., in curriculum). Members of the PMCC and the department chair are the only faculty currently teaching courses in which change has been implemented. Though change in instructional approach has occurred with all but one of these faculty, the focus was on changing students' study behavior and interaction with peers and faculty.

> **All students must become inducted into the "mathematics culture," so that student-to-student interaction reinforces their learning.**

REASONS FOR CHANGE AT NCA&TSU

North Carolina A&T State University is a public, comprehensive, land-grant university that is also a historically black institution. The current student body, including the undergraduate mathematics population, is about 87 percent African American. Beginning in 1992, degree requirements were changed in the professional mathematics degree curriculum in part to better prepare students for graduate school in the mathematical sciences and to encourage them to consider this choice. A major change made was to require both semesters of intermediate real analysis (Math 507, Math 508), and both semesters of abstract algebra (Math 511, Math 512), two proof-based mathematics sequences. The other two undergraduate degree curricula, engineering mathematics and mathematics education, require some but not all of the courses above. See figure 18.1 for changes in the program.

Changes in the Professional Mathematics Degree Curriculum at North Carolina A&T

1992–1993

Freshman Year

First Semester		Second Semester	
Course	Cr	Course	Cr
Math 131	4	Math 132	4
Chem 101,111	4	Chem102,112	4
Engl 100	3	Engl 101	3
History 100	3	History 101	3
C&I 100	1	FRST	1

Sophomore Year

First Semester		Second Semester	
Course	Cr	Course	Cr
Math 231	4	Math 350	3
Math 240 or alt.	3	Math 242	3
Phys 241,251	5	Phys 242,252	5
Humanities 200	3	Humanities 201	3
Speech 250	3	Health Ed.	2

Junior Year

First Semester		Second Semester	
Course	Cr	Course	Cr
Math 507	3	Math Elect.(300+)	6
Math 224	3	Phys 406	3
Math Elect.(300+)	3	FOLA	3
FOLA	3	Elective	4
Elective	3		

Senior Year

First Semester		Second Semester	
Course	Cr	Course	Cr
Math 505	1	Math Elect.(500+)	3
Math 511	3	Math Elect.(400+)	3
Math Elect.(500+)	3	Elective	9
Elective	8	Math Elect.	3

Total Credit Hours: 124

1997–1998

Freshman Year

First Semester		Second Semester	
Course	Cr	Course	Cr
Math 131	4	Math 132	4
Chem 101,111	4	Chem102,112	4
Engl 100	3	Engl 101	3
Soc. Sci. Elect.	3	Soc. Sci. Elect	3
PHED	2		

Sophomore Year

First Semester		Second Semester	
Course	Cr	Course	Cr
Math 231	4	Math 311	3
Math 240 or alt.	3	Math 331	3
Phys 241,251	4	Phys 242,252	4
Human. Elect.	3	Human. Elect.	3
Speech 250	3	Elective	3

Junior Year

First Semester		Second Semester	
Course	Cr	Course	Cr
Math 507	3	Math 508	3
Math 350	3	Math Elect. (300+)	3
Math 224	3	Math 440 or 460	3
FOLA	3	FOLA	3
Human. Elect.	3	Elective	3

Senior Year

First Semester		Second Semester	
Course	Cr	Course	Cr
Math 511	3	Math 512	3
Math 505	1	Math Elect.	3
Soc. Sci. Elect.	3	Soc. Sci. Elect.	3
Elective	6	Elective	5

Total Credit Hours: 124

Fig. 18.1

I taught Math 507 for the first time in fall 1993 and observed the following behaviors, which also occur in the Math 511–512 sequence:

1. Many students had not learned to write up solutions to problems in an organized step-by-step fashion prior to beginning the course.

2. Most students could not construct a proof. At that time calculus 3 had been the only prerequisite, taught procedurally, with little, if any, mention of proof.

3. Most students were inconsistent as resource persons to one another. Typically, students did not share notes, ideas, or problems. They mostly worked in isolation.

4. Many students did not keep organized notes or maintain a mathematics notebook.

5. Most students were used to imitating methods for solving standard problems, a much more instrumental approach (Skemp 1978). Thus, it was very new to be asked to master concepts that could not be grasped quickly through imitation. In fact, students would often go into a stall or paralysis and simply sit, not making even the first attempt at the work.

In short, there was no "mathematics culture" among the students. They did not talk about mathematics among themselves and rarely asked questions of the instructor outside of class. The students further along in the pipeline were not a resource for students enrolled in Math 507, but in fact reinforced the idea that somehow one hopes to survive real analysis, but one does not get anything out of the course. Math 507–508 was the dreaded course that no one could understand.

The faculty had difficulty dealing with such a response. One faculty member said of his students in a proof-based course, "They just sit there." Another advised, after the majority of the class had flunked a test, "Give out the test solutions and retest with a similar test," and said this was all he could think to do. But this "solution" was just imitation! Similar problems existed in the Math 511–512 course (abstract algebra). These anecdotal observations should not obscure the fact that this response on the part of students happened repeatedly in the upper-level courses until concerned faculty sought methods that would break the pattern and allow students to grow and develop in these courses. This included looking at whether the correct approach to studying these courses was communicated to students by the way faculty presented the material. For example, I gave out a questionnaire at the beginning of several proof-based courses I taught asking for students' opinions about how to study in a mathematics class. These results in part directed what devices we implemented.

A PLAN OF ACTION

Seeking a wider perspective, faculty members also sought information about mathematics departments that addressed similar difficulties by attending many talks at national and regional meetings. One successful program for lower-level mathematics courses, the Professional Development Program (PDP) at the University of California at Berkeley, organized an honors style program that brought in many African American and Hispanic students and was structured so that the students would work out all kinds of calculus problems in groups (Fullilove and Treisman 1990). This specifically developed the ability in the students to interact in mathematical discussions and to verbally discuss mathematics with both peers and instructors. It ended the isolated studying that had been observed among these groups but increased the amount and effectiveness of the studying in general. For example, an isolated student may be stuck on a problem and sit there alone, not asking for help from a peer, a teaching assistant, or a professor (this was observed to happen with minority students there). In PDP, a student had peers (fellow calculus students), older peers (undergraduate students who had successfully completed the calculus sequence), and graduate teaching assistants, and so the student could find quick assistance when stuck, enabling the student to do more examples and help others understand what he or she had come to understand. Students who participated fully were soon performing at a high level in their calculus courses, where previously the performance had been very poor. The lecture format was still in place in their classes, but they had learned how to study and communicate the mathematics.

Among the changes implemented by various instructors to encourage such effective studying among mathematics majors at NCA&TSU and to monitor its development were the following:

1. Having students maintain a journal
2. Starting courses with a review of logic
3. Giving daily quizzes on statements of definitions or theorems
4. Performing error analysis
5. Giving specific reading assignments
6. Encouraging group presentations
7. Offering extra credit in homework for maintaining a list of theorems and definitions and an orderly math notebook
8. Requiring office-hour attendance
9. Encouraging group work on studying concepts
10. Allowing oral tests on proofs

In addition to homework and tests, the changes above, if included, have an assigned value in the computation of the grade. Incorporating requirements that encourage study behavior that could lead to developing a more relational approach to doing mathematics, in fact, does bring about some development. For example, one of the Math 511–512 instructors regularly assigns group work where the students must figure out a proof or explain and illustrate a definition as a group and then present it to the rest of the class. The groups are regularly reassigned, and the results are a more developed ability to communicate the mathematics and a better understanding of concepts that they also had to explain to others. The lecture format is still in place.

To further illustrate, I taught Math 507–508 three consecutive years and tried several approaches in getting the students to work on learning definitions and theorems. The first strategy was to require daily quizzes on the statement of some specific theorem or definition. This ended the paralysis mentioned above, and it did help students learn to experience how the meaning would change when words were carelessly juxtaposed in a statement. However, because this solution is still a more instrumental approach (memorize and regurgitate), the students invariably would cram for the quiz and forget the definition in a few days rather than retain it and build on it.

The second year I taught this sequence, I added the requirement that students attend office hours at least once a week, even if they did not have a question. Most of the students came at least seven of the fifteen weeks. If they had no questions, I would ask them questions, attempting to make them think and use the definitions some were still attempting to cram. I also gave them extra credit on homework for maintaining a math notebook that included dated lecture notes and a running list of definitions and theorems. The third year, in addition to the quizzes and required office-hour attendance, I broke them up into reading groups in Math 507. Each reading group had to "present" a specified reading assignment to the class, rotating among three groups. It forced the students to struggle with the reading, to come in before class to ask questions about the reading, and to use and retain the material they were asked to state on quizzes. I had good results working with that 507 class. The second semester, just to see what had been internalized, I dropped the office-attendance requirement and the group reading assignments. The result was that the students did not read and study as before—the mathematical way of working had not been internalized and was not being reinforced by peers. The study behavior that had been developed still needed to be reinforced, if not through explicit requirements then at least through advisement and monitoring. However, in a proof course I taught the following year, the combination of requirements seems to have accomplished the development of a mathematics culture in a small group of students.

The proof course, Math 311 (mathematical logic and proof techniques), was taught for the first time in spring 1994 and was made a required prerequisite to Math 507–508 and Math 511–512 the following academic year. The course was developed by the PMCC but had to be approved by the mathematics department faculty and added to the curricula of the other two degree programs. Adoption was unanimous. The course now comes at the end of sophomore year for every mathematics major (all three degree programs), fostering camaraderie among them. The course uses Dan Fendel and Diane Resek's approach of emphasizing both exploration and proof. (All current members of the PMCC have taken a workshop on teaching mathematical proof from Fendel and Resek.) The texts used are *Foundations of Higher Mathematics: Exploration and Proof* by Fendel and Resek (1990) or *Foundations of Higher Mathematics* by Fletcher and Patty (1996). Spring 1997 yielded our first mathematically maturing class from Math 311. I taught this course. For this group, instead of telling them a specific definition to learn for a quiz, I gave them a block of text from which the definitions or theorems would come. The quizzes would occur about twice a week. Also, a well-known African American applied mathematician visited specifically to address the topic of how to study upper-level mathematics, and he had an enormous impact on the students. Among the additional approaches used was an oral test at the end of the course.

Each student (17 out of the original 25) was assigned a different theorem whose proof they had to discuss with me. Most of the theorems involved working with epsilon-delta proofs, but some of the theorems involved working with properties of functions. They were allowed to understand the proof in any way they could. They could work with one another. They could talk to graduate students or other faculty. They could read other proofs in other texts. And they could ask me questions. All these methods are what one does to learn mathematics anyway. I was able to question all the students individually about what they did to get to the point of understanding and then emphasized that this had to be their approach to every idea they encounter in Math 507, their next course. They made the transition to a more relational approach (Skemp 1978) as juniors in 1997–98, and they are now resources to their peers in the two following classes. A panel discussion was held in February 1998 where three of these juniors gave short discussions on reading and studying upper-level mathematics to the current sophomores in Math 311, and real communication is developing between members of the sophomore and junior classes.

The most interesting result with the current crop of juniors is that although they were introduced to proof through a variety of instructional methods, their current instructor uses a strictly no-frills lecture style that they will invariably encounter in graduate school, should they choose to attend. This instructor had expected one of the 507 students to continue with 508. Instead, he has eight students! One is a first semester graduate student, two are retaking who failed last year, and one is required to take the course by her degree program. The other four, in the other two degree programs, elected to take the dreaded Math 508, a first! The second most interesting result is that they told me that they should have begun learning to do proofs in calculus! They read (or attempt to read) the text before they go to lecture, and they are seen around the department, in classrooms, or in the student lounge clumped around doing mathematics homework problems! They put in very long hours in their studying. Again this is the beginning of a mathematics culture among the students if it can be duplicated in subsequent classes.

The department tries to do other things that encourage the students to get to know the faculty and develop both mentoring and peer relationships. In the fall of 1995, all faculty were brought into the advisement process. A student is assigned a single advisor for his entire academic career. An advisement committee recently developed a handbook for all undergraduate mathematics majors, which includes advice for how to study in the upper-level courses. Pi Mu Epsilon (national mathematics honor society), the North Carolina Council of Teachers of Mathematics (NCCTM) student chapter, and the Mathematical Association of America (MAA) student chapter foster close relations among our majors but also give them connection to the larger mathematics community. (The MAA student chapter was formerly a local math club called Digit Circle.) Participation in on-campus and off-campus undergraduate research programs is enthusiastically encouraged.

NEXT STEPS

NCA&TSU has produced probably five to six graduates from its undergraduate program who went on to earn Ph.D.'s in mathematics (several more in mathematics education). Currently there are two who have been admitted to candidacy in the Ph.D. program in mathematics at Howard University, four in the M.S. program in applied mathematics at NCA&TSU, and others in master's programs elsewhere. A senior has been accepted into a Ph.D. program in operations research, and two recent graduates applied to Ph.D. programs in the mathematical sciences for fall 1998. Three juniors, who have expressed interest in graduate school, have been accepted into 1998 summer research programs in Pennsylvania, Michigan, and North Carolina. One goal of our efforts is to regularly produce two to six students each year who go on to graduate school in the mathematical sciences to earn a Ph.D. rather than to continue the sporadic graduate school attendance that characterized the program prior to 1992.

Finally, some changes are in the works that are likely to be incorporated soon into the undergraduate programs:

1. Designate a section of each course of the calculus sequence (Math 131–132–231) to include proofs. These sections would not be exclusively for mathematics majors but would address their needs.

2. For those not ready for calculus, have a separate precalculus course for mathematics majors. This is logistically difficult.

3. Add senior-level reading courses to the list of courses, so that strong seniors headed to graduate school can work on courses that are common in the undergraduate curricula at other institutions but not offered as undergraduate courses at NCA&TSU.

4. Develop an honors program, adding problem sessions or seminars and increasing faculty contact hours with students through a variety of other mathematics-centered activities. This is a work in progress and is supported by a grant.

Implementing these changes, and continuing what has already occurred, would address the need for proofs in the calculus coursework for mathematics majors, address the need for foundation courses in the undergraduate curriculum, and address the need for pedagogy that includes intensive faulty-student interaction and encourages peer-interaction if we are to effectively prepare our majors and keep them in the mathematics pipeline. Although our current successes are preliminary and we will not know for years if we have been truly successful in developing more African American mathematicians, the current state of affairs is promising. Those of us involved with these efforts at NCA&TSU will continue in this direction.

REFERENCES

Asera, Rose, and Uri Treisman. "Routes to Mathematics for African-American, Latino, and Native American Students in the 1990s: The Educational Trajectories of Summer Mathematics Institute Participants." In *Changing the Culture: Mathematics Education in the Research Community*, vol. 5 of *CBMS Issues in Mathematics Education*, edited by Naomi Fisher et al., pp. 127–51. Providence, R.I.: American Mathematical Society; Washington D.C.: Mathematical Association of America, 1995.

Baldwin, James T. "Three Mathematical Cultures." In *Changing the Culture: Mathematics Education in the Research Community*, vol. 5 of *CBMS Issues in Mathematics Education*, edited by Naomi Fisher et al., pp. 17–30. Providence, R.I.: American Mathematical Society; Washington D.C.: Mathematical Association of America, 1995.

Fendel, David M., and Diane Resek. *Foundations of Higher Mathematics: Explorations and Proof*. Reading, Mass.: Addison-Wesley Publishing Co., 1990.

Fletcher, Peter, and C. Wayne Patty. *Foundations of Higher Mathematics*. 3rd ed. Boston: PWS Publishing Co., 1996

Fullilove, Robert, and Phillip Uri Treisman. "Mathematics Achievement among African-American Undergraduates at the University of California, Berkeley: An Evaluation of the Math Workshop Program." *Journal of Negro Education* 59, no. 3 (Summer 1990): 463–78.

National Research Council (NRC). *Everybody Counts: A Report to the Nation on the Future of Mathematics Education*. Washington, D.C.: National Academy Press, 1989.

Skemp, Richard. "Relational and Instrumental Understanding." *Arithmetic Teacher* 25 (1978): 9–15.

Summary

Some Final Thoughts on Changing the Faces of Mathematics

William F. Tate

The articles in this volume of Changing the Faces of Mathematics are part of a long history of discourse in African American education. One of the most important books in the literature on African American education is *The Miseducation of the Negro*. In his classic work on race and education in the United States, Carter G. Woodson ([1933] 1990) argued that one critical problem facing African American students in the mathematics classrooms of the segregated South was teachers ill-prepared to provide appropriate mathematics pedagogy. More than two decades after Woodson's treatise, *Brown v. Board of Education*, became the law of the land in 1954 and promised to improve the quality and nature of educational opportunities for African American students. The hopes and dreams of many African American parents for their children's education were linked to school desegregation (Grant 1995). Their hopes were built on the assumption that better qualified teachers and more rigorous curriculum options would be a product of *Brown*.

This important Supreme Court decision was followed by a large-scale effort to reform the nation's mathematics classrooms. Initiated in response to *Sputnik*, the "new math" reform movement sought to improve mathematics education in the United States, for it was thought that a good scientific education was key to a strong country (Kliebard 1987). However, the mathematics reform effort associated with *Sputnik* did very little to address the concerns of parents of students of color who were often residents in urban cities (Garcia 1995; Nieto 1995; Tate 1997). Those responsible for the reform argued their efforts should be limited to "college capable" students (Devault and Weaver 1970; Kliebard 1987). The code words *college capable* provided a signal to the education community that only a select few communities and students were to be served by the reform policy. This elitist political position on reform ignored the influence of a student's race or ethnic background on his or her opportunity to learn mathematics (Tate 1995). For example, many teachers in urban areas failed to receive the training required to understand and implement the new mathematics curriculum developed in the post-*Sputnik* era (Davis 1992; Darling-Hammond 1995). This is not to say efforts were not made to provide teachers an opportunity to learn the new mathematics programs; rather, the opportunities were limited and insufficient for the curricular and pedagogical change called for within the reform movement. Thus, for many urban school students—particularly African American students—the late 1950s and 1960s are best characterized as the era of "benign neglect" with respect to mathematics reform.

In the late 1960s and early 1970s, a new mathematics reform movement—"back to basics"—emerged that focused primarily on elementary and middle schools (National Council of Teachers of Mathematics [NCTM] 1980). This movement was an outgrowth of efforts to achieve equality of educational opportunity through compensatory education. The back-to-basics effort called for teaching a core set of rudimentary-level mathematics procedures and facts, often to the exclusion of more-advanced mathematical concepts. Moreover, the

> **For many urban school students— particularly African American students— the late 1950s and 1960s are best characterized as the era of "benign neglect" with respect to mathematics reform.**

back-to-basics movement was closely connected to minimum competency testing by the states in the late 1970s and 1980s and by proponents of the "effective schools movement." Although the basic-skills movement influenced the entire United States educational system, it had a dramatic impact on the mathematics curriculum and the nature of pedagogy in low-income urban schools (Strickland and Ascher 1992). On the positive side, the basic-skills movement did result in improved standardized mathematics test scores for students traditionally underserved (Secada 1992). In fact, the African American–white test-score gap has been slowly converging since 1965 (Hedges and Nowell 1998). The basic-skills movement demonstrated that when teachers and administrators rallied around a common goal in mathematics, were goal oriented, and were given the proper institutional support to achieve the goal, students would learn the content taught. Unfortunately, across every major national survey of high school students, African Americans are hugely underrepresented in the upper tails of the achievement distributions, and this underrepresentation does not seem to be decreasing. This phenomenon might be explained by teachers' expectations during this period.

Perhaps the success (albeit limited) of the basic-skills movement had to do with teachers' beliefs about their students. Many of the goals of the basic-skills movement were consistent with the teachers' perceptions of students' ability (Zeichner 1996; Knapp and Woolverton 1995). However, as the vision of what it means to be mathematically literate in our society has moved from the basic-skills curriculum to a more demanding standard, the limits of past pedagogical practice have become increasingly apparent. Teaching elementary and middle school children strictly low-level, basic mathematics skills throughout their grades K–8 school experience will not adequately prepare them for life in our democracy or the realities of a global economy. For the first time in the history of this country, all students are being challenged by state and local standards to learn mathematics at levels once reserved for "college capable" students (Massell 1992). This challenge places new demands on teachers, administrators, parents, and, of course, students.

> **As the vision of what it means to be mathematically literate in our society has moved from the basic-skills curriculum to a more demanding standard, the limits of past pedagogical practice have become increasingly apparent.**

These new demands are linked in many ways to activities within the National Council of Teachers of Mathematics (NCTM). In 1980, the NCTM published *An Agenda for Action*, which called for the implementation of a ten-year reform program. One goal of *An Agenda for Action* was to move the focus of school mathematics curricula beyond basic-skills objectives to a more problem-solving conception of mathematics content and instruction. Subsequently, but not as a direct result of *An Agenda for Action*, NCTM sponsored the development of mathematics curriculum and teaching standards (NCTM 1989; NCTM 1991). The Council gave three reasons for the creation and adoption of new mathematics standards: (1) to ensure quality, (2) to establish objectives for student learning, and (3) to catalyze change.

The importance of the new mathematics standards for African American students is obvious; previous reform efforts have not met the needs of certain groups of students. However, many questions remain about the "fit" between the new standards and the realities of African American students' school experience. The articles in this volume of Changing the Faces of Mathematics raise some of these questions and provide insight into reform-driven mathematics initiatives that are especially relevant to schools attempting to reconceptualize their mathematics programs. This volume represents an effort to contribute practical examples and principled ideas to the literature on African American students and mathematics education. I have not attempted to review all these examples and ideas; rather, my goal is to contribute a few additional thoughts in light of what I have read here.

FRAMING THE PROBLEM

How a social problem is framed can influence the type of intervention that is perceived as possible. This volume includes a variety of perspectives on how to positively influence African American students' opportunity to learn. Each builds on a particular paradigmatic perspective of mathematics education. Traditionally, the philosophies undergirding mathematics education are derived from psychology and mathematics (Kilpatrick 1992). Thus, it is not surprising that many of the papers frame the problem of African American students' performance in psychological terms. Strutchens, Cousins-Cooper, and Presmeg argued for the importance of examining stereotypes, expectations, and coping strategies. These chapters build on the literature in social psychology. Strutchens and Cousins-Cooper noted the strong influence stereotypes and expectations can have on students' achievement. This is also a theme in the chapters by Cooper, Oldham, and Dance and colleagues. Cooper noted that many of the graduate students at the University of Maryland recalled having a mentor with high expectations. Many of these mentors were instrumental in creating future graduate opportunities for the students. Similarly, Oldham discussed how introducing challenging mathematics curriculum opportunities was a central thrust of the North Carolina A&T faculty. Dance and colleagues described an atmosphere of challenge where problems are in contexts that interest the students and remediation is not done in isolation; rather, the review of essential skills is integrated into challenging investigations and problems. All three papers reflect high expectations by faculty for their students. This is not a trivial matter. There is growing evidence that suggests the black-white achievement gap, in part, is associated with expectations and stereotypes. For example, Steele (1997) found that African American and women students chosen at random in an experiment at the University of Michigan and put into an academic program described as "more demanding" actually performed better during and after their freshman year than other students in a regular or a remedial program.

Similarly, Treisman (1985) used this strategy in designing his successful cooperative group study in mathematics for college-aged African American students. He found that African American students placed in rigorous academic environments outperformed those in regular programs. An important feature of the academic environment was the opportunity not only to discuss problems from the mathematics class but also to create and extend the discourse about mathematics beyond the traditional opportunities found in calculus courses. The chapter by White captures this idea for the elementary school classroom. She provided examples of both limited and rich discourse opportunities in the mathematics classroom. Learning environments that support rich discourse provide important opportunities for students to learn more challenging mathematics. However, teacher expectations play a role in the construction of these learning environments. Studies from the area of literacy provide some additional insight. Gee (1987) suggests the explanation for the wide differences in literacy achievement between African American working- and lower-class students and white middle-class students is the nature of instruction experienced by each group. The latter group is treated as if they already have knowledge, and thus they experience a kind of apprenticeship where they are afforded the opportunity to perform activities they have not yet fully mastered. In this environment, the students are treated as if they come to school with knowledge and are competent in areas they are not. In contrast, the African American child is thought to be an empty vessel with little or no knowledge to build on. Thus, they must be "built up" with remediation. Unfortunately, remedial instruction is generally associated with low-level ideas, and these students have very little opportunity to learn more-complex and demanding skills.

Other literatures support the notion that high demands and expectations for African American students can lead to increased achievement trends for these students. For example, the research on course taking and high expectations is insightful. Hoffer, Rasinski, and Moore (1995) reported on the relationship between the number of mathematics courses that high school students of different racial and socioeconomic backgrounds completed and their achievement gain from the end of grade 8 to grade 12. The findings indicated that when African American and white students who completed the same courses were compared, the differences in average achievement gains were smaller and none were statistically significant. Further, none of the socioeconomic status (SES) comparisons showed significant differences among students taking the same number of courses. These findings can be interpreted to mean that much of the racial and SES differences in mathematics achievement in grades 9–12 is a product of the quality and number of mathematics courses that African American, white, and high- and low-SES students complete during secondary school. Unfortunately, in many schools the question of whether we expect African American students to take substantive mathematics has been answered in the negative.

Low expectations also influence how African American students are socialized into mathematics learning opportunities. Smith (1996) investigated the efforts of early access (eighth grade) to algebra on students' access to advanced mathematics courses and subsequent high school mathematics achievement. She found that early access to algebra has an effect beyond increased achievement and, in fact, may socialize a student into taking more mathematics. In essence, having credit for a year of algebra at the beginning of high school is a credential, regulating the expectations of school personnel and ultimately providing access to more-advanced coursework in mathematics. Understand the point: The credential increases both the students' and teachers' expectations about how much mathematics the student will take in high school, keeping students in the college-prep track longer and producing higher achievement results.

The importance of the Hoffer, Rasinski, and Moore and the Smith studies are that policy can be used to intervene. One method of intervention is to mandate specific courses at the eighth-grade and secondary school level. Of course, this option is not without problems. How do you help students make the transition from the elementary school mathematics curriculum to earlier access to algebra? This is especially important for students that have been underserved and, as a result, are not prepared for the transition. The chapter by Smith, Stiff, and Petree argued that providing students with problem-solving vignettes (PSVs) supported the opportunity to learn algebra by African American students who were the "least academically prepared." The design of the PSV was strongly associated with the idea that a real-life activity was more likely to promote students' understanding of mathematics. This theme is central to many of the chapters in the volume. I do not intend to discuss the various "real" applications that are advanced in the volume. However, note that the applications do vary on their level of mathematical sophistication and connection to anything real. For me what was more interesting were the arguments given for connecting mathematics curriculum to real events and situations. Two main arguments emerged.

The first argument put forth supporting reality-based instructional environments was derived from anthropological sources that have found cultural discontinuities between formal educational settings and African American students' lives and experiences (see, e.g., Foster [1991]; Ladson-Billings [1995]). Thus, educators have argued for schooling practices that are more congruent with African American students' lives. King (1994, pp. 27–28) stated:

[T]he culturally *Congruent* perspective focuses on transforming the educational process to align it more closely with the students' cultural knowledge and their indigenous ways of knowing, learning and being. The skills of social criticism are not necessarily addressed but it is presumed that transformed, culturally responsive and inclusive instructional approaches that drastically improve the education of African American students will generally benefit the whole society.

A second argument made by some of the authors was more closely connected to psychological sources that theorize that learning is dependent on the knowledge the learner brings to the experience, and pedagogy should build on students' conceptions (U.S. Department of Education 1994). The major thesis of this psychological perspective is that teachers' knowledge of students' thinking, when it is integrated, robust, and a part of the established curriculum, can affect the teaching and learning of mathematics (Fennema and Franke 1992). Thus, both the anthropological and psychological literatures support the relationship between teachers' understanding of children's experiences and pedagogical success. This is also an important theme of this volume.

THE CHALLENGE

Imagine if all teachers had high expectations for African American students and created challenging learning environments where they were guided by their knowledge of children's thinking and experiences. Would African American students' performance improve in mathematics? This is certainly an empirical question worth investigating. However, it requires that teachers respond to the challenge. The articles of this volume represent such a challenge. Each provides a principled idea to inform pedagogical and curricular decisions. Each idea must be examined closely by the potential reformer. After this examination, each educator must decide how to best implement the idea in his or her class. This is a difficult process that requires a great deal of thought and preparation. The challenge may seem great. However, the potential reward is well worth the effort.

REFERENCES

Darling-Hammond, Linda. "Inequality and Access to Knowledge." In *Handbook of Multicultural Education*, edited by James A. Banks and Cherry A. McGee Banks, pp. 465–83. New York: Macmillan, 1995.

Davis, Robert. "Reflections on Where Mathematics Education Now Stands and on Where It May Be Going." In *Handbook of Research on Mathematics Teaching and Learning*, edited by Douglas A. Grouws, pp. 724–34. New York: Macmillan Publishing Co., 1992.

Devault, M. Vere, and J. Fred Weaver. "Forces and Issues Related to Curriculum and Instruction, K–6." In *A History of Mathematics Education in the United States and Canada*, Thirty-second Yearbook of the National Council of Teachers of Mathematics, edited by Arthur. F. Coxford and Phillip S. Jones, pp. 92–152. Washington, D.C.: National Council of Teachers of Mathematics, 1970.

Fennema, Elizabeth, and Megan Franke. "Teachers' Knowledge and Its Impact." In *Handbook of Research on Mathematics Teaching and Learning*, edited by Douglas A. Grouws, pp. 147–164. New York: Macmillan Publishing Co., 1992.

Foster, Michele. "Just Got to Find a Way: Case Studies of the Lives and Practice of Exemplary Black High School Teachers." In *Readings in Equal Education: Qualitative Investigations into Schools and Schooling*, edited by Michele Foster, pp. 273–309. New York: AMS Press, 1991.

Garcia, Eugene E. "Educating Mexican American Students: Past Treatment and Recent Developments in Theory, Research, Policy, and Practice." In *Handbook of Research on Multicultural Education*, edited by James A. Banks and Cherry A. McGee Banks, pp. 372–87. New York: Macmillan, 1995.

Gee, James. "What Is Literacy?" *Teaching and Learning* 2 (1987): 3–11.

Grant, Carl A. "Reflections on the Promise of *Brown* and Multicultural Education." *Teachers College Record* 96 (1995): 707–21.

Hedges, Larry V., and Amy Nowell. "Black-White Test Score Convergence since 1965." In *The Black-White Test Score Gap*, edited by Christopher Jencks and Meredith Phillips, pp.149–81. Washington, D.C.: Brookings Institution Press, 1998.

Hoffer, Thomas, Kenneth Rasinski, and Whitney Moore. *Social Background Differences in High School Mathematics and Science Coursetaking and Achievement.* Washington, D.C.: National Center for Education Statistics, 1995.

King, Joyce E. "The Purpose of Schooling for African American Children." In *Teaching Diverse Populations: Formulating a Knowledge Base*, edited by Etta R. Hollins, Joyce E. King, and Warren C. Hayman, pp. 25–56. Albany, N.Y.: State University of New York, 1994.

Kilpatrick, Jeremy. "A History of Research in Mathematics Education." In *Handbook of Research on Mathematics Teaching and Learning*, edited by Douglas A. Grouws, pp. 3–38. New York: Macmillan Publishing Co., 1992.

Kliebard, Herbert M. *The Struggle for the American Curriculum 1893–1958.* New York: Routledge & Kegan Paul, 1987.

Knapp, Michael, and Sara Woolverton. "Social Class and Schooling." In *Handbook of Research on Multicultural Education*, edited by James A. Banks and Cherry A. McGee Banks, pp. 548–622. New York: Macmillan, 1995.

Ladson-Billings, Gloria. "Toward a Theory of Culturally Relevant Pedagogy." *American Educational Research Journal* 28 (Fall 1995): 465–91.

National Council of Teachers of Mathematics. A*n Agenda for Action: Recommendations for School Mathematics of the 1980s.* Reston, Va.: National Council of Teachers of Mathematics, 1980.

———. *Curriculum and Evaluation Standards for School Mathematics.* Reston, Va.: National Council of Teachers of Mathematics, 1989.

———. *Professional Standards for Teaching Mathematics.* Reston, Va.: National Council of Teachers of Mathematics, 1991.

Massel, Diane. "Setting Standards in Mathematics and Social Studies." *Education and Urban Society* 26 (1994): 118–40.

Nieto, Sonia. "A History of the Education of Puerto Rican Students in U.S. Mainland Schools: 'Losers,' 'Outsiders,' or 'Leaders'?" In *Handbook of Research on Multicultural Education*, edited by James A. Banks and Cherry A. McGee Banks, pp. 372–87. New York: Macmillan, 1995.

Secada, Walter G. "Race, Ethnicity, Social Class, Language, and Achievement in Mathematics." In *Handbook of Research on Mathematics Teaching and Learning*, edited by Douglas A. Grouws, pp. 623–60. New York: Macmillan Publishing Co., 1992.

Smith, Julia B. "Does an Extra Year Make Any Difference? The Impact of Early Access to Algebra on Long-Term Gains in Mathematics Achievement." *Educational Evaluation and Policy Analysis* 18 (Summer 1996): 141–53.

Steele, Claude M. "A Threat in the Air: How Stereotypes Shape Intellectual Identity and Performance." *American Psychologist* 52 (June 1997): 613–29.

Strickland, Dorothy S., and Carol C. Ascher. "Low-Income African American Children and Public Schooling." In *Handbook of Research on Curriculum*, edited by Phillip W. Jackson, pp. 609–25. New York: Macmillan Publishing Co., 1992.

Tate, William F. "Brown, Sputnik, and Mathematics Reform: Lessons from the Past." In *Readings on Equal Education: Forty Years after the Brown Decision*, edited by Charles Teddlie and Kofi Lomotey, pp. 251–64. New York: AMS Press, 1997.

———. "School Mathematics and African American Students: Thinking Seriously about Opportunity to Learn Standards." *Educational Administration Quarterly* 31 (August 1995): 424–48.

Treisman, Uri P. "A Study of the Mathematics Achievement of Black Students at the University of California at Berkeley." Doctoral diss., University of California at Berkeley, 1985.

U.S. Department of Education. *Issues of Curriculum Reform in Science, Mathematics, and Higher Order Thinking across the Disciplines.* Washington, D.C.: U.S. Government Printing Office, 1994.

Woodson, Carter G. *The Mis-education of the Negro.* 1933. Reprint, Trenton, N.J.: African World Press, 1990.

Zeichner, Kenneth M. "Educating Teachers to Close the Achievement Gap: Issues of Pedagogy, Knowledge, and Teacher Preparation." In *Closing the Achievement Gap: A Vision for Changing Beliefs and Practices*, edited by Belinda Williams, pp. 56–76. Alexandria, Va.: Association for Supervision and Curriculum Development, 1996.

2